Collins

CONCISE COURSE

CSEC®
English A

Dr Saadiqa Khan, Angela Lalla and Dorothy L. Warner

Julia Burchell, Mike Gould and Beth Kemp

William Collins' dream of knowledge for all began with the publication of his first book in 1819.
A self-educated mill worker, he not only enriched millions of lives, but also founded a flourishing publishing house. Today, staying true to this spirit, Collins books are packed with inspiration, innovation and practical expertise.
They place you at the centre of a world of possibility and give you exactly what you need to explore it.

Collins. Freedom to teach.

Published by Collins
An imprint of HarperCollins*Publishers*

The News Building, 1 London Bridge Street, London SE1 9GF, UK

1st Floor, Watermarque Building, Ringsend Road, Dublin 4, Ireland

Browse the complete Collins catalogue at
www.collins.co.uk/caribbeanschools

© HarperCollins*Publishers* Limited 2021

10 9 8 7 6 5 4 3 2 1

ISBN 978-0-00-845857-7

Concise Course CSEC® English is an independent publication and has not been authorised, sponsored or otherwise approved by **CXC®**.

CSEC® is a registered trade mark of the **Caribbean Examinations Council (CXC®)**

British Library Cataloguing-in-Publication Data
A catalogue record for this publication is available from the British Library.

Authors: Julia Burchell, Mike Gould and Beth Kemp
Series consultants: Dr Saadiqa Khan, Angela Lalla and Dorothy L. Warner
Publisher: Elaine Higgleton
Product manager: Catherine Martin
Development editor: Lucy Hobbs
Editorial project manager: Beth Franklin
Copyeditor: Sonya Newland
Proofreader: Catherine Dakin
Cover designer: Kevin Robbins and Gordon MacGilp
Typesetter: QBS Learning
Artwork: QBS Learning
Production controller: Lyndsey Rogers
Printed and bound by Grafi ca Veneta S. P. A.

MIX
Paper from responsible sources
FSC™ C007454

This book is produced from independently certified FSC™ paper to ensure responsible forest management.

For more information visit:
www.harpercollins.co.uk/green
Acknowledgments are at the back of the book

Contents

**Download answers for free at www.collins.
co.uk/caribbeanschools**

Introduction

The Collins Concise Revision Course for CSEC® English A will help you to prepare for your CSEC® examinations so you are ready to tackle Paper 1 and Paper 2 with confidence.

The course is divided into two sections, with one section focusing on each paper.

Paper 1

- This section is designed to help you understand the skills and knowledge that underpin the Paper 1 examination questions.
- Each chapter addresses one of the syllabus skills and abilities to be assessed, asking you to read and respond to the range of texts you may meet in your Paper 1 exam.
- Each chapter ends with a 'Test yourself' set of practice exam-style questions. This includes guidance on where you might have gone wrong with that particular type of multiple-choice question.
- The final chapter offers a range of exam-style questions to help you practise your skills and improve your exam performance.
- Answers to all the tasks are included at the end of the book.

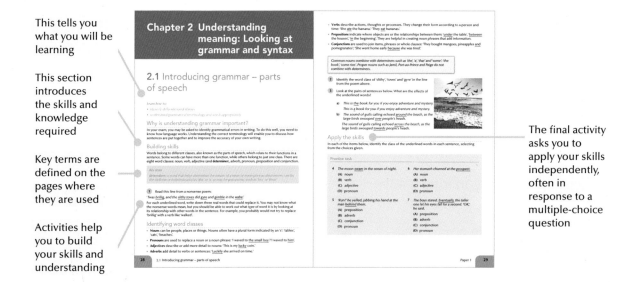

This tells you what you will be learning

This section introduces the skills and knowledge required

Key terms are defined on the pages where they are used

Activities help you to build your skills and understanding

The final activity asks you to apply your skills independently, often in response to a multiple-choice question

Paper 2

- The Paper 2 section includes a chapter on each examination question. The chapters recap and model the skills and knowledge needed to produce each type of writing, moving from scaffolded practice activities to full examination-style tasks.
- Each chapter ends with a 'Test yourself' unit, with a full practice question and two annotated sample responses to exemplify competent and superior performance.
- The final chapter offers a complete paper to help you practise your skills and improve your exam performance.
- Answers to all the tasks are included at the end of the book. (For marking guidance and sample answers for the final practice paper, please visit collins.co.uk/caribbeanschools)

This tells you what you will be learning

This section introduces the skill or concept in focus

Activities help you to build your skills and understanding

Revision tips suggest additional ways to prepare for the exam

A sample response illustrates the features of competent achievement

A sample response illustrates the features of superior achievement

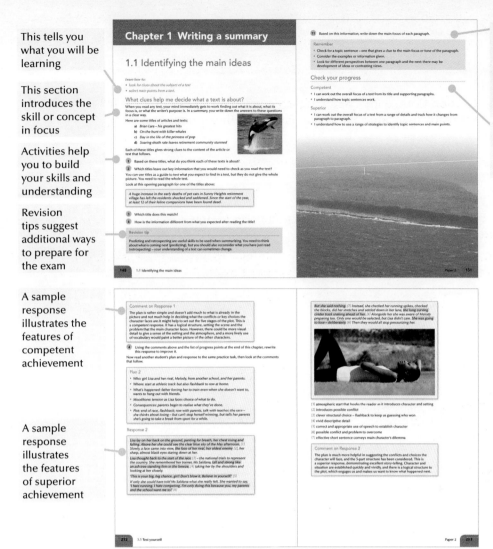

The final activity asks you to apply your skills independently, often in response to an exam-style task

These checklists help you to assess your own work

School-Based Assessment

This tells you which stage of the School-Based Assessment the unit focuses on

This explains the particular skills or knowledge relevant to this stage of the SBA

This introduces key ideas/ways of working through example SBA topics

Activities help you develop your own ideas so that you learn to work independently and in a group

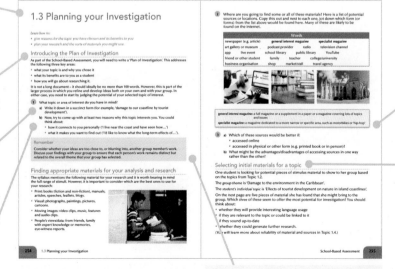

Key terms or vocabulary specific to the SBA are clearly defined or explained

Key headings help break down the process of completing your SBA into manageable 'chunks'

Tips help you avoid potential pitfalls when producing your SBA

A Glossary at the end of the book collates all the key literary and linguistic terminology, to support you in your revision.

Introducing Paper 1

Introducing Paper 1

This part of the coursebook introduces the core skills you will need to demonstrate in your Paper 1 exam in addition to the techniques you will need to answer questions effectively. In order to support and develop your understanding of the critical reading skills needed, you should read widely both for entertainment and informative purposes, asking yourself what the writer's key points are, what their main purpose is, and how particular effects are achieved.

Chapters 1 and 2 explore skills related to working out the meanings of words and phrases through vocabulary, grammar and syntax knowledge. Chapter 3 explores the particular skills you need to find explicit and implicit information and to distinguish between fact and opinion. This part then moves on to discuss poetry, fiction and non-fiction prose texts from a diverse range of authors, including John Keats, Derek Walcott, Charles Dickens, Edith Wharton and Edwidge Danticat.

You will be challenged to consider ideas such as how a text can have both main themes and sub-themes, whether a text shows bias, how writers use techniques such as figurative language, and the particular devices writers use to persuade you or promote a particular viewpoint. Each section from 1 to 9 ends with an Apply the skills task, which allows you to practise a particular question type or skill from Paper 1.

Each chapter ends with extended practice tasks to ensure you have a chance to apply what you have learned.

The section as a whole is completed with a full practice paper, based on Paper 1 question styles.

Chapter 1 Understanding meaning: Looking at word choice and idiom

1.1 Introducing literal meaning

Learn how to:
* *work out the literal meaning of individual words.*

Why is being able to work out literal meaning important?

You may be asked to work out the **literal meaning** of individual words in a text extract or sentence.

Building skills

Read the following extract, from a website about Cuban buildings.

> **Cuba's Colonial Architecture**
>
> *Colonial architecture in Havana may not be as decorative as that found in other Spanish colonies such as Peru, but it has a simple, solid elegance. Old Havana is, without doubt, the finest showcase of colonial architecture in Cuba. Its features are seen all over the island, however.*
>
> From www.insightguides.com

Imagine that you have been asked to find a **synonym** for the word 'decorative' in the extract above, but you are not sure what the word means. Your choices are:

    a)   beautiful

    b)   ornamental

    c)   detailed

    d)   attractive

The following steps can help you arrive at a definition.

1   **Fill in the blank:** Imagine the word is not there and try to fill in the blank by finding a word that would make sense in the sentence.

2   **Read around the gap:** Reading around the blank you have created, you can see words such as 'simple' and 'solid', which seem to be descriptions of structures.

3   **Look at the sentence structure:** The use of 'may not be as...but' suggests that the missing word is a positive one.

4   **Think about similar words that you know:** 'Decoration' is a word used to describe things that we add to something to make it look better, but decoration is not usually necessary to make something work or function.

Now look again at your choices. Do any of them seem to be a positive word that could be used to describe an unnecessary but attractive quality of a building? Use a checklist or table to compare which word 'fits' with most of your ideas.

	Positive	Unnecessary	Attractive	Buildings
beautiful	✓			✓
ornamental	✓	✓	✓	✓
detailed	✓		✓	✓
attractive	✓		✓	✓

 1 What is the synonym for 'decorative'?

Revision tip
....

Remember the letters FRLT (Fill, Read, Look, Think) to recall the steps for working out literal meaning.

Apply the skills

Read the next paragraph of the extract about Cuban buildings and their design.

The strongest influence on Cuban colonial architecture came, of course, from Spain, in particular from Andalusia, where the so-called Mudéjar style – a fusion of Christian and Arabic architectural traditions that developed in medieval Spain – predominated at the time of the colonization of Cuba.

Many of the early buildings in Havana were built by Mudéjar craftsmen, who came by ship from Seville and Cádiz and adapted the styles they knew to suit the conditions in the Caribbean: primarily the hot climate and the relative paucity of materials. The talent of these craftsmen lay above all in carpentry. Woods such as mahogany and cedar were abundant in Cuba at that time, and were used to construct ceilings, doors, columns, and railings, as well as furniture.

Practice task
....

2 Look at the three words underlined in the extract. Work out what each word means using the method outlined in this topic.

The table below may help you consider similar words.

Word	Similar words
predominated	dominate
paucity	pauper, city
construct	structure, construe

1.2 Introducing non-literal language

Learn how to:

- *recognise a range of non-literal language techniques*
- *consider whether an implicit idea is being suggested.*

Why is being able to recognise non-literal language important?

You may be asked to identify examples of **implicit** or **non-literal meaning**. You may also be asked specific questions about a text which rely on you having understood the writer's feelings or attitudes which are 'hidden' in their word choices.

> *Key terms*
>
> ***implicit meaning:*** *meaning that has to be inferred or deduced; implicit meaning often reveals opinions or feelings or can lead you to draw a conclusion about an author's intention or viewpoint*
>
> ***non-literal language:*** *also called figurative language, this is used in ways that go beyond a literal meaning to create an additional effect*

Building skills

The table below contains some examples of non-literal language and the effect they have. How many are you familiar with? Can you think of any others?

Non-literal language use	Effect
simile	suggests sensory qualities of the item being described
metaphor	suggests sensory qualities of the item being described
personification	gives life (and often, therefore, a greater sense of connection) to inanimate objects; can suggest sensory qualities
hyperbole	exaggerated expression
onomatopoeia	where the word used represents or closely resembles the actual sound
idiom	a saying or phrase that becomes well known in everyday speech
pun	creates humorous effect by exploiting different meanings of words

Considering the effect of non-literal language

You may be asked to explain the effects of the words a writer has chosen. There is a range of effects, but they can be summed up in three main ways:

- impact (e.g. strength of an idea/humour)
- sensory appeal
- emotion.

1 Consider these examples of non-literal language use. Which of the three effects do they create?

    a) *Swish, the broom swept the polished deck gently in her soft hands.*

    b) *The porch light was an oasis in the darkness of the stormy night.*

    c) *If we do not fight to the last breath then we will lose our Post Office for good.*

Language often creates more than one effect at the same time.

Apply the skills

Practice task

Read the following blog about visiting Jamaica.

> So you don't want to spend 24 hours a day on the beach? You're the type of traveller who gets tired of reggae and cold drinks being forced on you every five minutes, after about an hour? Do not despair! Jamaica can offer you all that you need to keep that adrenalin pumping and those muscles aching with overuse. What is her solution? Hiking of course!
>
> **If you're brave, then why not try the Cockpit Country Trails?** Located on the north-western part of the island, Cockpit Country is a challenging area as it features steeper hills. Make your way to the Barbecue Bottom Road, which runs north–south and from there you'll find two old historic trails: the Troy Trail and the Quick Step Trail. These trails are not easy to find and are seldom used, so a knowledgeable local guide is absolutely essential on these routes. Don't think you can go it alone!
>
> If that doesn't float your boat, then try heading underground! After a steep climb you'll reach the mouth of the cave and from then on it's spot the bats and duck the stalactites (which sparkle like diamonds, by the way) as you enjoy a break from the glaring sun outside.
>
> Remember, this area is said to be haunted by spirits and duppies, so keep your wits about you! You might even need one of those sodas by the time you get back to the pool side!

2   Identify five uses of non-literal language in the extract.

3   Explain in a short sentence the effect that each choice has on the reader.

1.3 Understanding nuance

Learn how to:

• *consider nuance when giving synonyms or working on sentence-completion activities.*

Why is understanding nuance important?

In your exam, you need to be sensitive to **nuance**. You should consider it when choosing vocabulary to add to sentence-completion tasks and when providing synonyms and **antonyms**. Nuance is one of the ways in which writers and speakers make their language choices fit their audience and **purpose**. It is also a way to reveal attitudes and emotions. You may need to choose it as a technique or identify it as one.

> **Key terms**
>
> **nuance:** *the precise meaning of a word; this may be very subtly or slightly different from that of another similar word (e.g. consider the difference between 'large' and 'enormous' or 'pleasant' and 'delightful')*
>
> **antonym:** *a word with the opposite meaning to the original word*
>
> **purpose:** *the main aim of a piece of speech or writing*

Building skills

It is important to be aware of the precise meanings of words, even when they appear to be very similar.

1 Draw a spider diagram like the one below, grouping together words linked to the concept of dislike.

2 Arrange the words that you have collected on a line of intensity. Start on the left with the word that expresses the weakest level of dislike. The word on the far right should express the most intense level of dislike.

3 Repeat the process with one of the following words.

• happiness   • brightness   • darkness   • confusion

Often the 'power' of nuance comes from its **connotations**. To consider the connotations of words, you should spend some time thinking about how individual words make you feel and what ideas they conjure up.

4 Copy and complete the following table to consider the sensory and emotional associations of the words in the first column.

Word	Sensory associations (linked to sight, sound, touch, taste)	Emotional associations (linked to feelings)
hideous	deformity	fear
gorgeous		
spacious		
cramped		

5 Create your own table of connotations for the words you came up with in Item 3.

Another aspect of nuance is the **register** that a word is drawn from. When choosing synonyms or doing sentence-completion tasks, try to keep the register consistent or the word you choose will seem inappropriate.

Look at the following sentence-completion task.

The doctor diagnosed my sister with a _____ case of mononeucleosis.

a)	bad	**c)**	wicked
b)	severe	**d)**	horrible

Each of the word choices expresses the idea that the attack of mononucleosis is not a mild one. However, b) seems to be the most formal and best matches the use of 'diagnosed' and 'mononeucleosis'.

> *Key terms*
>
> *connotation: a sensory or emotional association that a word or phrase has in addition to its literal meaning*
>
> *register: the level of formality of a text or, in some cases, the use of a particular type of language (e.g. legal jargon or medical terminology)*

6 Choose one of the words below to complete the sentence.

Playfully, the pup _____ its master and scampered happily across the road.

a) evaded

b) escaped

c) dodged

d) defied

Apply the skills

Complete the following sentences, selecting carefully from the choices given.

7 He was always immaculately dressed at interviews and was _____ well-presented.

a)	quite	**c)**	consciously
b)	scrupulously	**d)**	carefully

8 The garden was a _____ of manicured wild and exotic flowers native to the island, nestling like a gift on the hillside.

a)	wilderness	**c)**	haven
b)	oasis	**d)**	bouquet

9 The politician's voice _____ from the walls like bats from the eaves of a cottage.

a)	reverberated	**c)**	bounced
b)	sprang	**d)**	recoiled

10 'You can't hurt me,' the little boy shouted, 'I'm _____.'

a)	invincible	**c)**	magical
b)	superman	**d)**	protected

1.4 Understanding register

Learn how to:
- *make word choices based on the level of formality needed*
- *recognise when register is being used to match audience and purpose.*

Why does understanding formality matter?

In your exam, you may be asked to select words to complete sentences or provide synonyms and antonyms for words. In doing so, you need to consider the register of any words you select or match. You may also be asked to indicate the audience or purpose of a text.

Building skills

In some areas of communication a range of words may match different registers. For example, when greeting someone you have many options, including:

- 'Good morning'
- 'Hello'
- 'Hi'
- 'Wassup?'

1 Write down three other sets of words that offer different levels of formality.

Certain verbs have a polite form. For example, 'Could you?' is considered more polite than 'Can you?'

2 Write down three other verbs that offer different levels of formality.

Informal expressions are often shortened versions of formal statements. For example, 'Would you pass me the newspaper?' can be shortened to 'Pass me the paper.'

3 Write down three more shortened sentences.

Informal sentences often lose the subject at the start of a sentence. For example, 'I can't wait to see you!' becomes 'Can't wait to see you!'

Abbreviations, such as 'I'm' for 'I am' or 'we'll' for 'we will', are considered to be informal and are not used in official writing. Formal vocabulary choices tend to be longer, more complex words such as 'co-operate' rather than 'help' or 'convenient' rather than 'easy'.

4 Make a list of formal and informal word pairs.

5 Read the advert below. A few details that give clues to its register have been underlined. Annotate these with explanations of what they show.

MESSY PLAY DAY!

Hey! Don't sit at home whilst the kids grizzle around you!

Join us for a messy play day – and we'll even clean up afterwards.

Everything provided – just bring your budding artists!

11am Community Hall Friday 7th June

Apply the skills

Complete the following sentences, choosing words of the appropriate formality. Look out for the features listed in this topic to help you to identify the register of the sentence before you make your choice.

Practice task

6 To conceal her true identity, the woman _____ herself carefully.

    a) hid

    b) disguised

    c) dressed

    d) concealed

7 '_____the sun cream now!' Susan yelled. 'It's getting hot here.'

    a) I would like

    b) Pass

    c) Let me have

    d) May I have

8 The parents were _____, which inflamed the situation.

    a) irritated

    b) cheesed off

    c) irate

    d) grumpy

9 Candidates are _____ that interviews will begin at 9 a.m.

    a) told

    b) warned

    c) to note

    d) advised

10 Read the following passage. At whom is it directed?

> *The provision of a range of creative play equipment should be considered as research suggests this to be an excellent predictor of future creativity in language usage. Social workers Thomas, Martin and Burchell (2011) suggest that the availability of paper, crayons, play-figures and simple musical instruments can be used to raise future achievement significantly.*

    a) parents/carers

    b) playgroup leaders

    c) high school teachers

    d) parents

1.5 Identifying synonyms

Learn how to:

• *replace specific words with a synonym.*

Why are synonyms important?

In your exam, you may be asked to choose the correct synonym to complete sentences. Choosing the correct synonym for a word shows that you have considered and understood the precise meaning and desired impact of a sentence.

Remember

Be careful when selecting a replacement for a given word – even a word with a similar meaning may have a nuance that adds a hint of emotion that may not match the original. A similar word can also create the wrong register.

Building skills

Finding a synonym when you're not sure of the meaning of the original word

You can use the four-step approach you studied in Topic 1.1 to work out the literal meaning of the word for which you are being asked to find a replacement.

Read the following extract.

> *Trade winds bring steady sea breezes in to the Caribbean from the north-east all year round. These temper the heat of the rays of the sun, so the weather in the Windward Islands will always feel milder than that in the Leewards and the north-eastern sides of most islands will see milder temperatures than the south-west corners.*

Imagine you have been asked to find the synonym for 'temper' in line 2. You are given the following choices:

    a)   bad mood   **b)**   adjust   **c)**   weaken   **d)**   cool

You may never have seen or heard the word 'temper' before in this context.

Apply Step 1, which is to cover the word. You may think that a good word to fit the space would be 'adjust'.

Test this understanding with Step 2, which is to look at the rest of the sentence or text.

For Step 3, look at the sentence structure and ask yourself what sort of word it is (noun, verb, adjective, adverb). This should help you to identify likely choices in the possible answers you are shown. Look at the annotations below, which show how your thoughts might develop as you go through Steps 2 and 3.

> Step 2: The winds seem to make the heat of the sun less intense. Does 'temper' mean reduce or lessen?

Trade winds bring steady sea breezes in to the Caribbean from the north-east all year-round. These temper the heat of the rays of the sun, so the weather in the Windward Island will always feel milder than that in the Leewards...

> Step 3: Is this a verb? It seems to be, as the subject is the winds and they do something to the sun.

Step 4 is to think of similar words that might help. For example, you may have heard people talk about tempered steel – a type of metal that has been processed to change its strength. This could help you to consider the idea of the wind reducing the heat of the sun and lead you to the conclusion that 'adjust' is the correct word.

Apply the skills

Practice task

1 Find a synonym for the underlined word in this sentence.
Aruba's weather stays <u>moderate</u>, however, due to a constant ocean breeze.

   a) mild   **c)** undramatic

   b) tame   **d)** reasonable

2 Find a synonym for the underlined word in this sentence.
In contrast, Dominica has a <u>lush</u>, tropical, heavily precipitated forest; average rainfall in the interior can be over 300 inches per year.

   a) overgrown   **c)** luxurious

   b) beautiful   **d)** flourishing

3 Find a synonym for the underlined word in this sentence.
While weather patterns <u>vary</u> from island to island in the Caribbean, the one thing that is consistent about Caribbean weather is its year-round beauty.

   a) change

   b) are unreliable

   c) range

   d) are unpredictable

1.6 Identifying antonyms

Learn how to:

- *find antonyms for a given word.*

Why are antonyms important?

You may be asked to choose the correct antonym to go with words given in complete sentences in your exam. Choosing the correct antonym for a word shows that you have thought about and understood the precise meaning and desired impact of a sentence.

Building skills

Finding an antonym when you are not sure of the meaning of the original word

You can use the same process to identify an antonym as you did to find the synonym. When you have worked out the literal meaning of the word, add an extra step and find a word that means the opposite.

Read the following extract.

> *The weather is <u>milder</u> today even though a storm is supposed to be passing by sometime soon. The sun isn't quite as harsh and the winds are hardly moving the palm fronds as I look out of my window past the shutters and down to the still sea. With any luck I'll be able to get out and fish for a while before any trouble begins.*

Find an antonym of the word 'milder' in the extract above. Choose from:

- **a)** harsher
- **b)** hotter
- **c)** wilder
- **d)** more severe

Here is an example of how you might jot down down your thoughts around the text as you work through the steps to find an antonym for 'milder'.

Step 1: If I obscure this word then I think a word to describe the quality of the weather is needed. Could it be hot or cool?	Step 2: Read around the gap: In the sentences that follow it mentions the weather having changed, which makes me think that the word describes a change of some kind.

The weather is <u>milder</u> today even though a storm is supposed to be passing by sometime soon. The sun isn't quite as harsh and the winds are hardly moving the palm fronds as I look out of my window past the shutters and down to the still sea. With any luck I'll be able to get out and fish for a while before any trouble begins.

<table>
<tr><td>Step 3: Consider the sentence structure: 'milder' may mean the weather after a storm, which is usually calm.</td><td>Step 4: Think of similar words. I have heard the word 'mild' used to describe tastes that are not too strong or spicy.</td></tr>
</table>

Step 5: I think that 'milder' describes calmer weather after the storm. I am now thinking that either option a) or c) would be an antonym for it. b) is too specific about temperature.

Practice task

1   What is an antonym for 'still' as used in the extract above? Choose from the following:

   a)   moving

   b)   undulating

   c)   travelling

   d)   fidgety

Write down your thoughts, as you follow the five steps.

Remember

You may also need to match the register of the rest of the sentence.

Revision tip

Pick ten words at random every day and work out their antonyms.

Apply the skills

Practice task

2   Find four antonyms for the underlined word in this sentence. Then show how you would decide which one is most appropriate.

   Aruba's weather stays <u>moderate</u>, however, due to a constant ocean breeze.

3   Find four antonyms for the underlined word in this sentence. Then show how you would decide which one is most appropriate.

   In contrast, Dominica has a <u>lush</u>, tropical, heavily precipitated forest; average rainfall in the interior can be over 300 inches per year.

4   Find four antonyms for the underlined word in this sentence. Then show how you would decide which one is most appropriate.

   While weather patterns <u>vary</u> from island to island in the Caribbean, the one thing that is consistent about Caribbean weather is its year-round beauty.

1.7 Identifying clichés and idioms

Learn how to:

• *recognise clichés and idioms.*

Why are clichés and idioms important?

You may be asked to identify sentences that contain **clichés** or **idioms**. You may also be asked to identify the use of informal language, of which idioms and clichés are a feature.

> *Key terms*
>
> *cliché: an unoriginal expression that has lost its effectiveness through overuse*
>
> *idiom: a well-known phrase or wise saying, sometimes involving a metaphor that may not be easy to understand*

Building skills

Identifying idioms

Look out for phrases that do not seem to be logical or to make sense. Often there is a **metaphor** at the heart of an idiom, but it is not always easy to work out what the comparison is or why it is being used. For example, 'I smell a rat' means that you suspect something is not right.

> *Key term*
>
> *metaphor: a comparison in which one thing is said to actually be another*

1 Work out what these idioms mean.

   a) *She's a thorn in my side.*

   b) *I've got cold feet about this.*

   c) *I'm all ears!*

Identifying clichés

Look out for sentences or phrases that you have heard many times. Also identify phrases that make generalizations rather than comment on a specific moment – for example, 'absence makes the heart grow fonder', rather than 'he missed her so badly nothing could stop him glancing over at her chair every few minutes'.

> Remember
>
> A cliché can also be an idiom, but it is usually an expression that is particularly overused or slightly too general for the context.

2 Explain why each of the following is a cliché.

  a) *It's a win-win situation.*

  b) *That jigsaw is a piece of cake.*

  c) *We must draw a line in the sand.*

3 Which of the sentences below contain a cliché or idiom?

  a) *Who are the hot favourites this year?*

  b) *Life was difficult – but she would just have to take it one day at a time.*

  c) *She wanted the ground to open up and swallow her.*

  d) *You're barking up the wrong tree!*

  e) *He pulled the wool over my eyes!*

  f) *The pilot was confident; he had an ace up his sleeve.*

  g) *'All hands on deck!' shouted Mum as the delivery arrived.*

  h) *The sun shone like a fireball in the sky.*

  i) *I scrabbled at the wrapping, all fingers and thumbs today.*

  j) *My Gran always said not to air my dirty laundry in public.*

  k) *I hope they don't judge a book by its cover because I look terrible today!*

  l) *It's raining cats and dogs.*

  m) *Just turn left and, Bob's your uncle, you're there.*

4 Rewrite each of the phrases from Item 3 in a more original way.

Why are idioms and clichés sometimes inappropriate?

Sometimes idioms and clichés introduce a visual image that clashes with the literal meaning being described. For example:

John was so scared of the dog that it was as if the cat had got his tongue.

The idiom 'the cat had got his tongue' means he was unable to speak, but in this case the word 'cat' clashes with 'dog' and makes this choice of idiom inappropriate.

Idioms and clichés may also be inappropriate if they suggest a light-heartedness or lack of thought. For example, if a competitor is seriously injured in a race but still finishes it, the commentator would not use the cliché 'All's well that ends well', as it sounds insensitive to the injured competitor.

Apply the skills

5 The following sentences contain inappropriate use of idiom or cliché. Identify the inappropriate phrase in each sentence and explain why it would be best avoided.

  a) *It has been the day from hell for everyone at the funeral home.*

  b) *The nanny said that completing the crossword was like taking candy from a baby.*

  c) *You could cut the air with a knife when the twins were around.*

  d) *Reaching this trial verdict is as easy as pie for the jury!*

1.8 Recognising redundancies

Learn how to:

• *recognise redundancy.*

Why is being able to recognise and avoid redundancy important?

In the exam, you may be asked to identify sentences that contain **redundancy**.

Building skills

Recognising redundancy in a text

To identify examples of redundancy in a text:

• Pay attention to **nouns phrases** that are a combination of two words, such as 'free gift' or 'unconfirmed rumour'.

• Look for sentences with a second clause that seems to repeat the meaning of the first, such as, 'The parents cried as they watched the race, and they wept as the students ran.'

If you are unsure whether you have found a redundant phrase, ask yourself what each of the words mean and whether they share any definitions. If they do, then you may have found an example.

Remember

Writers use repetition of concepts to make their writing more memorable and persuasive. This means that the redundancy is often intentional and effective. Ask yourself whether the sentence is intended to have **rhetorical** impact, or whether any new information is included.

Key terms

redundancy: when more than one word is used even though the meaning is already clearly made by the first word (e.g. 'an added bonus')

noun phrase: a noun that is modified by additional information, often adjectives (e.g. 'hollow eye-sockets')

rhetorical: written or spoken to produce an effect rather than to convey information

1. Read the following paragraph. Identify at least five redundant phrases.

> *When I got home from shopping I realised that I had purchased a variety of different items but had not obtained the most important, vital thing: yoghurt. It was absolutely essential that I had some as I had intended to combine together some fresh fruit and yoghurt to make a delicious tasty dessert for dinner. How had I managed to forget the most critically important ingredient. Without it the final result would not be as good and I was mentally planning where I could get some, while at the same time dreading another trip out.*

2. Which of the following sentences contain an example of redundancy?

 a) *We need to eliminate this virus in our homes, our residences, our havens!*

 b) *It is impossible to complete such a difficult jigsaw.*

 c) *I scoured the internet for any evidence of my past history.*

 d) *The sun scorched the daisies, devouring, consuming them with its heat.*

 e) *I believe that they entered the home under false pretences.*

 f) *Some of the graduating students, who were ecstatic with their results, were very happy.*

 g) *We were doubtful about the agent's motives.*

 h) *James asked quietly whether he could discreetly leave the meeting as he had an appointment.*

 i) *The round moon shone in the sky.*

 j) *Sitting alone, she was by herself as the record played.*

3. Rewrite each sentence in a more efficient way.

Apply the skills

Practice task

For each of the following sentences, select the option below that best describes each of them.

 a) The sentence is too wordy, that is, repetitive or contains redundancies.

 b) The sentence is acceptable as it stands.

 c) The sentence is incorrect grammatically.

 d) The sentence contains clichés or misused metaphors.

4 *Not one of the staff or employees knew the price.*

5 *Hatred for him bubbled in her like a gentle spring.*

6 *John threw the ball and it hit the earth with impact.*

7 *There was not a soul about, nobody to help her.*

Test yourself

Instructions: The original sentence in this section is followed by four sentences labelled a), b), c) and d). Choose the one NEAREST IN MEANING to the original sentence. Be sure to read all four options before you select your answer.

1   The raucous noise of the motorbike revving up was excruciating in the peacefulness of the early morning.

   a)   The noise of the motorbike starting was very loud.

   b)   The morning quiet emphasised how loud and unpleasant the noise of the motorbike starting was.

   c)   The motorbike engine disturbed the peace with its loud noise.

   d)   The horrible noise of the motorbike engine starting was even more painful in the quiet part of the day.

Instructions: Each sentence in this section has ONE underlined word. Choose from the four options the word that is nearest in meaning to the underlined word.

2   The gardener was an <u>insatiable</u> gossip and would talk about his clients all day if she encouraged him.

   a)   unrivalled

   b)   never satisfied

   c)   never ending

   d)   malicious

3   The children drank <u>copious</u> amounts of fizzy drinks during the journey and felt quite ill by the time they arrived.

a) small

b) expensive

c) unhealthy

d) considerable

Instructions: Each sentence in this section has ONE underlined word. Choose from the four options the word that is the closest opposite to the underlined word.

4   It is best to choose a breed of dog that <u>suits</u> your lifestyle and income, if you want one as a pet.

a) compliments

b) clashes with

c) contradicts

d) inhibits

5   She was extremely <u>fastidious</u> and insisted on having several sets of plates and cutlery to match every type of dish.

a) carefree

b) careless

c) careful

d) fussy

Instructions: Some of the following sentences are unacceptable because of inappropriate grammar, idiom or vocabulary. No sentence contains more than one inappropriate element.

Select the ONE underlined part that you feel is inappropriate and choose the appropriate letter A, B, C. If the sentence is acceptable as it stands, choose D.

6   It was only <u>raining cats and dogs,</u> <u>so</u> she didn't <u>need</u> an umbrella. <u>No error</u>
                      A   B   C   D

7   The cliff path was <u>very extremely dangerous</u> and <u>had claimed</u> one life already <u>that</u> year.
                              A   B   C

No error
  D

Where might you have gone wrong?

Item 1

b) is correct.

You may have chosen option a) or c) but these do not mention the effect of the timing of the bike's noise. Option d) does, but is not precise about it.

Item 2

b) is correct.

You may have thought that 'never ending' was an appropriate synonym, and it does express much of the meaning because it implies that the gossiping will not end. However, answer b) adds the notion of satisfaction, that the gossiping is a need that cannot be staunched and so is the closest alternative. It also suggests that the gossiping is fulfilling an appetite in the man as food or drink does, which adds an extra nuance.

Item 3

d) is correct.

You may have guessed as several of the words would certainly complete the sentence, however, only one suggests large quantities.

Item 4

b) is correct.

You may have got confused and chosen a synonym instead of an antonym. You may also have had difficulty choosing between b) and c), as both suggest opposition, which is an antonym for something 'suiting' someone. However, 'contradict' is more often used to suggest speech or logic, while 'clashes with' fits better with the idea of a pet and a lifestyle.

Item 5

a) is correct.

You may have had difficulty deciding between a) and b), but the nuance attached to 'careless' is a lack of thought verging on laziness or intentional lack of thought, whereas 'carefree' suggests an awareness but lack of tension, which is a more appropriate antonym.

Item 6

a) is correct.

You may have remembered that this is an idiom used to describe rain, but as it indicates when rain is very heavy, it cannot be used here and is an error.

Item 7

a) is correct.

'Very' and 'extremely' both suggest degree and do not need to be used side by side, which means that (A) is an example of redundancy and poor grammar.

Chapter 2 Understanding meaning: Looking at grammar and syntax

2.1 Introducing grammar – parts of speech

Learn how to:

- *identify different word classes*
- *understand grammatical terminology and use it appropriately.*

Why is understanding grammar important?

In your exam, you may be asked to identify grammatical errors in writing. To do this well, you need to know how language works. Understanding the correct terminology will enable you to discuss how sentences are put together and to improve the accuracy of your own writing.

Building skills

Words belong to different classes, also known as the parts of speech, which relate to their functions in a sentence. Some words can have more than one function, while others belong to just one class. There are eight word classes: noun, verb, adjective (and **determiner**), adverb, pronoun, preposition and conjunction.

> *Key term*
>
> **determiner:** *a word that helps determine the nature of a noun or noun phrase; determiners can be the definite or indefinite articles 'the' or 'a' or may be possessive, such as 'her' or 'their'*

1 Read this line from a nonsense poem:

' 'Twas <u>brillig</u>, and the <u>slithy toves</u> did <u>gyre</u> and <u>gimble</u> in the <u>wabe</u>.'

For each underlined word, write down three real words that could replace it. You may not know what the nonsense words mean, but you should be able to work out what *type* of word it is by looking at its relationship with other words in the sentence. For example, you probably would not try to replace 'brillig' with a verb like 'walked'.

Identifying word classes

- **Nouns** can be people, places or things. Nouns often have a plural form indicated by an 's': 'tables', 'cats', 'beaches'.
- **Pronouns** are used to replace a noun or a noun phrase: 'I waved to <u>the small boy</u>'/'I waved to <u>him</u>.'
- **Adjectives** describe or add more detail to nouns: 'This is my <u>lucky</u> coin.'
- **Adverbs** add detail to verbs or sentences: '<u>Luckily</u> she arrived on time.'

- **Verbs** describe actions, thoughts or processes. They change their form according to a person and time: 'She <u>ate</u> the banana.' 'They <u>eat</u> bananas.'
- **Prepositions** indicate where objects are or the relationships between them: '<u>under</u> the table', '<u>between</u> the houses', '<u>in</u> the beginning'. They are helpful in creating noun phrases that add information.
- **Conjunctions** are used to join items, phrases or whole clauses: 'They bought mangoes, pineapples <u>and</u> pomegranates'; 'She went home early <u>because</u> she was tired.'

> Common nouns combine with determiners such as 'the', 'a', 'that' and 'some': 'the book', 'some rice'. Proper nouns such as Jamil, Port-au-Prince and Paige do not combine with determiners.

2 Identify the word class of 'slithy', 'toves' and 'gyre' in the line from the poem above.

3 Look at the pairs of sentences below. What are the effects of the underlined words?

a) *This is <u>the</u> book for you if you enjoy adventure and mystery.*

This is <u>a</u> book for you if you enjoy adventure and mystery.

b) *The sound of gulls calling echoed <u>around</u> the beach, as the large birds swooped <u>over</u> people's heads.*

The sound of gulls calling echoed <u>across</u> the beach, as the large birds swooped <u>towards</u> people's heads.

Apply the skills

In each of the items below, identify the class of the underlined words in each sentence, selecting from the choices given.

Practice task

4 *The moon <u>swam</u> in the ocean of night.*

a) noun
b) verb
c) adjective
d) pronoun

5 *'Run!' he yelled, jabbing his hand at the man <u>behind</u> them.*

a) preposition
b) adverb
c) conjunction
d) pronoun

6 *Her stomach churned at the <u>prospect</u>.*

a) noun
b) verb
c) adjective
d) pronoun

7 *The boys stared. <u>Eventually,</u> the taller one let his eyes fall for a second. 'OK,' he said.*

a) preposition
b) adverb
c) conjunction
d) pronoun

2.2 Introducing syntax and structure

Learn how to:

- *organise texts using sentences and paragraphs*
- *identify problems with conjunctions and word order.*

Why are syntax and structure important?

For a text to make sense, it must be constructed logically. In the exam, you may be asked to identify sentences with errors in their construction.

In English, phrases and clauses can be linked in different ways to prioritise different parts of a sentence and give slightly different meanings. In the exam, you may be asked to interpret texts, to show that you are able to infer writers' meanings based on the choices they have made in constructing texts. Being able to analyse **syntax** and **structure** will help you do this.

> *Key terms*
>
> **syntax:** *the arrangement of words and phrases to create well-formed sentences*
>
> **structure:** *the way that writing is arranged; in the case of poetry, the order of words, the way they are punctuated and organised into lines*

Building skills

There are three main types of sentence. An example of each is shown below.

Simple sentence:

Simple sentences make strong statements [1].

[1] **main clause**

Compound sentence:

Compound sentences are formed from two (or more) main clauses [1] and [2] allow you to present two ideas of equal value [3].

[1] main clause

[2] conjunction

[3] main clause (note that the subject is the same as in the first clause but is not repeated)

Complex sentence:

Complex sentences, including one or more subordinate clauses [2], allow you to add detail to a main clause [1].

[1] main clause

[2] **subordinate clause** (in this case an embedded clause, inserted into the main clause)

Sometimes punctuation is used to join clauses in compound and complex sentences, but you can also use conjunctions. Be careful when using conjunctions and ensure they work properly in the sentence.

1 In which three of the sentences below is there a poor choice of conjunction? For each one, choose a more appropriate conjunction.

    a) *I came to your summer fair yesterday although I am disgusted with how it was run.*

    b) *He ran across the playground because he had heard a scream from behind the shed.*

    c) *They could have gone to the festival except he had mentioned it sooner.*

    d) *I wish I had done that as I would definitely have loved it.*

    e) *He wanted to get everything sorted today, whereas unfortunately people just kept getting in the way.*

Sentences can also be categorised by their function or purpose. The table below describes some sentence functions.

Function	Description	Examples
statement (declarative)	Requires a subject (pronoun or noun phrase), which generally comes before the verb.	*Although it's late, there is still time to act.* *There are too many suffering for us to ignore them.*
command (imperative)	Has no subject directly stated ('you' is understood); usually begins with a verb.	*Act now to obtain your free copy.* *Click below for more information.*
question (interrogative)	Often starts with a **wh word** or a verb; the main verb may come before the subject.	*How do you make bread?* *Is it time to go yet?*
exclamation (exclamatory)	Not a complete sentence.	*Homework is a total nightmare!* *Not on your life!*

2 Three of the sentences below contain errors in phrasing or punctuation. Identify the sentences and correct the errors.

a) *To what extent is Shakespeare still relevant to the modern world.*

b) *It is possible that people might disagree on this issue for decades to come.*

c) *Why we still arguing about this same point?*

d) *What a terrible waste of a day that was.*

e) *Please clear up this mess.*

Building knowledge of paragraphing

3 Which of these factors are reasons to start a new **paragraph**?

a) You are starting to write about a different topic or sub-topic.

b) You have written ten lines.

c) You have not started a new paragraph for a while.

d) You are writing about a different time.

e) You are writing about a different place.

f) You are writing about a different person or using a different speaker.

> *Key term*
>
> *paragraph: a distinct section in a piece of writing that signals a change of idea or point being made, change of person or perspective or a change of time or location*

Look at this example of the beginning of an argument text (an opinion article) and the comments on each paragraph.

Paragraph 1	Comment
School uniforms should be a thing of the past. They belong in a dusty old cupboard, along with the cane and chalk. Although many would argue otherwise, uniforms do not contribute to order, but cause discipline problems.	The opening paragraph clearly sets out the writer's views in a general way, while also setting the tone of the article by using strong terms and seeking to engage the reader directly.
Paragraph 2	**Comment**
How do they cause discipline problems? *Having strict rules about clothing leads to students breaking these rules in a multitude of ways.* Ties tied too loosely, shirts not tucked in, skirts of the wrong length: all little rebellions against the uniform code.	The second paragraph focuses specifically on one aspect of the argument, and offers evidence for that claim.
Paragraph 3	**Comment**
Furthermore, these little rebellions lead to unnecessary clashes between teachers and students and waste class time. Many lessons in schools that are strict on uniform begin with a series of instructions or even sanctions related to uniform rules.	The third paragraph picks up that evidence and develops a further argument from it.

Each paragraph in a text focuses on one idea. The **topic sentence** expresses that idea clearly, while the rest of the paragraph offers evidence or further details.

In all extended writing, it is important that paragraphs are linked and follow on logically from each other. This is an important way of achieving **cohesion** in your writing. Cohesive devices include:

- pronouns linking to previous statements: 'the problem is simple...Although it seems...'

- consistent **verb tenses**: 'the problem is simple... Although it seems...'

- conjunctions and adverbials making links: 'the problem is simple...Although it seems...'.

> *Key terms*
>
> *topic sentence: the sentence that sums up the main idea of a paragraph; the topic sentence is often, but not always, at the start of the paragraph*
>
> *cohesion: the successful linking of ideas in a text so that it flows well*
>
> *verb tense: defines when an action is happening (e.g. present tense: 'I arrive at 11 a.m.'; past tense: 'I arrived at 11 a.m.'; future tense: 'I will arrive at 11 a.m.'*

4 Look at the table above containing the first three paragraphs of an article about school uniform. Which words, phrases and ideas provide connections from one paragraph to the next?

5 Rewrite the following paragraph to make it clearer and more consistent.

> *She paused for breath, looking around to check where she is now. Suddenly she realises she didn't know this place at all; she's never been there before. Panic gripped her and she didn't know what to do next. Who could help her? Glancing around, she sees a woman with a small child and decides to ask her for directions.*

Apply the skills

> **Practice task**
>
> **6** Select the option a), b), c) or d) that BEST describes each of the sentences below.
>
> **i)** The necklace glittered with a rainbow of brightly coloured jewels.
>
> **ii)** He was convinced that he would never understand the explanation although it was highly complicated.
>
> **iii)** I am writing to ask why your company does not include details of work experience opportunities on your website?
>
> **a)** The sentence is too wordy – that is, repetitive or contains redundancies.
>
> **b)** The sentence is acceptable as it stands.
>
> **c)** The sentence is incorrect grammatically.
>
> **d)** The sentence contains clichés or misused metaphors.

2.3 Understanding pronouns

Learn how to:

* *identify and avoid pronoun errors.*

Why are pronouns important?

Pronouns are often used incorrectly because colloquial speech has different patterns from formal written Standard English. In the exam, you may be asked to identify sentences that contain grammatical errors, which might include errors in the use of pronouns.

Building skills

Subject pronouns are usually used before a verb, when the subject is carrying out the action.

1 Copy the subject pronoun grid below and fill in the empty boxes.

first person	singular	to refer to just yourself	I
first person	plural	to refer to a group that includes you	
second person		to refer to another person whom you are talking to/ addressing directly	you
	plural	to refer to a group of people whom you are talking to/ addressing directly	you
	singular masculine	to refer to a single male person you are talking about	he
third person		to refer to a single female person you are talking about	she
third person	singular neutral	to refer to a single thing or animal you are talking about	it
third person		to refer to a group you are talking about (rather than to)	they

2 Choose a subject pronoun to fill in each of the blanks in the following statements.

    a) *The man turned towards them…looked like…wanted to speak but didn't know what to say.*

    b) *Levi, Brianna and I are coming this afternoon…will be arriving at about three.*

    c) *Jodi, Lisa and Leanne all have driving tests next month…could all be on the road soon.*

Object pronouns are used when the pronoun is receiving the action of the verb, directly or indirectly:

* First person singular: 'I have a new phone. My mum gave it to me.'
* First person plural: 'We have a new pet rabbit. Our mum bought it for us.'
* Second person: 'You have a new phone. Did your mum give it to you?'
* Third person singular masculine: 'He has a new phone. His mum gave it to him.'
* Third person singular feminine: 'She has a new phone. Her mum gave it to her.'
* Third person plural: 'They have a new pet rabbit. Their mum bought it for them.'

3 Identify the sentences below that have pronoun errors and correct the errors.

   a) *He ran across the road.*

   b) *Him ate the chicken really fast.*

   c) *I saw she yesterday.*

   d) *You can't do that.*

   e) *Them are going to the party with us.*

Sometimes other words get in the way and make it more difficult to tell whether there is an error. Look at this sentence:

Between you and I, something should be done about that mess at the end of the street.

This is incorrect, because the preposition 'between' means that both pronouns should be in the object form: 'you' and 'me'.

Apply the skills

Practice task

4 Select the option a), b), c) or d) that BEST describes each of the sentences below.

   i) *Jamie's mother couldn't open the jar so she asked he to do it for her.*

   ii) *Paulette asked to go to the party with Justine. They would not be home too late, so him agreed that they could go.*

   iii) *She stared at them, really envying they clothes.*

   a) The sentence uses the subject pronoun incorrectly.

   b) The sentence is acceptable as it stands.

   c) The sentence uses the object pronoun incorrectly.

   d) The sentence fails to use the possessive determiner.

2.4 Understanding verbs and tenses

Learn how to:
- *use verb phrases accurately*
- *identify verb errors.*

Why are verbs important?

The verb is the core of a sentence. It indicates a state, action, thought or process. In your exam, you need to use verbs precisely. You may need to decipher verbs in a piece of writing, to identify errors and explain meaning.

Building skills

Sentences must contain a **finite verb** to make sense. In a multi-verb phrase, one will be a **main verb**. This tells you what action or process is happening. Any other verbs will be **auxiliary verbs**, helping to indicate the tense. In this case, the auxiliary verb is finite – it agrees with the subject.

(She) was [1] leaving [2].   *(She) was [2] leaving [1].*

(She) left [1].   *(She) left [1].*

[1] finite verb   [1] main verb

[2] non-finite verb   [2] auxiliary verb

Key terms

finite verb: a verb that has been conjugated for tense and subject agreement (and is therefore limited in terms of time and person it can refer to)

main verb: in a multi-verb phrase, the verb that reveals what action or process is happening (e.g. 'She was <u>leaving</u>.')

auxiliary verb: a verb that helps indicate the tense of another verb (e.g. 'was' in 'She <u>was</u> leaving.')

non-finite verb: a verb that is not conjugated to agree with a subject; infinitives (e.g. 'to eat', 'to dance') and participles (e.g. '<u>Dancing</u> his way to the table…') are non-finite

---

1 Which of the examples underlined below is not a finite verb?

    a) *The sun gloriously <u>shining</u> in the sky.*

    b) *The sun <u>shone</u> gloriously over the ocean.*

    c) *Over the ocean <u>shines</u> the sun.*

Remember

Common errors include:

- missing out parts of the verb 'to be' ('I am', 'you are', 'he is', 'she is', 'we are', 'they are')
- missing verb endings (i.e. not 'agreeing' the verb with its subject, particularly for third person verbs in the present tense).

2 Look at the two versions of each sentence below. Which version of each is correct?

a) *He talks so quickly*   *He talk so quickly.*

b) *She is a pretty girl.*   *She a pretty girl*

c) *There be many problems.*   *There are many problems.*

Building an understanding of tenses

The table below gives examples of some of the main verb tenses.

simple present	*I jump, he jumps*	These tenses use a finite form of the main verb, i.e. the main verb shows tense and subject agreement.
simple past	*I jumped, she jumped*	
present continuous	*I am jumping, he is jumping*	These tenses use a finite form of the auxiliary verb together with the main present participle.
past continuous	*I was jumping, she was jumping*	
present perfect	*I have jumped, he has jumped*	These tenses use a finite form of the auxiliary together with the main past participle.
past perfect	*I had jumped, she had jumped*	

3 Which of these clauses can go together? Use the verbs they contain to guide you.

a) *If I had more money,*   *I could have done more interesting things.*

b) *If I had had more money,*   *I will do more interesting things.*

c) *If I get more money,*   *I could do more interesting things.*

Apply the skills

Practice task

4 Look at the following text. Which of the three options below is NEAREST IN MEANING to the original sentence? Be sure to read all three choices before you select your answer.

> *Susan did not attend the prom despite weeks of planning because she had had an argument with Saskia and Sharmaine with whom she had planned to go.*

a) Susan was unable to go to the prom due to an argument with Saskia and Sharmaine, whom she was planning to go with.

b) Saskia and Sharmaine, who had promised to go to the prom with Susan, argued with her so that she would not go to the prom which they had been planning for weeks.

c) Susan would have attended the prom, as she had been planning to for weeks, if she had not argued with Saskia and Sharmaine, who had promised to go with her.

2.5 Understanding prepositions

Learn how to:
- *. use prepositions effectively*
- *identify errors with prepositions.*

Why are prepositions important?

Prepositions – words like 'to', 'at', 'on', 'in', 'under' and 'across', help make meanings precise. In your exam, you will need to use language accurately yourself, but you may also be asked to identify errors in the use of prepositions.

Building skills

1 Identify the prepositions in the following paragraph.

> *Mrs Shelley works in the accounting department at Fitzgerald & Millers, the law firm in town. Her walk there every morning, along busy roads, takes 20 minutes. She always goes to the coffee shop next door to get her lunch, as she says their coffee is the finest on the island.*

Remember

Pay attention to the words *around* prepositions. For example, a pronoun after a preposition is more likely to be an object than a subject: 'Mum gave it to me/him/her' *not* 'Mum gave it to I/he/she'.

2 Which of the following examples use prepositions inaccurately or have errors in the use of other words because of prepositions?

  a) *He goes to school by foot every day, even though it is several miles.*

  b) *The students divided the work equally between them.*

  c) *He looked far too much like a troublemaker, between you and I.*

  d) *That film was in the TV last week as well, I'm sure of it.*

  e) *Thank you for your order from our store. You can check the status of your order by visiting our site and logging into your account at any time.*

  f) *Put that down carefully – remember, it was we Gran gave that to and we should look after it.*

Prepositions can be confusing because they do not always follow the same pattern and their literal meaning may make them seem wrong when in fact they are correct.

3 Which prepositions are generally used in Standard English to convey the following?

  a) travel, e.g…foot/the bus/the train/the plane (but…bus/train/plane)

  b) media/technology, e.g…the radio/TV/internet/phone

4 Which of the following 'ask' sentences demonstrate the correct use (or non-use) of prepositions?

  a) *I asked to my manager to give me a raise.*

  b) *I am asking for a large pond to be built in the community garden.*

  c) *I asked my husband to take the bin out five times before he finally did.*

  d) *I tried asking about the exam dates but it was no good.*

5 What is the difference in meaning between the following pairs of sentences?

  a) *The bird was killed with a rock.*   *The bird was killed by a rock.*

  b) *I went to Grand Lake Etang last year.*   *I went into Grand Lake Etang last year.*

  c) *He ran across the park.*   *He ran around the park.*

Apply the skills

Practice task

6 Look at the following sentences. Do they contain inappropriate grammar, idiom or vocabulary or are they acceptable as they stand? No sentence contains more than one error.

Select the ONE underlined part that you feel is inappropriate and choose the appropriate letter A, B or C. If the sentence is acceptable as it stands, choose D.

  a) *Travelling <u>by</u> bus is an excellent choice <u>of</u> transport, which will support both the*

       A   B

  environment and health if combined <u>to</u> some walking. <u>No error</u>

                                  C   D

  b) *The importance <u>of</u> daily practice cannot be stressed enough, since many thousands of people*

                    A

  are experiencing benefits all <u>among</u> the world and introducing calm <u>into</u> their lives. <u>No error</u>

                              B   C   D

  c) *The sub-committee had been discussing <u>to</u> the problem all morning and still were yet <u>to</u>*

                                          A   B

  reach an agreement, despite people bringing <u>up</u> many valid and interesting points. <u>No error</u>

                                            C   D

2.6 Understanding punctuation

Learn how to:

- *develop your skills with punctuation*
- *identify errors in punctuation.*

Why is punctuation important?

Correct punctuation is a key part of accurate communication. In the exam, you will not only need to punctuate your own writing correctly, you may also be asked to identify errors of punctuation in a piece of writing.

Building skills

How would you rate your confidence with punctuation? Use the table below to help you decide how you can improve.

Level of confidence	Your revision priority
I find punctuation confusing/have never really understood it properly.	Check and practise the basic rules (**commas**, **full stops**, **apostrophes**, **question marks** and **exclamation marks**, then speech punctuation).
I know the basics when I think about it, but I make some mistakes in my writing.	Remind yourself to double check punctuation when writing. Allow time for this and specifically look at punctuation. Revise punctuation rules just to make sure.
I am fine with most punctuation, but am not sure about more complicated usage.	Check and practise rules for speech punctuation, **colons**, **semicolons**, **brackets** and **dashes**.
Punctuation is not something I worry about as I usually get it right.	Check the activities here, but prioritise other areas in your revision.

The table below shows where punctuation marks can be used.

at the end of a sentence	full stop, question mark, exclamation mark	Getting punctuation right is very important. Can you help? Just do it!
inside speech marks	comma, full stop, question mark, exclamation mark	'I'm leaving now,' he said. He said, 'I'm leaving now.' Are you going now?' he asked. 'I'm leaving now!' he exclaimed.
with a list	comma, semicolon, colon	sun, sea and sand the shifting sands; the unrelenting sun and the crowds of tourists I've got everything, I think: purse, keys and phone.
to separate phrases or clauses in a sentence	comma, semicolon, colon, dash, brackets	To be on time, try catching an earlier bus. I think, and I could be wrong, that we should not be doing this. It was the hottest summer on record; I had had enough. I've eaten it all: everything that was left for me. I think – and I could be wrong – that we should not be doing this. I think (and I could be wrong) that we should not be doing this.

1   Write an explanation of the rules for at least one of the rows in the table above. For example, for the first row you could write:

A full stop is used at the end of a statement. A question mark must be used at the end of a question and an exclamation mark at the end of an exclamation.

Remember

Apostrophes are used to show either omission or possession with a noun, but never with a pronoun – e.g. Joanne's but not her's.

2   Write out each of these sentences, choosing the correct option from the two alternatives given.

    a)   *The goat hurt it's/its leg.*

    b)   *Joelle and Deneice both play for the local girls'/girl's soccer team.*

    c)   *He wouldn't/would'nt have gone if she hadn't/had'nt sent him 17 texts.*

Apply the skills

Practice task

3   Select the option a), b), c) or d) that BEST describes each of the sentences below.

    i)   *I am busy with revision; so I cannot go out tonight.*

    ii)   *She stared at him in horror. 'Surely you cannot be serious' she said.*

    iii)   *The two things I know about this issue are: it is a problem for families and it is getting worse.*

    iv)   *The politician's argument is clear; he is not going to do anything about it.*

    a)   A punctuation mark is missing.

    b)   The sentence is acceptable as it stands.

    c)   The punctuation is incorrect.

    d)   There is one too many punctuation marks.

2.7 Developing spelling skills

Learn how to:
- *develop your skills in spelling*
- *identify errors in spelling.*

Why is spelling important?

Your spelling creates an impression of you, so it is important to spell accurately in your exam. You may also be asked to identify misspelled words in a piece of writing.

Building skills

You may feel like your spelling ability is fixed by now – people say things like 'I am a poor speller', as if it is something you *are*, not something you *do*. However, spelling is a skill that can be learned, practised and improved.

Revision tip

To practise your spelling skills, look for patterns in words when you are reading. All reading counts: advertising, food packets, internet articles (but beware of personal pages, which may themselves contain errors).

Here are some basic spelling rules:

- To make a noun ending in 'y' plural, change the 'y' to 'i' then add 'es', unless there is a vowel before the 'y' ('babies', 'delays'). The word 'monkey' is an exception to this.
- Most nouns ending in 'f' change to 'v' then add 'es' in the plural. Those ending in 'ff' just take an 's' ('calves', 'sniffs').
- Nouns ending in 's', 'ss', 'ch', 'x', 'z', 'ch' or 'sh', add 'es' in the plural ('foxes', 'businesses').
- When adding an ending that starts with a vowel (e.g. '-ing' or '-er') to a one-syllable word with a single vowel plus a consonant at the end (e.g. 'shop', but not 'book'), the consonant is doubled ('shopping', 'booking'). This also happens with two-syllable words when the stress falls on the second syllable ('begin' – 'beginner', 'occur' – 'occurring').
- Generally, drop the silent 'e' before adding endings beginning with a vowel ('hoping', 'imaginable'), unless the word ends in 'ce' or 'ge', thus keeping the sound soft ('outrageous').
- When adding suffixes to words ending in 'y', the 'y' generally changes to an 'i' ('happy' – 'happiness', 'greedy' – 'greedily').

1. Write eight sentences. Each sentence should use at least one of the words in the box below, paired with one of the endings. Make sure you apply the appropriate spelling rule from the list above.

Words
adventure   beauty   big   box   bus   cliff   company   courage   difficulty
disaster   dry   faith   force   knife   large   manage   notice   refer
sense   sit   tall   trolley   watch   wolf   write

Endings
-able   -er   -est   -ful   -ible   -ing   -ish
-ly   -ous   -s

2. Which of the following sentences contain errors in commonly confused words? Correct these errors.

a) *If there not going to check every single one, their is no point checking any.*

b) *I do not know why you're going over this again.*

c) *If only he'd listened to me, he two would have avoided this.*

Apply the skills

Practice task

3. In the following sentences, one of the words may be misspelled. Choose the misspelled word from the three options A, B or C. If no word is misspelled, choose option D.

a) *Having carefully <u>concidered</u> all the requirements of her boss, the <u>secretary</u> was confident*
    A
    B

she had selected <u>appropriate</u> accommodation for the upcoming conference. <u>No error</u>
    C
    D

b) *I am afraid that I can no longer <u>concern</u> myself with your requests for <u>advise</u>. Please seek*
    A
    B

<u>encouragement</u> elsewhere. <u>No error</u>
    C
    D

c) *The school's <u>biennial</u> celebrations will commence with the founder's concert. We*
    A

<u>anticipate</u> a high level of performance this year following the highly <u>successful</u> offerings
    B
    C

earlier in the term. <u>No error</u>
    D

d) *In light of the current <u>disaster</u>, it would be <u>innappropriate</u> to <u>solicit</u> further donations for*
    A
    B
    C

any other region. <u>No error</u>
    D

Test yourself

Instructions: The original sentences in this section are followed by four sentences labelled a), b), c) and d). Choose the one NEAREST IN MEANING to the original sentence. Be sure to read all four options before you select your answer.

1 He might have been able to leave the party early, if he had not felt compelled to talk to everyone after spending so long talking to people at the start.

   a) He did not want to leave the party until he had spoken to everyone, even though it took him a great deal of time to get around to them all.

   b) He spent so much time talking to people at the start of the party that he then felt he had to talk to everyone. This made him unable to leave the party early.

   c) Because he spoke to so many people at the start of the party, he was unable to get away early.

   d) It was his duty to talk to everyone at the party and this made it unlikely for him to be able to leave early.

2 Despite how it appears on the news, many young people take an active interest in their country's politics.

   a) Politics is not interesting to young people, but there are some who care a lot about it.

   b) Although it does not seem exciting, young people should care about politics.

   c) Young people might care more about their country's politics if it looked better on the news.

   d) The news shows that not many young people care about politics, but this is not an accurate picture.

Instructions: Revise each of the following sentences according to the directions that follow it. You may delete or include words, but do not change the meaning of the original sentence. Look at the options a), b), c) and d) for the word or phrase that must be included in your revised sentence.

3 The children tried their hardest to complete every item in the mathematics exam in the time allotted, but were unable to do so.

   Begin the sentence with: *Despite trying their hardest…*

   a) can not

   b) would not be able to

   c) could not

   d) could not have

4 'It's an absolute disgrace,' Mr Mountjoy said. 'I've lived here all my life and have never seen such a mess.'

   Begin the sentence with: *Mr Mountjoy said that…*

   a) has not seen

   b) has never seen

   c) would never have seen

   d) had never seen

5   He hid the evidence because he wanted to avoid detention.

Substitute 'so that' for 'because'.

a)   he avoided

b)   he might avoid

c)   he avoids

d)   he will avoid

Instructions: Select the option a), b), c) or d) that BEST describes each of the sentences.

a)   The punctuation is incorrect.

b)   The sentence grammar is incorrect.

c)   The sentence is acceptable as it stands.

d)   There is one too many punctuation marks.

6   In my opinion, your decision to amend the plans are misguided because you have not considered the views of the residents.

7   The difficulties we are facing might have been avoided, if he has followed the instructions from the start.

8   Although many troubles lay ahead of them, the travellers strode bravely into the jungle, they were sure that together they could face anything.

9   Despite working all through the night, the clinician was unable to determine the cause of the outbreak and had to institute a quarantine with immediate effect.

Where you might have gone wrong

Item 1

b) is correct.

The secret to questions such as this is to untangle the meaning carefully. The instructions tell you to select the answer that is NEAREST IN MEANING, so it is clear that one will be more nearly like the first than the others and it is likely that they will all be quite similar, so it really is a process of elimination. You need to focus on the smaller words to check the precise meanings. For example, d) is probably the easiest to eliminate because of the word 'duty' – this implies it is somehow his job or responsibility to talk to everyone, which it does not seem to be. He 'felt compelled' in the original, which should tell you that in fact he was not compelled. This was just his own impression. So, a) and c) are closer to the original meaning than d), but b) covers all the main points and gives the same reason for his feeling he could not leave.

Item 2

d) is correct.

d) is the closest to the original meaning. a) is the next closest. b) and c) are opinions related to the topic, but they do not convey the same meaning.

> ### Remember
>
> In items like 1 and 2, look for the *closest* meaning.

Item 3

c) is the answer.

These questions require you to think through what the sentence would look like if you changed it as per the instructions. Often they will require changes in the verb, such as the tense or person, or they may require a preposition or pronoun change. The verb has to be 'can' rather than 'would' because of changing from 'to be able to'. It also has to be in the past tense, so c) is the only option.

Item 4

d) is the answer.

This question requires a shift from **direct speech** to **reported speech** and therefore, as well as moving from the **first person** to the **third person**, you would need to change from present to past tense. The full version would be something like: 'Mr Mountjoy said that it was an absolute disgrace. He had lived there all his life and had never seen a mess like it.'

> *Key terms*
>
> *direct speech: the actual words spoken by someone, indicated by use of speech marks*
>
> *reported speech: someone else's account of what was said, without speech marks*
>
> *first person: when a story is told or an account is given from the point of view of the person or people who had the experience (using 'I' or 'we')*
>
> *third person: when a story is told or an account is given from the point of view of a person relating the experiences of others (using 'he' or 'she')*

Item 5

b) is the answer.

This one requires 'might' to indicate that avoiding detention is something that he wants to happen, but it is not a definite outcome. 'Will' would be too certain and the use of 'avoid' on its own, in any tense, would also seem too predetermined.

Remember

For items like 4 and 5, try the sentence out in your mind first.

Item 6

b) is the answer.

This one is incorrect grammatically because the verb 'are' does not agree with its subject 'your decision'. It should be: '...your decision (to amend the plans) is...'.

Item 7

b) is the answer.

This is incorrect grammatically because the tenses between the two clauses do not match. The first clause begins in the present tense with 'the difficulties we are facing' but the focus is on 'might have been avoided' which is the past tense, so the conditional 'if' clause should match that with 'if he had followed the instructions'.

Item 8

a) is the answer.

Although all the words and agreements are correct, the second comma should not be there as there are two sentences. There should be a full stop before 'They were sure...' as you should not have a comma between main clauses.

Item 9

c) is the answer.

This sentence is acceptable as it stands.

Remember

For items like 5–9, make sure you read through the whole question carefully.

Chapter 3 Extracting information from information texts

3.1 Recognising facts and other types of information

Learn how to:

- *recognise a fact.*

Why is being able to work out what is factual important?

The Paper 1 exam will feature five types of writing. The third is informative writing and the last is a visual extract. Both are likely to contain **facts** that you may be asked to pick out. In questions on argumentative texts, you may be asked about uses or misuses of facts to support opinions.

> **Key term**
>
> **facts:** *pieces of information that can be proven with evidence*

Building skills

Identifying facts

Certain types of writing tend to be more factual than others. For example, informative texts rely on facts more than promotional or personal writing, which will have a specific (positive) angle.

To quickly identify facts in a piece of writing, look for:

- Information containing numbers, such as quantities or percentages: 'There are 60 per cent more snakes than people on the island.'

- Dates or times: 'The 26th of each month is the day of the highest number of car accidents in Georgetown.'

1 Read the text below, which is from a blog about hoax phone calls. Find four facts in the text.

Does your phone keep ringing yet, when you answer, there's no one there? 75 per cent of phone owners have reported this as an issue in a recent survey, commissioned by local telephone provider GreenRing.

If this sounds familiar to you, then whatever you do, don't ring back! While the number looks like an innocent three-digit area code for the Caribbean, it's actually a premium-rate line.

> *A key point about these calls is that they only ever let the phone ring once before disconnecting. This tells you that it's a robo caller on the other end of the line, not your long lost Auntie Betty. Apparently, you're 65 per cent more likely to return a missed call than you are to ring them if they leave a message.*

Being sure you have found a fact

The easiest way to check that you have identified a fact is to ask: 'How could it be proved?' This means thinking about who could prove it and/or with what kind of evidence.

Look at this sentence:

Pink Sands on Harbour Island is the prettiest beach in the Caribbean.

The statement sounds very definite, but the point cannot be proved, because whether something is pretty or not is a personal point of view, not a fact. Adjectives like this often signal to the reader that an opinion is being given. An example of a factual statement is: 'Pink Sands on Harbour Island is the only beach to turn pink at sunset.' This fact could be proved by a survey of all of the beaches at sunset.

Remember

- Facts do not go with words such as 'should' or 'ought' or 'I believe'! These suggest that you are reading an opinion.
- You cannot have the opposite view of a fact.

2 How would you 'prove' that the four facts you found in Item 1 are factual? Consider whether each one links to a specific event (what) or person (who), whether the event happened at a specific place (where) or time (when) or for a specific reason (why). Write an explanation for each one.

Apply the skills

3 **a)** Find four facts in the travel article below.

b) Explain how you would prove each one.

Vampire bat

You might be afraid of facing a vampire bat, but you'll only come across one in the Caribbean if you're travelling in Trinidad. These bloodsuckers may be small (only about 3 inches long and weighing 1.5 ounces), but don't be fooled – they'll still try to attack you (or any other mammal) in your sleep. Don't worry, though. They can only drink about an ounce of blood in one sitting, so they won't bleed you dry!

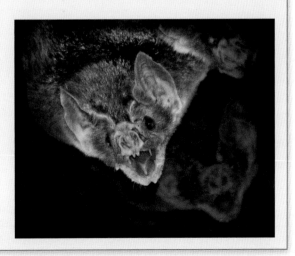

3.2 Extracting literal information from a text

Learn how to:
- *select information as required*
- *extract information in order to answer a question.*

Why is being able to extract **literal information** important?

The Paper 1 exam will feature five types of writing, containing facts that you may be asked to pick out. In items on argumentative texts, you may also be asked about uses or misuses of facts to support opinions.

> **Revision tip**
> ....
> Remember to read the item very carefully, focusing on which ideas you are being asked to identify in the text.

> *Key term*
> *literal information: information that is factual or without any implied meaning*

Building skills

Using structure to find information quickly

Certain features of texts can help you find information quickly. Headings and subheadings are examples of this. For example, you might see the question 'How wide is a frigatebird's wingspan?' and the text may have three subheadings: 'Habitat', 'Life cycle' and 'Key facts'. To answer the question, you would know to look in the 'Key facts' section, as wingspan is not related to where the bird lives or how it breeds.

1 Where would you look to find out about their nests?

Using the words of the question to provide search clues to the answer

Questions usually give you specific words that you can search for in the text in order to find the answer. For example, if the question says 'How did the people of St Kitts first discover fresh water?' then you would look for the word 'fresh water' in the text. The answer is likely to be close by.

2 What is the key word in this question?

What is the height of the Pico Duarte summit?

Eliminating possible answers from a selection

In this part of the exam, you will be answering multiple-choice questions. Be aware that some of the incorrect answer options may still feature words or ideas from the text. You need to check each possible answer carefully against the extract to eliminate the misleading ones.

3   Read the following extract, then answer the item below.

> ### Solenodon
>
> *The Hispaniolan solenodon is one of the most weird and wonderful creatures you'll ever come across. There are only two species in the world – this and the Cuban solenodon. This animal's most unusual feature is its very long snout, which is attached to its head in a ball-and-socket joint, which makes it incredibly flexible and it digs for insects. The solenodon is one of the few mammals that paralyses its prey with toxic saliva.*

What is the most unusual feature of a solenodon?

   a)   its prey

   b)   its snout

   c)   its saliva

   d)   its head

(Hint: The key word here is 'most'.)

Apply the skills

Read the following extract, then answer the items below.

> ### Mongoose
>
>
>
> *One animal you'll see plenty of on St John is the mongoose. If you come across them raiding local bins, they might sit up and stare at you in the manner of a meerkat. But while they may look adorable, mongoose are a real problem on the island. So how did this Indian creature find its way to the Caribbean? When Danish settlers came to the region, rats came along with them. The rats had no predators and they flourished in the warm climate, growing fat on sugar from the plantations. As the rats got out of hand, the planters realised they needed to introduce a predator to bring them under control, so they decided to import mongoose. It was a good idea in theory but it failed in practice – the rats spent their days asleep in the trees and only came out at night, where the mongoose couldn't get at them. Instead, they found different prey, including birds and lizards. They thrived on their new diet and are now a bigger problem than the rats ever were.*

4   Why did the rats flourish?

   a)   They were fed by locals.

   b)   They had no predators.

   c)   They were healthier in St John.

   d)   They were looked after well.

5   What did the planters decide to do?

   a)   Kill the rats.

   b)   Introduce a predator.

   c)   Put down poison.

   d)   Leave the rats alone.

6   How does the writer feel about the mongoose?

   a)   He admires them.

   b)   He dislikes them.

   c)   He thinks they look sweet.

   d)   He is neutral.

3.3 Using implicit information

Learn how to:

- *use implicit information to draw conclusions.*

Why is being able to work out what is implied important?

Some questions will ask you specific things about a text. In order to answer these, you may need to have understood what the writer is implying.

Building skills

Drawing conclusions by combining information

Sometimes you may be given several pieces of information. You will need to use this information *together*, to draw conclusions or infer information.

Average high temperatures

Location	Jan	Feb	Mar	Apr	May	Jun	Jul	Aug	Sep	Oct	Nov	Dec
Antigua	82	82	83	84	85	86	87	87	87	86	85	83
Aruba	86	87	87	88	89	90	89	90	91	90	90	87
Bahamas	77	77	79	82	85	87	89	89	88	85	82	79
Barbados	83	83	84	85	86	86	86	86	86	86	85	84
Belize	82	82	85	87	89	88	88	88	87	86	84	82

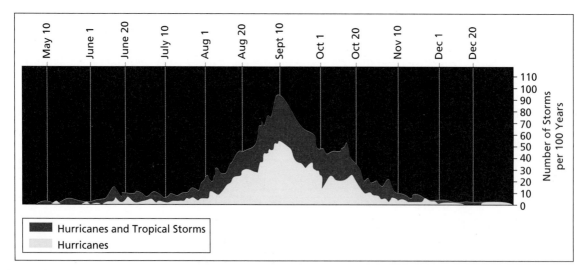

Which of the five destinations shown in this table would be the warmest to visit in June?

To find the answer to this question using the table and the graph above, you would focus on the table and look down the column of data for June. When you had found the highest number, you would track across to the destination column to find the one that matched it: Aruba.

1. Using the two sets of information, recommend a place and time for a holidaymaker who enjoys warmth but not rain.

Drawing conclusions by recognising connotations

Single words can carry an association, often called a connotation. This may be a 'parcel' of sensory detail that a word conveys, or it may be an emotive association. Sometimes writers use a series of words or phrases with similar connotations, which can help you understand their attitude or point of view. (Look back to Topic 1.4 to remind yourself about connotation and nuance.)

2 The information below is from a website offering advice on when to visit the Caribbean. What do the two underlined words add to your understanding of the conditions described?

> *No destination is particularly likely to be right in the path of disaster from a storm or hurricane. But storms and hurricanes that pass through the region affect islands and coastlines over large areas. A tropical storm can <u>dump</u> large amounts of rain even at its outer edges.*
>
> *One way to avoid getting <u>entangled</u> in a tropical storm is simply to stay away from the Caribbean, and especially the islands most likely to be hit, during September and October in particular. Another way of preparing for the possibility is to buy travel insurance.*

3 What would you infer about the writer's attitude towards storms from this extract?

a) He sees them as highly dangerous.

b) They are a minor inconvenience.

c) He is quite casual but realistic about them.

How did you reach your conclusion?

Apply the skills

Practice task

Look at the two sets of information below.

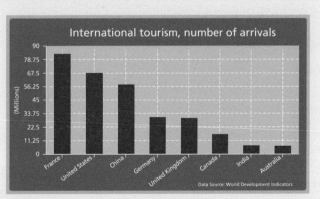

4 Using this information, what can you infer about:

a) worldwide tourist preferences

b) tourist preferences within Europe?

3.4 Extracting information from a non-prose source

Learn how to:

• *select information from tables, diagrams, charts and images.*

Why is being able to extract information from non-prose sources important?

You may be asked specific questions about the literal meaning of information contained in a range of sources other than prose. You could also be asked to identify implicit meanings contained in such sources or across a number of sources.

Building skills

Reading from tables

Tables are useful for recording large amounts of information (usually numbers).

Look at the following table recording the hobbies of a group of 100 teenagers.

Hobby	Number of students
Beach/Swimming	26
Fishing	7
Social networking	22
Computer/Internet hosted games	15
Athletics	30

It is a fact that 30% of the students enjoyed athletics as a hobby.

1 Which other facts could you work out by comparing the results?

You can also work out the idea that fishing is the least popular activity within the group by comparing all of the results and identifying the lowest.

2 Which other implicit ideas could you work out by comparing the results?

Tables are also useful when comparing results across different groups.

Look at the following table that records the hobbies of a group of 100 teenagers but reports the results by gender.

Hobby	Number of male students	Number of female students
Beach/Swimming	8	18
Fishing	7	0
Social networking	3	19
Computer/Internet hosted games	14	1
Athletics	20	10

3 Which new facts could you work out by comparing the results?

4 Which new implicit ideas could you work out by comparing the results?

Reading pie charts

Pie charts are ideal for working out proportions.

- Look at the pie chart on the right recording the agricultural exports from the USA to the Dominican Republic.

  This chart is useful for giving you a rough idea of amounts. From it you can estimate which commodity makes up almost a quarter of the exports. You can work out which is the smallest and largest export by comparing the size of the segments for each export.

U.S. Agricultural Exports to Dominican Republic, 2014

Source: FAS Global Agricultural Trade System

5 What are the limitations of this kind of information?

Reading bar charts

Bar charts are useful for assessing quantity and also for making comparisons over time.

Look at this bar chart showing the number of tourists visiting Cuba between 1990 and 2015.

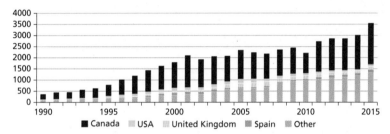

It is important to look at the information given on the axes of bar charts to make sure that you know what you are reading.

You can easily see that numbers of visitors are growing. You can also work out the growth trends for each country if you read across the chart from left to right focusing on one colour at a time.

6 Which country has consistently increased the number of tourists visiting Cuba?

Apply the skills

Practice task

7 Study the following charts about Jamaica.
What can you infer about tourist preferences from your study of the two sets of information?

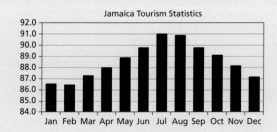

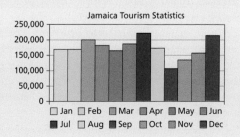

3.5 Recognising main and subordinate ideas

Learn how to:

* *recognise the main idea in a text*
* *recognise the secondary ideas in a text.*

Why is being able to work out the main and subordinate idea important?

You may be asked specific questions about a text that rely on you understanding the writer's overall purpose or main idea. You may also be asked to identify a main idea and **subordinate ideas**, or more minor events that lead to a main event. You may simply be asked to identify the main idea within a sentence or paragraph.

Building skills

Identifying the main idea of a whole text

Main ideas are often summed up in headings, **topic sentences** or revisited in summary sentences at the end of a paragraph or text. The main idea of a text is usually related to its overall purpose and the writer's attitude or viewpoint.

1 This headline from an article in a local paper makes the main idea of the article clear by placing it first. What is the subordinate idea?

Extra Money for Local Sport – Harbour Vale Centre to Benefit

> **Key terms**
>
> **subordinate idea:** *an idea that is an example or part of a bigger or main idea (also called a secondary idea)*
>
> **topic sentence:** *the sentence that sums up the main idea of a paragraph, often placed at the start*

Identifying subordinate ideas

Subordinate ideas are often given in the form of an example or they add detail to support the main idea. Sometimes the supporting details will be in the same sentence as a main idea.

2 Read the first few sentences of the article mentioned above. How do they relate to the main idea?

> *I am delighted that our national government has finally seen sense and decided to invest in local sport. The sports centre at Harbour Vale, for example, has been neglected for far too long. The all- weather football pitches and basketball courts are tatty and unloved. The surfaces are bumpy, and the lines practically invisible – how anyone manages to have a proper game is difficult to say! The long-awaited money will pay for pitches to be relaid, new markings, an upgrade of changing areas and even a new self-service café to replace the unhealthy drinks and snack machines. Young people will at last have a sports centre to be proud of.*

You could structure your answer in the following way:

The first sentence repeats…

The second sentence echoes the…

Then the writer adds detail with…

Apply the skills

Practice task

Read the text on this web page from a longer website extract.

● ● ●   ↻ ⚲ ⌂

Getting around in Grenada
There are few ways of getting around on the island.

Buses – Taxis – Water Taxis – Ferry – Car Rental
The best and cheapest Transportation is the public Mini Bus!

Our buses drive around the entire island.
It's a lot of fun, because as you drive, you are entertained by typical Caribbean music.
On the buses, you will meet some of the friendliest and most helpful people in the entire Caribbean.

The Local Bus

The bus stops wherever it is needed. They drive regularly from Grand Anse to St. George's. The drive takes about 5 minutes, and costs only $1.50 EC per person.

In St. George's, the capital, there is a central bus station, where you can find buses to different parts of the island.

Taxis

---

3   Which of the following best describes the main idea?

   a)   to promote Grenada to tourists

   b)   to help local bus services gain more customers

   c)   to give information on different ways to travel

   d)   to give information about the cost of travel on Grenada

4   How do the main heading and subheadings help you to work this out?

5   Focus on each section of the page in turn.

   a)   Identify the main and subordinate ideas in each section.

   b)   Explain how they relate to each other.

3.6 Identifying sequences in a text

Learn how to:

* *recognise the order of events and ideas in a text.*

Why is being able to recognise a sequence important?

You may be asked specific questions that test your understanding of the order of events or ideas in a text. You may also be asked to draw inferences about how events have influenced each other (cause and effect).

Building skills

Spotting that time order is being used

When writing chronological order, a writer will often use dates or times to signal the stages of development.

1 Pick out the dates from the passage below. What do they suggest about the way the text is ordered?

> *Traditionally, and in fact right up until the 1900s, we <u>used</u> natural sources of fuel that were cheap and abundant. However, modernization (and tourism) has led to a heavy usage of diesel and oil, which has to be imported at a high cost. In 2001, the islands of the Caribbean region consumed a combined total of 2.2 quadrillion Btu of energy. Oil is the dominant fuel, accounting for about 92 per cent of total 2001 energy consumption. We <u>need</u> to be looking towards renewable sources of energy as well as recent developments in natural gas technology in order to fend off a crisis, and it looks as if there are many ideas for the late 2000s.*

Another way to tell whether something happened in the past is to look at the tense the writer uses. If the writer is describing current events, they will use the present tense. The past tense is used to describe events that have already taken place.

2 Look at the underlined words in the extract above. List the words that show you which tense is being used in the rest of paragraph.

Remember

Time-sequence words can be replaced by nouns such as 'dawn', 'dusk' or other words that suggest a time of day (for example, 'moonlight', 'sunrise' or 'sunset').

Drawing conclusions by recognising sequences

In items that ask you to identify the event that started something off, look for words such as 'in the beginning', 'initially', 'at the start'.

If you are asked to find an idea in an article that seems most powerful, influential or effective (a cause and effect relationship), look for words such as 'importantly', 'fundamentally' or phrases such as 'this led to', 'as a result'.

3   Read the following article about lionfish. Write down the words that suggest sequences or
     cause and effect relationships.

*Lionfish are a bit of a nightmare!
To start with, they can cause
damage to all sorts of
environments: sea grasses,
mangroves and coral reefs.
An equally serious issue is that
they also prey on important fish
and shellfish.*

*As a result, whole ecosystems
can be affected, which in turn
leads to an economic knock-on
effect. But even worse is the
knock-on effect on tourism, because as coral reefs are destroyed there are few
places to visit. Plus, who wants to tread on one of these venomous horrors?*

Apply the skills

Read the following informative extract about changes in the sea, then answer the items below.

*Instead of the thriving reefs that one would have seen only a few years back,
there are now ghost forests of bleached white skeletons covered in slime. As
the greenhouse gas carbon dioxide increasingly gets absorbed by the ocean's
surface waters, it creates carbonic acid, which changes the pH of the sea,
making it more difficult for coral polyps and other shell-forming organisms to
produce their rigid homes.*

*When corals die (Earle said fully half of the world's reefs are already gone, or in
steep decline) the fish and other organisms that breed among them die off as
well. Equally important, reefs are an invaluable line of defense against storm
surges and destructive waves. Without these natural seawalls, beach erosion and
damage to low-lying coastal areas during hurricanes can spiral out of control.*

From www.truth-out.org

4   Which factor has led to the coral dying off?

  a)   slime on the coral

  b)   hurricanes

  c)   carbon-dioxide absorption

  d)   fish dying

5   What does coral die-off lead to?

  a)   death of sea mammals

  b)   coastal erosion

  c)   hurricanes getting out of control

  d)   economic problems

Read the following informative article about the chikungunya virus, then answer the items that follow to test your understanding of the text.

U.S. mosquitos spreading chikungunya, the excruciatingly painful disease that tore through the Caribbean?

Health officials urged residents to prevent mosquito bites but said there was no cause for alarm.

5 *'There is no broad risk to the health of the general public,' said Dr. Celeste Philip, a public health official with the Department of Health.*

Chikungunya virus is rarely fatal. Infected people typically suffer fever, severe joint pain and swelling, muscle aches, headaches or rash. 'Chikungunya' is derived from the Kimakonde word meaning 'that which bends up,' which describes the debilitating pain
10 *infected people suffer. Patients usually recover in about a week, although some people suffer long-term joint pain. There is no vaccine and no specific treatment.*

This virus is not spread person to person, but rather by the bite of the Asian tiger mosquito (Aedes albopictus) or the yellow fever mosquito (Aedes aegypti). That's why health officials believe the virus is spreading here – the two cases had not recently left
15 *the country.*

The infected Floridians were described as a 41-year-old woman in Miami-Dade County who began experiencing symptoms on June 10, and a 50-year-old man in Palm Beach County, who first noticed symptoms July 1.

Philip said both are doing well.

20 *More than 230 chikungunya cases have been reported in Americans this year, but all the others were travellers believed to have been infected elsewhere.*

Now that chikungunya is in the United States, CDC officials think it will behave like dengue virus, with imported cases causing occasional local transmissions but not widespread outbreaks.

25 *Mosquito control and avoidance are the best current options, they said.*

From http://news.nationalpost.com

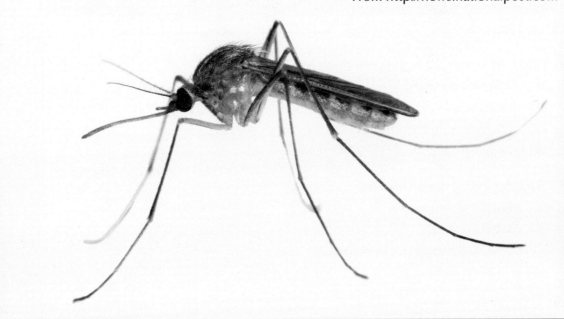

1 Indicate which of the following options is true with a tick.

   The virus is rarely fatal but:

   a) occasionally kills

   b) causes short-term health issues only

   c) causes severe pain

   d) can cause long-term issues

2 Indicate which of the following options is true with a tick.

   The virus is spread:

   a) person to person

   b) by mosquito bites

   c) by the bite of two kinds of mosquitos

3 Based on the article, which adjective best describes the chikungunya virus?

   a) deadly

   b) dangerous

   c) unpleasant

   d) irritating

4 The word 'debilitating' in line 9 means:

   a) can kill

   b) weakening

   c) very painful

   d) unwelcome

5 The main intention of the writer is to:

   a) urge action by scientists

   b) advise tourists to the Caribbean

   c) outline the dangers of the virus

   d) reassure citizens of the USA

6 What is the main idea of this article?

   a) The virus is very dangerous and must be controlled

   b) How to avoid infection

   c) The virus has spread to a new place

   d) A vaccine must be developed

7 Is this virus new?

   a) To America only

   b) Yes

   c) No

   d) To the Caribbean only

Where might you have gone wrong?

Item 1

b), c) and d) are true.

You may have misunderstood 'rarely fatal' and thought that it meant that deaths did occur. You may have missed mentions of pain and recovery in paragraph 3 or not understood fully what 'long-term' meant.

Make sure that you read carefully and use the reading strategies suggested in Chapter 1 to work out what unfamiliar words may mean.

Item 2

c) is true.

You may have misread the text, as it uses the phrase 'person to person'. You may also have felt that 'by mosquitos' is true. However, in fact it is only two kinds of mosquito that spread the virus.

Ensure that you read for precise meanings and take particular notice of numbers, dates and percentages when dealing with factual information.

Item 3

c) is correct.

You may have considered the virus to be dangerous, but the article uses a time sequence to make it clear that it is not life-threatening or an epidemic, which rules out ideas of danger and the word 'deadly'. However, it does mention pain and some long-term effects, and 'irritating' does not seem a strong enough term to describe this.

Make sure that you consider the precise meanings of words before selecting them.

Item 4

b) is correct.

You may not have been familiar with this word or may not have read around it to eliminate a). Alternatively, you may have guessed that the virus would be unwelcome and so chosen d).

Using your knowledge of similar words, you could have worked out that the prefix 'de' usually means to take something away. Reading the surrounding text may have revealed that the virus has a short-term effect, and perhaps the image of 'bending up' might have led you to 'weakening'.

Item 5

d) is correct.

You may have felt that the article outlines dangers, but actually it downplays the dangers of the virus and barely mentions a vaccine. Early on, 'residents' are mentioned and later 'spreading here' is stated, suggesting an American target audience.

Pay close attention to the sequences of words, in this case the locations mentioned – Caribbean, Florida, USA – to help you work out who the writer is targeting.

Item 6

c) is correct.

You may have been distracted by b), as the article gives information about prevention measures. You may personally feel that a vaccine is needed and have chosen d). However, treatment of the virus and prevention would not be issues if it had not spread, which leads you to c) as the correct choice.

Ask yourself where the root of pieces of information are, whether they are examples, secondary issues or the main idea.

Item 7

a) is correct.

You may not have known where to find an answer to this question.

Careful reading of time sequences will show you that the writer has written 'Now that chikungunya is in the United States', which suggests that it was not there before. Scan time sequences carefully to ensure you answer accurately.

Chapter 4 Gaining insights from literature: Poetry

4.1 Understanding literal language in poetry

Learn how to:

• *identify the literal meaning of individual words.*

Why is being able to identify literal meaning important?

You may be asked to identify the precise **literal meaning** of individual words in a text extract or sentence. In order to do this, you need to use a number of techniques, some of which will be familiar to you if you have worked through Topics 1.1 and 3.2. However, although the techniques are similar, the effects of words in poetry can be richer and more varied.

> *Key term*
>
> **literal meaning:** *the dictionary definition of a word, without any nuance or connotation taken into account*

Building skills

How can you work out literal meanings?

You can use several techniques for working out literal meanings, which are explained in the table below.

Technique	Example
Check the **context** of the word – what clues are there from the vocabulary around it in the poem?	A poem about a storm might have a **semantic field** related to conflict or war.
Check the word's position in the text – where is it placed?	A poem's ending might focus on regret or looking forward, or draw a conclusion of some sort.
Think of similar words or phrases.	The word 'battalion' (a group of soldiers) is linked to 'battle', 'battling', 'embattled', etc.
Consider the word alongside synonyms to gauge its strength or weakness, or how positive or negative it is.	A poem about rain might refer to someone being 'drenched' – how is that stronger or weaker than 'wet', 'damp' or 'sodden'?

1 Use any of these techniques to work out the literal meaning of the underlined words in this short poem about a storm.

<u>Embattled</u>, I shelter underneath the towering oak,

A giant with branches, it reaches high to angry skies,

Where <u>furious</u> clouds cast arrows and <u>spikes</u> of rain,

That fall around me and spear the ground.

How can you work out the effects of a word or phrase?

Understanding the meaning of a word is one skill; understanding its *effect* is a different one. For example, in the verse above, the poet calls the tree 'a giant'.

Writers select particular words for three main reasons:

- impact
- sensory appeal
- to convey emotion.

The literal meaning of 'giant' is a huge person or creature, often seen in fairy tales.

Three students are discussing the effect of the poet using this word:

Frankie: The poet means the tree is, like, *so big*, like bigger than any other tree, right? He couldn't believe it.

Shola: Yeah, but he used the word 'giant', like the tree was kind of scary…

Jerome: Totally, like it was alive. A monster.

2 a) Who do you agree with? Are any of the students completely right about the effect of using the word 'giant'?

b) What else comes into your mind when you read the description?

3 For which of these three reasons did the poet use the word 'giant': impact, sensory appeal or to convey emotion? Was it just for one reason – or more?

Read the following poem. In it, the poet speaks to an elderly cat that has been in his neighbourhood for many years, but whose fur looks as fine as it did in its youth.

To a Cat

Cat! who has pass'd thy grand **climacteric**,
How many mice and rats hast in thy days
Destroy'd? How many tit-bits stolen? Gaze
With those bright languid segments green, and prick
Those velvet ears – but prythee do not stick
Thy latent talons in me – and tell me all thy **frays**,
Of fish and mice, and rats and tender chick;
Nay, look not down, nor lick thy dainty wrists, –
For all the wheezy asthma – and for all
Thy tail's tip is nick'd off – and though the fists
Of many a maid have given thee many a maul,
Still is thy fur as when the lists
In youth thou enter'dst on glass-bottled wall.

John Keats

climacteric: most vital and healthy point

frays: short for 'affrays'

---

4   Look at the words that are underlined in the poem.

     a)   Think about possible alternatives to each word chosen (for example, Keats used 'destroy'd' rather than 'killed' or 'eaten').

     b)   Consider each word in turn and make a table like the one below.

Word: 'Destroy'd'	Alternatives: 'killed', 'eaten', 'hunted'
Impact	The precise meaning of this word suggests total destruction, as if the prey has been made unrecognizable.
Sensory appeal	Leads us to imagine that the cat is extremely strong and aggressive.
Emotion conveyed	Creates a sense of awe and perhaps even dislike towards the cat.

     c)   When you have drawn a table for each of the underlined words, ask yourself whether any ideas or concepts are repeated or whether any patterns emerge.

In this poem, there are many words to describe the effects of time on the cat. Not only does it show the way the cat appears calm and appealing, but also a sense of its power to cause pain and suffering.

Apply the skills

Reread the poem, then answer the following items.

5   The cat's claws are described as:

     a)   sharp

     b)   openly dangerous

     c)   potentially harmful

     d)   retracted

6   The poet thinks that the cat is:

     a)   beautiful and vibrant

     b)   attractive with a few signs of ageing

     c)   just as it was when he first saw it

     d)   ageing rapidly

7   The word 'segments' suggests that the cat's eyes are:

     a)   small

     b)   identical

     c)   curved

     d)   level with each other

8   When the poet uses the phrase 'for all' he means:

     a)   before

     b)   especially

     c)   when

     d)   even though

4.2 Understanding figurative language in poetry

Learn how to:
- *recognise figurative techniques*
- *recognise the effect of figurative techniques.*

Why is being able to recognise and analyse figurative language important?

You may be asked specific questions about a word or phrase which require you to tell how a particular word or phrase is used figuratively and the effect created.

Poetry is often rich in figurative language. Read the following verses from the poem 'Laventille' by Derek Walcott.

Laventille

It huddled there
steel tinkling its blue painted metal air,
tempered in violence, like Rio's **favelas**,

with snaking, perilous streets whose edges fell as
its **Episcopal** *turkey-buzzards fall*
from its miraculous hilltop

shrine,
down the impossible drop
to **Belmont, Woodbrook, Maraval, St. Clair**

that shine
like peddlers' tin trinkets in the sun.
From a harsh

shower, its gutters growled and gargled wash
past the Youth Centre, past the water catchment,
a rigid children's carousel of cement;

we climbed where lank electric
lines and tension cables linked its raw brick
hovels like a complex feud,

where the inheritors of the **middle passage** *stewed,*
five to a room, still clamped below their hatch,
breeding like felonies

Derek Walcott

favelas: slums or shanty-towns

Episcopal: relating to bishops

Belmont, Woodbrook, Maraval, St. Clair: other communities, near Laventille

middle passage: the middle stage of the transatlantic slave trade; the sea journey undertaken by enslaved people from West Africa to the West Indies

---

Building skills

Identifying figurative techniques common in poetry

Walcott uses a number of common figurative techniques, which are described in the table below.

Technique	Definition
imagery	Language that powerfully evokes the senses, e.g. 'steel tinkling'.
contrast	Ideas created by placing opposing images together, e.g. 'miraculous hilltop' and 'raw brick hovels' – emphasising the poverty below and the almost heavenly sight above.
simile	One thing compared to another using 'like' or 'as', e.g. the streets and roofs that 'shine like peddlers' tin trinkets in the sun'.
metaphor	A more direct comparison, saying something *is* something else, e.g. the steel drums of Laventille 'tempered in violence' ('tempered' means changed or hardened).
extended metaphor	A comparison that is repeated and developed in several ways. Here, Walcott refers to the inhabitants of Laventille being like enslaved people on a ship, trapped and chained. He extends the metaphor later in the poem.
personification	An inanimate object is described with human qualities, e.g. the town 'huddled'.
symbolism	An object or key setting is used consistently to represent a concept or theme. Here, the 'tin trinkets' could be seen to represent poverty – people or things that are thin and deemed worthless.

1   Look again at the poem. What sort of technique is being used in the following examples? (Be aware it may be more than one.)

   a)   'snaking, perilous streets'

   b)   'a rigid children's carousel of cement'

   c)   'like a complex feud'

2   What other powerful or striking images stand out? What effect does each have?

3   The mass of power lines which link the shacks (the 'hovels') in which the poor live are described as being 'like a complex feud'.

   A 'feud' is a violent, long-lasting quarrel between families or groups of people. Why do you think Walcott has chosen this simile?

4 Read the following extract from a narrative poem and identify as many figurative techniques as you can.

> Kasinath the new young singer
> fills the hall with sound:
> The seven notes dance in his throat
> like seven tame birds.
> His voice is a sharp sword slicing
> and thrusting everywhere,
> It darts like lightning – no
> knowing where it will go when.
> He sets deadly traps for
> himself, then cuts them away:
> The courtiers listen in amazement,
> give frequent gasps of praise.
>
> From 'Broken Song' by
> Rabindranath Tagore

Remember

You can identify a simile easily because the comparison includes the words 'as' or 'like'.

Considering the effect of figurative language

Writers select the words that they use for three main reasons: impact, emotion and sensory appeal.

5 Find the two similes in the poem above.

    a) How is the description of a singer given impact by these similes? Are these the images normally associated with beautiful singing? What effect does the word choice have on the reader?

    b) What does Tagore want to convey about the singer's voice? Consider the connotations of the four images created. What kinds of ideas do they bring with them (for example, 'tame birds' carries with it the idea of beautiful song, but also captivity and vulnerability)?

    c) What emotions does the figurative language create? How does this make you feel about the singer?

6 Using your answers to Item 4, write a short paragraph summarizing your ideas about the overall effect of Tagore's figurative language.

Literal and figurative language combined

A lot of language is figurative as well as literal. In poetry, it is important to see descriptions as part of the overall picture. For example, a poem about a sick old man might refer to a 'flickering candle'. This could mean a literal candle that the old man is holding, but it could also be a metaphor for life about to end.

7 You are about to read a poem about an unspoilt island. In it, the poet refers to the 'waning sun'. Without reading the poem, what is:

    a) the literal meaning of this phrase

    b) its possible figurative meaning?

If you are not sure, you can check when you read the whole poem.

Apply the skills

Read the following poem, then answer the items on pages 72–73. The poet is describing a much-loved place, which he hopes will not undergo the kind of changes that have occurred elsewhere.

Skeete's Bay, Barbados

One always missed the turning, but found, in time
The broken sign that pointed crookedly, loath to
Allow another stranger here. Perhaps this Tom
Or Dick has plans for progress that will tow
5   The boats away and make them 'quaint'; that will tame
This wild coast with pale rheumatics who tee

Off where sea-egg shells and fisherman
Now lie with unconcern. Naked children
And their sticks flush crabs from their holes
10   and a bare-legged girl, dress in wet folds
Wades slow towards a waning sun.

And the sea tossed angrily
For it knew that freedom here was short.
It remembered other coasts
15   Made mod by small-eyed men in big cars

And as before it knew she'd vanish
The bare-legged girl; the children and their crabs
Would leave; a better world would banish
them to imitation coconut trays

20   But those small eyes reflecting dollar signs
Have not yet found the crooked finger to this peace;
And down the beach the women bathe their sons
Who'll never talk, like Pap, of fishing seasons past.

Only memory will turn down this way
25   When some old man somewhere recalls his day
On this beach where sea-egg shells once lay.

Robert Lee

8   Which feature of figurative language is this an example of: 'the sea tossed angrily'?

   a)   extended metaphor

   b)   simile

   c)   metaphor

   d)   personification

9   Why does the poet describe the bay now and as it might be?

   a)   to show progress

   b)   to explain how change happens

   c)   to shock the reader

   d)   to create a contrast to reflect on

10   Why does the poet write 'small eyes' (reflecting dollar signs)? Tick answers you agree with.

   a)   to link to the 'small eyed' men earlier in the poem

   b)   to suggest that the men don't see the true beauty of the place

   c)   to make the men seem unappealing

   d)   to suggest that the men have no power

11 Which feature of figurative language is this an example of: 'sea-egg shells'?

   a) simile

   b) personification

   c) symbolism

   d) apostrophe

12 Robert Lee uses Skeete's Bay:

   a) as a symbol for modernization

   b) to represent his childhood

   c) to voice his fears for the future of the Caribbean

   d) to show how nice unspoilt places are

4.3 Understanding sound effects in poetry

Learn how to:

- *recognise sound techniques*
- *recognise the effect of sound techniques.*

Why is being able to analyse sound effects important?

You may be asked specific questions about a word or phrase which rely on you having understood that it is a **sound effect**. You may be asked to identify the technique being used or the effect of its use.

> *Key term*
>
> **sound effect:** *the rhythms and sounds by which letters within words, whole words and combinations of words create meanings*

> **Revision tip**
>
> Create a list of sound effects and learn them by using a mnemonic made from their initial letters. Add examples of each technique.

Building skills

Identifying common sound techniques in poetry

1. Poets use many sound effect techniques. Copy the table below and add more examples.

Technique	Definition
rhyme	Where sounds used in two or more words match, e.g. 'Only memory will turn down this way/When some old man somewhere recalls his day.'
rhythm	Where the length of words, the number of stressed syllables in a word or a line, or the punctuation used creates a regular pattern, e.g. 'I wandered lonely as a cloud' (Wordsworth) has four stressed syllables.
onomatopoeia	Where a word's sound reflects the actual sound that it is describing, e.g. the words 'growled' and 'gargled' from 'Laventille' describe the sound of the gutter water.
alliteration	When words close to each other have the same initial letter, e.g. 'Thrush's eggs look little low heavens' (G. M. Hopkins).
consonance	When words close to each other repeat the same consonant sound, e.g. 'whose edges fell as/its Episcopal turkey-buzzards fall' (Walcott).
assonance	When words close to each other repeat the same vowel sound, e.g. 'tin trinkets', 'impossible drop' (Walcott).
sibilance	When the repetition of 's' sounds in words close together creates a 'hissing' effect, e.g. 'He sipped with his straight mouth/Softly drank through his straight gums, into his slack long body' (D. H. Lawrence)

2 Read the following poem and identify any sound effects in it.

The Sea

The sea is a hungry dog,
Giant and grey.
He rolls on the beach all day.
With his clashing teeth and shaggy jaws
5   Hour upon hour he gnaws
The rumbling, tumbling stones,
And 'Bones, bones, bones, bones!'
The giant sea-dog moans,
Licking his greasy paws.

10 And when the night wind roars
And the moon rocks in the stormy cloud,
He bounds to his feet and snuffs and sniffs,
Shaking his wet sides over the cliffs,
And howls and hollos long and loud.

15 But on quiet days in May or June,
When even the grasses on the dune
Play no more their reedy tune,
With his head between his paws
He lies on the sandy shores,
20 So quiet, so quiet, he scarcely snores.

James Reeves

Considering the effect of sound effects in poetry

Remember that writers select words for their impact, sensory appeal and emotion. For example, read aloud the lines from D. H. Lawrence's 'Snake':

He sipped with his straight mouth,
Softly drank through his straight gums, into his slack long body...

The rhythm of the poem makes the reader read it slowly because of the long second line.

3 What does this suggest about:
   a) the snake's movements
   b) the snake's own shape or form?

Some of the ways in which sound effects work in these areas in 'The Sea' are outlined below.

Impact:

- Repetition of sounds can make the words they are a part of more memorable; for example, rhyme at the end of a line. Think whether any lines from 'The Sea' have stuck in your mind because they rhyme.

- Alliteration often increases the volume and pace of our reading, which imprints it on our minds more effectively. Did your chosen lines feature alliteration?

4 Find two examples of alliteration in 'The Sea'. What do they add?

5 Think of an unusual metaphor to describe a tropical storm. Then write a few lines about it, including alliteration and rhyme.

Sensory appeal:

- Specific sound effects such as onomatopoeic words help transport the reader to the scene. Pick out the onomatopoeic words from the poem.

- Alliteration, consonance and sibilance can each be repeated to create an ongoing sound effect. Think about how 'howls and hollos' help to create an ongoing echoing bark.

- Rhythm can create a sense of movement – for example: 'He rolls on the beach all day / With his clashing teeth and shaggy jaws'. Try saying 'clashing' and 'shaggy' out loud and think about the kind of motion you picture as you say them.

6 Write two lines of a poem that describes the sound of a tropical storm. Use onomatopoeia, rhythm and letter patterns.

Conveying emotion:

- A fast rhythm, using lots of short syllables, can create a sense of energy and perhaps threat.

- Alliteration of 'hard' consonants can often create an angry 'voice'.

- Alliteration of soft consonants can create a sense that someone is sad or subdued.

- Long assonance can create a sad, eerie or relaxed mood.

7 How does the poet use sounds to present the dog in three different ways in the three verses of the poem?

Read this extract from a poem about a very high cliff. It was written at the start of the 19th century, so some of the language is quite challenging!

***From* Beachy Head**

Advances now, with feathery silver touched,
The rippling tide of flood; glisten the sands,
While, inmates of the chalky clefts that scar
*Thy sides **precipitous**, with shrill harsh cry,*
Their white wings glancing in the level beam,
*The **terns**, and **gulls**, and **tarrocks**, seek their food,*
And thy rough hollows echo to the voice
*Of the gray **choughs**, and ever restless **daws**.*

precipitous: extremely steep

terns, gulls, tarrocks: sea birds

chough: a type of crow

daw: jackdaw, a type of crow

Charlotte Smith

8 How does Smith use sound words and phrases to convey:
  - the tide as it comes in (think about onomatopoeic words or phrases)
  - the sounds of the different birds (think about assonance or alliteration).

9 There are lots of 'sound echoes' in the poem – places where a sound on one line is mirrored by a similar one nearby ('harsh' and 'scar', 'sides' and 'cry'). Why do you think Smith uses this technique to describe the sea, the birds and the cliffs?

10 **a)** Write the last line of a poem about a tropical storm. Use sound effects to create an angry tone.

  b) Now try to soften the tone and write the last line of a poem in praise of the storm.

Apply the skills

Read the following poem, then answer the items that follow. Before you do so, you could try to:

- identify particular uses of sound effects in the poem (for example, quickly listing examples of alliteration, using the grid on page 74 to help you)
- consider which senses and emotions they appeal to
- think about the individual impact of words, phrases or lines *and* the overall impact.

Wind-rush

I'd like to set out a storm
watching it like the dream it is
watching the sea come
emptying its folds of boats

Watching towering palmtrees fall
across the backs of running cattle
watching the wind carry trees
and drop them on top of shack roofs

Hearing leaves of branches whistle –
I won't miss how breezeblow madness
batter and beat the place up island-wide
knocking things over with sea raging and raging

How island-wide bugle-blow of wind
batter and mash-up the place

break up big limb and banana leaf-them
in nothing but a day of wind-rush –
screaming
         plundering
             crying

James Berry

11 Which of the following is an example of onomatopoeia from the poem?

    a) 'fall'

    b) 'miss'

    c) 'batter'

    d) 'break up'

12 The third verse uses a series of repeating 'b' sounds to emphasise the wind's power. What is this an example of?

    a) alliteration

    b) assonance

    c) consonance

    d) onomatopoeia

13 What sound does the alliterative 'bugle blow' make you hear?

    a) a deep resounding boom

    b) a high-pitched, piercing note or series of notes

    c) a repetitive whistle

    d) a continuous hum

14 How do the final three words of the poem change or maintain the rhythm of the poem?

    a) They slow it down, drawing out the pain through a series of unstressed final syllables.

    b) They speed it up, accentuating the wind's power.

    c) They continue the same rhythm, with the '-ing' verbs mirroring all the other verbs.

    d) They break up the rhythm, so it sounds jumpy and disjointed.

15 The title 'Wind-rush' has another meaning – one referring to the ship that brought the first West Indian immigrants to the United Kingdom in 1948. James Berry missed that boat but came to England on the next one. Which of these statements best describes what the sound effects and devices tell us about the poet's feelings?

    a) They bring back fond memories from childhood.

    b) They evoke unpleasant memories of powerful storms.

    c) They warn people of the dangers of storms.

    d) They show how much he misses island life.

4.4 Understanding structure in poetry

Learn how to:

- *identify the structure of a poem*
- *recognise a range of structural techniques.*

Why is being able to recognise and analyse structure important?

You may be asked specific questions about **structure** such as word order or line length. You may also be asked to identify a technique being used or the effect of its use.

> *Key term*
>
> *structure: the way that things are arranged; in the case of poetry this means the order of words, the way they are punctuated and organised into lines*

Building skills

Identifying structures used in poetry

The most obvious way that poetry is structured is into verses or stanzas. Often these will signal a change of topic or mood, in the same way that paragraphs do in prose.

Line length is also an example of structure in poetry. You can describe the length of lines by counting the number of words and syllables that they contain. Look out for dramatic changes such as a short line in among several long ones.

Another aspect of structure is the pattern made by syllables *within* a line or verse. This is often referred to as the metre. Sometimes you may be able to recognise a pattern, such as iambic pentameter (five stressed and five unstressed syllables in each line).

Considering the effect of structure in poetry

Read the following poem.

> **Well Done**
>
> *Six year old*
> *And no one had ever told me I was good at something*
> *But one time*
> *Let me tell you what got my heart jumping*
> *Let me take you right back to the start*
>
> *I love Mrs Evans because she taught me art*
> *Most of the lessons I sat around because I thought they were boring*
> *Me and my mate did an impression of someone snoring*
> *I got sent outside the class*
> *Paper and pencil I did some drawing*
>
> *Not well looked after*
> *But I was full of laughter*
> *I was always trying to be dafter*
> *Than Darren on the next table*
> *Sometimes life was like my desk, a bit unstable*

So there I am sat outside the geography class again
I've only got a pencil because I'm not allowed a pen
I can doodle and poodle
I can draw more than a score
I can sketch someone sketchy
I can paint the front door
I can dribble and scribble
I can create a cartoon
I can even draw the curtains to rub out the moon

The paper, the pencil and me
Sometimes my efforts were blunt, upfront
Sharply spoken but I kept a clear mind
See I used up two pencils a day
Not because I wrote a lot
Because I sharpened them all away
Mrs Evans was in the front telling everybody to
LEARN LEARN LEARN
I stood behind her going
TURN, TURN, TURN

See I loved art lessons cos learning was fun
Specially when I got the work back and it said 'Well done'
Oh no! Jelly belly, I've got this weird feeling inside
The teacher said 'you better watch out boy because you're gonna burst with pride'
I said 'Oh no Mrs Evans I don't like this feeling'
And I wet myself and cried.

So when people say 'Well done' I tend to shy away
But you can always rest assured that they'll always remember what you say
So whether you're a teacher, a parent, social worker or a mum
Just remember the importance of telling the young ones Well done
And in the future when it may feel they're swimming against the tide
They'll look back to those few seconds and how it made them feel so good inside.

Dreadlock Alien

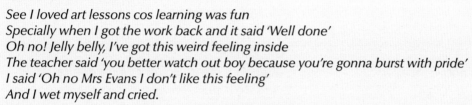

1 **a)** Write a heading or title for each verse. Try to include a sense of the topic being covered and also whether or not the poet is speaking in the present or recalling something from the past.

  b) Why do you think the poet chose to start each new verse when he did?

Building or breaking a pattern in the number of syllables or line lengths affects the pace and rhythm of those lines. This in turn will create or change a mood or emotion.

2 Pick out the lines from 'Well Done' that have fewer syllables in them. What is the effect of this technique?

Very regular patterns normally create a sense of confidence and positivity, whereas frequent changes and breaks suggest confusion or thoughtfulness.

3 Reread the fourth verse of 'Well Done'.

   a) What do you notice about the number of syllables and words in each line?

   b) What is the mood created as you read?

When surrounded by long lines, a short line will stand out and gain emphasis.

4 Why does the sixth verse end with a short line?

Apply the skills

Read the following poem, then answer the items that follow. The poem is written as a conversation between a couple.

Our Love Now

I said,
  observe how the wound heals in time,
  how the skin slowly knits
  and once more becomes whole.
  The cut will mend, and such
  is our relationship.

I said,
  observe the scab above the scald.
  The red burnt flesh is ugly,
  but it can be hidden.
  In time it will disappear.
  Such is our love, such is our love.

I said,
  remember how when you cut your hair,
  you feel different, somehow incomplete.
  but the hair grows – before long
  it is always the same.
  Our beauty together is such.

I said,
  listen to how the raging storm
  damages the trees outside.
  The storm is frightening
  but it will soon be gone.
  People will forget it ever existed.
  The breach in us can be mended.

She said,
  Although the wound heals
  and appears cured, it is not the same.
  There is always a scar,
  a permanent reminder.
  Such is our love now.

She said,
  Although the burn will no longer sting
  and we'll almost forget that it's there
  the skin remains bleached
  and a numbness prevails.
  Such is our love now.

She said,
  After you've cut your hair,
  it grows again slowly. During that
  time changes must occur,
  the style will be different.
  Such is our love now.

She said,
  Although the storm is temporary
  and soon passes,
  it leaves damage in its wake
  which can never be repaired.
  The tree is forever dead.
  Such is our love.

Martyn Lowery

---

5   Why has Lowery set out the poem in two parallel columns?

   a)   To make it look different.

   b)   To show different viewpoints.

   c)   To create the effect of a dialogue.

   d)   To show how different the couple's perceptions are.

6   Why has Lowery made the verses in each column the same length?

   a)   It creates a calm tone.

   b)   It suggests that the woman can match everything the man says.

   c)   It is as if she does not want to add anything new.

   d)   The last ones are longer to end the debate.

7   Why has Lowery made the female narrator's lines shorter than the man's?

   a)   Hers are shorter so as not to encourage him.

   b)   She just answers him factually.

   c)   His words are more authoritative so contain more information.

   d)   Her lines are more emotional than his.

4.5 Identifying themes in poetry

Learn how to:
- *recognise when a theme is being built up*
- *recognise the techniques used to suggest a theme.*

Why is being able to recognise and analyse themes important?

You may be asked specific questions about the **theme** of a poem which rely on you having recognised that theme as it developed. You may be asked to identify the techniques being used to create it. You may also be asked what you think the purpose of a poem is and, to answer this, you will need to understand its theme.

> **Key term**
>
> **theme:** *a topic or idea that is explored in a piece of writing*

Building skills

Identifying themes and sub-themes

The theme of a poem can often be summed up in one word, such as love, nature or pollution. However, it is often helpful to be more specific: the joys of love, the beauty of nature, the increase in pollution. Some poems may deal with several sub-themes related to a larger theme: the joys and pains of love, the beauty and dangers of nature, the growth and dangers of pollution.

> **Revision tip**
>
> Using the main theme words of 'love', 'conflict', 'relationships', 'death', create a list of words for each that might be their sub-themes. For example, the list for 'conflict' might start with 'war' and 'battle'.

> **Remember**
>
> The theme is not necessarily what a poem is *about*; it is what it makes you *think about*.

1 Look at the following four extracts from poems. What is each of them about? Match them to the four subjects listed below.

(1)	(2)

Grandfather
advised me:
Learn a trade
I learned
to sit at desk
and condense
No layoff
from this
condenser
	I'm pillowed and padded, pale and puffing
	lifting household stuffing–
	  carpets, dishes
	  benches, fishes
	I've spent my life in nothing.

(3)	(4)

Winter's after me–she's out
with sheets so white it hurts the eyes.
Nightgown,
pillow slip blow thru my bare catalpa trees,
no objects here.
	My man says the wind blows from the south,
	  we go out fishing, he has no luck,
	  I catch a dozen, that burns him up,
	I face the east and the wind's in my mouth,
	but my man has to have it in the south.

a) winter

b) wind direction

c) choosing a job

d) everyday life

2 Now match each poetry extract to one of these themes:

a) the harshness of nature

b) clinging to beliefs, even in the face of contrary evidence

c) the meaninglessness of domesticity

d) the decline of trades and crafts

How similar are the subject and theme of each poem? What are the links between the two?

Considering the techniques used to build themes

When trying to identify themes in a poem, a good place to start is by looking at the nouns (and its title). These will name places, people and objects, and give you an idea whether a specific setting or event is being written about and who is the focus of the poem. Decide whether or not they are concrete nouns or abstract ones. This may suggest whether the poem is about an idea, an emotion or an actual event or person. When you have looked at the nouns, go through the same process with the verbs.

Next, look at the vocabulary used. Is it drawn from a **semantic field** that you recognise? This may lead you to realise that the poet is exploring a particular emotion or event.

Key term

semantic field: a group or set of words that relate to a topic or subject

3 Read the short poem below. Using the steps outlined above, decide on its theme and sub-theme.

> *Sorrow moves in wide waves,*
> *   it passes, lets us be.*
> *It uses us, we use it,*
> *   it's blind while we see.*
> *Consciousness is illimitable,*
> *   too good to forsake*
> *tho what we feel be misery*
> *   and we know will break.*
>
> From 'Sorrow Moves in Wide Waves' by Lorine Niedecker

Linking theme and purpose

Poems are written for many reasons and, ultimately, only the poet will know why they put pen to paper. However, not all poems are written for personal reasons and it is possible to suggest the purpose of a poem. Here are some possible purposes:

- to express emotions
- to express opinions
- to share experiences
- to share emotions
- to educate/inform
- to show the 'we are not alone'
- to provoke debate.

The theme of a poem can help you work out the poet's purpose.

4 What could the purposes be of the following poems? Match each one to what you consider to be the most likely purpose:

(1) a love sonnet		**a)**	to inform and provoke debate
(2) a poem about loss of the rainforests		**b)**	to share feelings with the reader
(3) an elegy to a recently dead parent		**c)**	to share information and entertain
(4) a ballad telling a story of a local crime		**d)**	to express difficult emotions

Apply the skills

Read the following poem. Then answer the items below.

> ### All That's Bright Must Fade
>
> *All that's bright must fade, –*
> *The brightest still the fleetest;*
> *All that's sweet was made*
> *But to be lost when sweetest.*
> 5 *Stars that shine and fall;*
> *The flower that drops in springing;*
> *These, alas! are types of all*
> *To which our hearts are clinging.*
>
> *Who would seek or prize*
> 10 *Delights that end in aching?*
> *Who would trust to ties*
> *That every hour are breaking?*
> *Better far to be*
> *In utter darkness lying,*
> 15 *Than to be blest with light and see*
> *That light for ever flying.*
>
> Thomas Moore

Practice task

5 **a)** Look at the title of the poem. What clues does it contain about the content or theme of the poem?

b) List the nouns used in the first six lines of the poem. Do they suggest a possible theme?

c) Is there a difference between the nouns used in lines 1–6 and lines 7–12? Do they suggest a possible theme?

6 How is the image in the final couplet different from the images that have come before it? What new sub-theme does this introduce?

7 Which of the following would you choose as the main theme of the poem?

a) love

b) life and death

c) the pain of unrequited love

d) the impermanence of beauty

Test yourself

Read the following poem, then answer the items below. The poem describes what the poet would give to her loved one as a Valentine. As her choice is unusual, she justifies it by pointing out why it is appropriate.

Valentine

Not a red rose or a satin heart.

I give you an onion.
It is a moon wrapped in brown paper.
It promises light
5   *like the careful undressing of love.*

Here.
It will blind you with tears
like a lover.
It will make your reflection
10 *a wobbling photo of grief.*

I am trying to be truthful.

Not a cute card or a kissogram.

I give you an onion.
Its fierce kiss will stay on your lips,
15 *possessive and faithful*
as we are,
for as long as we are.

Take it.
Its platinum loops shrink to a wedding-ring,
20 *if you like.*

Lethal.
Its scent will cling to your fingers,
cling to your knife.

Carol Ann Duffy

1   What does Duffy suggest she will give her partner as a Valentine's gift?

   a)   a rose

   b)   a satin heart

   c)   an onion

   d)   the moon

2   Duffy says that the onion is a moon. What figurative device is this an example of?

   a)   simile

   b)   hyperbole

   c)   metaphor

   d)   personification

3   Why does Duffy describe the onion as 'a moon wrapped in brown paper'?

    a)   to suggest it has two colours

    b)   to suggest it is white inside with a thin brown outer 'skin'

    c)   to suggest it has an outer layer

    d)   to show it is a gift

4   How many of the senses does the poem appeal to?

    a)   four

    b)   five

    c)   two

    d)   three

Where might you have gone wrong?

Item 1

c) is correct.

You may have read the first line and, as they are quite normal Valentine's gifts, chosen a) or b). You may have read on and seen that a lot of the poem is about a moon and thought this was the theme so chosen d). However, close reading shows that the poem starts with 'Not a red rose or a satin heart' before saying 'I give you an onion'. Always read the whole poem before answering any items.

Item 2

c) is correct.

You may have worked out that Duffy is comparing the onion to the moon and thought it was an example of a simile a). However there is no 'as' or 'like' so it is not a simile. A hyperbole is an exaggeration, which this is not, and as the onion is not compared to a human, this is not personification. The words 'It is' signal that a metaphor is being used.

Item 3

b) is correct.

In this case, you need to choose the answer that is most accurate or precise, because it could be argued that all four are potentially correct statements about the onion. However, this item asks you to explore Duffy's reasons for her description. a) is factually correct but does not account for Duffy's use of 'wrapped in'. c) and d) do not include reference to the colours she describes. b), which combines the idea of the layers and the colours, is the correct choice.

Item 4

a) is correct.

Almost all the senses are evoked by the poem: we can picture the appearance of the onion, we can smell it at the end, taste it in line 14 and feel it in line 19. However, no sense of sound is evoked.

Chapter 5 Gaining insights from literature: Prose

5.1 Understanding figurative language in prose

Learn how to:
- *recognise figurative techniques*
- *recognise the effect of figurative techniques.*

Why is being able to recognise and analyse figurative language important?

You may be asked specific questions about a word or phrase which rely on you having understood that it is an example of figurative language. You may also be asked to identify the technique being used or the effect of its use.

> ### Remember
>
> The figurative techniques used in poetry and prose are largely the same, so you do not need to learn a new list of techniques. However, bear in mind that some techniques are less common in poetry than in prose.

Building skills

Identifying figurative techniques common in literary prose

1. Write down the definitions of the following words.
   a) simile
   b) metaphor
   c) personification
   d) symbolism
   e) pathetic fallacy

2 Read the extract below. It is about a young boy, Pip, who has stolen food and drink from home in order to feed an escaped convict who has threatened him if he does not return with supplies. Identify five examples of figurative techniques.

It was a rimy morning, and very damp. I had seen the damp lying on the outside of my little window, as if some goblin had been crying there all night, and using the window for a pocket-handkerchief. Now, I saw the damp lying on the bare hedges and spare grass, like a coarser sort of spiders' webs; hanging itself from twig to twig and blade to blade. On every rail and gate, wet lay clammy; and the marsh-mist was so thick that the wooden finger on the post directing people to our village – a direction which they never accepted, for they never came there – was invisible to me until I was quite close under it. Then, as I looked up at it, while it dripped, it seemed to my oppressed conscience like a phantom devoting me to the Hulks.

The mist was heavier yet when I got out upon the marshes, so that instead of my running at everything, everything seemed to run at me. This was very disagreeable to a guilty mind. The gates and dykes and banks came bursting at me through the mist, as if they cried as plainly as could be, 'A boy with Somebody-else's pork pie! Stop him!' The cattle came upon me with like suddenness, staring out of their eyes, and steaming out of their nostrils, 'Holloa, young thief!' One black ox, with a white cravat on – who even had to my awakened conscience something of a clerical air – fixed me so obstinately with his eyes, and moved his blunt head round in such an accusatory manner as I moved round, that I blubbered out to him, 'I couldn't help it, sir! It wasn't for myself I took it!' Upon which he put down his head, blew a cloud of smoke out of his nose, and vanished with a kick-up of his hind-legs and a flourish of his tail.

From *Great Expectations* by Charles Dickens

Considering the effect of figurative language

Remember that writers select particular words for three main reasons:

* impact
* sensory appeal
* conveying emotion.

3 Look again at the extract from *Great Expectations*.

    a) How is the description of the mist given impact by the figurative language?

    b) How are our senses stimulated by the passage? How do its sights, sounds and sensations help the reader to imagine the scene?

    c) Consider the connotations of the images created. Do certain words carry with them ideas and emotions in addition to their literal meanings?

It can be helpful to create a table like the one below to work through the effects of language in a piece of writing.

Words from the extract	Sensory associations (what it makes you see/hear/feel/taste)	Emotional associations (what it makes you feel)
'goblin had been crying there all night'	droplets of water	fear (of supernatural)
'like a coarser sort of spiders' webs'		
'like a phantom devoting me to the Hulks'		

4 Overall, how do these techniques make you feel about the journey Pip is on and how he is feeling?

Apply the skills

Read this extract from *Ethan Frome*, then answer the items that follow. The passage describes a journey taken by the narrator with the main character of the novel, whom he has recently met.

> *Abreast of the schoolhouse the road forked, and we dipped down a lane to the left, between hemlock boughs bent inward to their trunks by the weight of the snow. I had often walked that way on Sundays, and knew that the solitary roof showing through bare branches near the bottom of the hill was that of Frome's **saw-mill**. It looked **exanimate***
> 5 *enough, with its idle wheel looming above the black stream dashed with yellow-white spume, and its cluster of sheds sagging under their white load. Frome did not even turn his head as we drove by, and still in silence we began to mount the next slope. About a mile farther, on a road I had never travelled, we came to an orchard of starved apple-trees writhing over a hillside among outcroppings of slate that nuzzled up through the snow*
> 10 *like animals pushing out their noses to breathe. Beyond the orchard lay a field or two, their boundaries lost under drifts; and above the fields, huddled against the white immensities of land and sky, one of those lonely **New England** farm-houses that make the landscape lonelier.*

15 *'That's my place,' said Frome, with a sideway jerk of his lame elbow; and in the distress and oppression of the scene I did not know what to answer. The snow had ceased, and a flash of watery sunlight exposed the house on the slope above us in all its plaintive ugliness. The black **wraith** of a deciduous creeper flapped from the porch, and the thin wooden walls, under their worn coat of paint, seemed to shiver in the wind that had risen with the ceasing of the snow.*

From *Ethan Frome* by Edith Wharton

saw-mill: a workshop where wood is cut and turned into timber logs for building

exanimate: lifeless

New England: a north-eastern region of the USA

wraith: a ghost or spectre

Practice task

5 The sheds are described as 'sagging under their white load'. This creates an effect of:

a) dazzling light

b) weary pressure

c) frosty sharpness

d) strong defiance

6 What technique is used in line 9 to describe the way the slate rocks poke through the snow?

a) pathetic fallacy

b) personification

c) hyperbole

d) simile

7 The description of the 'wraith-like' creeper in the final sentence gives the impression that the house is:

a) haunted

b) secretive

c) dying or decaying

d) welcoming

8 The writer's main purpose with this extract is to:

a) create a dramatic incident

b) develop characters

c) explain information

d) create atmosphere

5.2 Identifying tone in prose

Learn how to:

- *identify tone and feeling*
- *recognise the techniques used to create tone and feeling.*

Why is being able to recognise and analyse tone important?

You may be asked specific questions about tone. You may be asked to identify the technique being used to create tone or the effect of its use. If you can gauge the tone of a text, it will also help you to work out its purpose.

Remember

Tone is not the same as mood. The mood of a piece of writing influences how *the reader* feels.

Building skills

Identifying tone in prose

In order to identify tone, you need to be familiar with a wide variety of words that can be used to describe it. Tone can be described by any word that conveys an emotion or feeling.

1 Look up the definitions of the following words:

    a) melancholic

    b) ironic

    c) sarcastic

    d) condescending

2 Read the following extract from *Ethan Frome*. How would you sum up the narrator's tone? Could you use one of the words above, or is the tone here different?

> *I went after him into a low unlit passage, at the back of which a ladder-like staircase rose into obscurity. On our right a line of light marked the door of the room which had sent its ray across the night; and behind the door I heard a woman's voice droning querulously.*
>
> *Frome stamped on the worn oil-cloth to shake the snow from his boots, and set down his lantern on a kitchen chair which was the only piece of furniture in the hall. Then he opened the door.*
>
> *'Come in,' he said; and as he spoke the droning voice grew still...*
>
> *It was that night that I found the clue to Ethan Frome, and began to put together this vision of his story.*
>
> From *Ethan Frome* by Edith Wharton

Sometimes the tone is obvious from the choice of words, which may link directly to emotional states of the characters. In the extract above, the phrase 'I found the clue' suggests that the narrator is curious and thoughtful. However, sometimes tone is created in more subtle ways.

3 In the extract on page 92, you learned from the narrator of Frome's useless workshop and his run-down house. Now the narrator mentions 'the worn oil-cloth' and the 'kitchen chair' in the hall. What sort of tone is created by these references?

Recognising the techniques that create tone in prose

Tone is often implicit, so it can be difficult to identify. You can look for implicit tone in:

• word choice: the precise meaning, nuances and connotations of the words selected

• figurative language: the 'extras' that the writer uses in addition to the literal meaning of words

• sound and structure: the way that the writer uses sound effects, paragraphs, sentences and punctuation.

> **Revision tip**
>
> You can use the mnemonic WFS (word choice, figurative language, sound and structure) to help you remember what to look for when skim-reading extracts in search of clues to the tone.

Read the following extract, taken from a piece of travel writing, then answer the WFS items below. The writer has just described the arrival of a ship in harbour and the crowds of people who have gathered to meet it.

All at once the reason for this air of expectancy became clear, for down the gangway a scarcely recognizable figure was advancing at the head of a uniformed **retinue**. *It was one of our shipmates, the* **high proconsular dignitary**, *no longer the colourless and larva-like figure we had known on the journey, but a superb metamorphosis in white and gold and brass, arriving here to take over his new appointment as* **Prefect**. *His hat and cuffs glittered with bullion, and on his bosom alongside another* **decoration** *of bright green, the Legion of Honour made a red splash. It was difficult to believe that it was same man.*

From *The Traveller's Tree:
A Journey Through the Caribbean*
by Patrick Leigh Fermor

retinue: a group of staff who attend an important person

high proconsular dignitary: a government officer

Prefect: a government leader for an area

decoration: a medal

4 Word choice:

    a) What emotion(s) does the writer name?

    b) What does 'scarcely recognizable' suggest about the figure?

    c) Find three colours used to describe the Prefect as he appears on the gangway.

    d) What other words or phrases suggest that his appearance is unexpected?

5 Figurative language:

    a) What does 'colourless and larva-like' suggest about the figure?

    b) Are these complimentary descriptions?

6 Sound and structure: what is the meaning of the final sentence in the paragraph?

How would you sum up the writer's tone?

a) complimentary

b) amused

c) astonished

d) bemused

Apply the skills

Read the following extract, then answer the items that follow. This passage is from the same travelogue, as the narrator is introduced to some new tastes. How does he feel about them?

With slow enjoyment we ate the fruit we had bought in the market. The bananas were gigantic but commonplace. The sour-sops were about the size of a child's football, tapering into the shape of a pear, and covered with dark rind roughened with innumerable little hooked briers. The fruit inside was semi-liquid and snow white, expelling an aroma faintly resembling peardrops, and wringing our dusty palates with a delicious and slightly acid astringency. The paw-paw, which we next opened, was roughly the same size, but the soft rind was a smooth, patchy gold in colour, mottled with green and rusty brown. We halved it lengthways, and discovered two deep oblongs of a dewy, coral-coloured fruit of a consistency miraculously poised between solidarity and liquescence; much sweeter than the sour-sop, and, I thought, even better. Its sweetness is mitigated and, as it were, underlined by the faintest tang of something sharper – was it creosote or turpentine? – but so slight that one loses the identity of the taste while attempting to define it. Pushing the ruins aside, we each chose an avocado pear: dark green or violet globes the size of cricket balls, enclosed in a hard and warty carapace.

From *The Traveller's Tree: A Journey Through the Caribbean*
by Patrick Leigh Fermor

7 How would you sum up the writer's tone when describing the fruit?

   a) fascinated

   b) pleased

   c) hungry

   d) greedy

8 It is clear that the writer is impressed by the taste of the paw-paw. Which figurative technique does the writer use to suggest this?

   a) exaggeration

   b) onomatopoeia

   c) simile

   d) use of sensory detail

9 What aspects of structure are used to show how overwhelmed by the new tastes and textures the writer feels?

   a) lists

   b) a summary sentence at the end

   c) long, multi-clause sentences

   d) exclamation marks

5.3 Understanding structure in prose

Learn how to:

• *identify the techniques used by writers to structure prose texts*
• *recognise the effects of these structural techniques.*

Why is being able to recognise and analyse structure important?

You may be asked specific questions about word order, punctuation, sentence structure or paragraphing. This may lead to questions about sequencing of ideas or the way information is revealed. You may be asked to identify a technique being used or its effect.

Building skills

Identifying common structures in prose

Prose is often organised into chapters. For example, Mary Seacole's biography is divided into 109 chapters. Each chapter outlines a different period of her life, in chronological order. Here is one of the chapter headings:

CHAPTER IX

VOYAGE TO CONSTANTINOPLE–MALTA–GIBRALTAR, AND WHAT I THOUGHT OF IT – VISIT TO SCUTARI HOSPITAL – MISS NIGHTINGALE

Sometimes chapter headings are intended to arouse our curiosity or hint at drama to come.

Within chapters, prose is organised by paragraphs. These are used to signal a change of place, time or perspective.

1. How do you think the paragraphs will be organised within Chapter IX of Seacole's biography?

The third level of organisation in prose is sentences. There are three types of sentence: simple, compound and complex. For more on these sentence types see Paper 1, Topic 2.2.

2 Identify the different sentence types used in the extract below.

> *Sasha climbed faster. He was not far behind her, but at least his fingers were no longer grasping at her ankles. At least she couldn't hear his breath wheezing as he struggled to breathe and climb. She continued to climb. Faster she went.*

There are many grammatical rules relating to structure. For example, a conjunction such as 'but', or 'because' should not be used to start a sentence and you should try not to end a sentence with a preposition (for example, 'a type he'd never heard of'). Often we only notice these rules when a writer breaks them!

Revision tip

....

If you are asked about structure, consider the three organisation levels:

- **overall** (the way a whole text is split up)
- **internal** (the way paragraphs are organised)
- **sentence** level

Remember this as OIS.

Revision tip

....

When studying structure, think about devices in prose such as flashback or *in media res*. (For more about these, see Paper 2, Topic 3.1 in Paper 2.)

Considering the effect of structure in prose

Read the extract below from a short story. In it, a man is telling a story from his childhood to his grandson.

> *'I walked a little way further through the woods and came to a place where some rock ledges were sticking out and I could see a skinny possum sticking his sharp little nose out of a small hole on the cliff ledge. I took careful aim with my rifle and killed the poor little starved possum. I said, "I'm sorry to kill you, little fellow, but you were suffering from hunger just like my folks are."*
>
> *'My conscience pricked me something fierce as I picked up the poor little thing. "Maybe I done you a favour," I told the dead creature as I carried him through the deep snow. Eating him would be better than nothing, but being so hungry had made me feel humble and caring. As I walked, I thought about the prayer I had made, and although He hadn't given me a deer or a rabbit, but instead a pitiful little possum, I recalled what Mammy had told me one time. "God always gives us just what we need – not what we ask for."*
>
> *'I looked down at the little possum. Its eyes were closed and I cried as I realised it would never see another bright summer morning when the woods are green and flushed with life, when squirrels and rabbits play their games. Tears poured down my face at the thought of him never again eating grapes off the summer vines. I sat down for a while and cried, but it was so cold, the tears froze on my cheeks.' A tear rolled down Grandpa's face as he went on with his story.*
>
> From *Starvation Hollow* by Stanley McQueen

3. Why does the writer choose to start new paragraphs where he does?

4. a) In the third paragraph, why does the writer choose to start the sentence with 'Tears': 'Tears poured down my face at the thought of him never again eating grapes off the summer vines.'

   b) How could this sentence be reordered? What is the effect of the new word order?

Apply the skills

Read the following extract from a ghost story, then answer the items that follow. In this passage, a child, Jack, is settling down for the night when he encounters a ghost.

The shadow ran back and forth across the ceiling like an animal, but Jack wasn't nervous. It was just a shadow. The woman who died here must have fallen asleep sometimes watching that shadow, he thought. For some reason the thought comforted him. He lay on top of the bedclothes, wide awake for hours, mildly frightened by what he'd experienced that day, but
5 *also excited by it, and enjoying the mixture of darkness and moonlight in the room.*

He had nearly drifted off to sleep when he felt a pressure. It came from the foot of the bed, as if someone had carefully sat down without wanting to disturb him. It was the slightest of pressures, almost nothing. Jack barely noticed it. And if he'd already fallen asleep perhaps he wouldn't have noticed the sigh either, a long sigh against his right ear, followed by a
10 *caress that reached across his shoulders and down onto his throat.*

It was like a mother's caress, but it was not his mother.

Jack screamed. A small, thin woman, face as pale as a white candle, was draped across his bed.
15 *Her arm was extended tenderly towards him. Her eyes, in the moonlight, were black as a bird's. Clearly startled that Jack could see her, she backed off. Her arms*
20 *drifted, her body appearing to rise gradually off the bed.*

Jack lunged for the door. Even before he reached it, he was struggling to find air. By the next
25 *breath, he was hyperventilating – inhaling too rapidly for enough oxygen to enter his lungs.*

From *Breathe: A Ghost Story* by Cliff McNish

5 Which part of the novel do you imagine that this extract is from?

  a) the end

  b) early, but not right at the start

  c) the middle

  d) the beginning

6 What is the effect of the very short third paragraph?

  a) it leaves the reader hanging

  b) it signals a change in mood

  c) it calms the reader

  d) it emphasises Jack's fears

7 Why does the writer start the fourth paragraph with the simple sentence 'Jack screamed'?

  a) to make the reader feel sorry for him

  b) to emphasise the scream

  c) to give the reader time to think

  d) to foreground his fear

5.4 Identifying themes in prose

Learn how to:

- *recognise when a theme is being built up*
- *recognise the techniques used to suggest a theme.*

Why is being able to recognise and analyse themes important?

You may be asked specific questions about the theme of a text that rely on you having recognised it as it built up. You may be asked to identify the techniques being used to create it. You may also be asked what you think the purpose of a text is; to comment on this you will need to have accurately identified its theme.

Building skills

Identifying themes and sub-themes

The theme of a text can often be summed up in one word – for example, war, family, courage. However, it is often helpful to be more specific: the horror of war, the trials and tribulations of family life, the courage of those who are ill. Some texts may include sub-themes related to a larger theme, such as the role of women in war, life at home in war time, the men left behind.

> **Remember**
>
> Literary prose tends to be longer than poetry, but themes are shown in similar ways. Prose may be structured to tell a story or chart a life. It may still develop a theme by continually prompting the reader to consider an issue or realise a particular universal truth.

1. Read the following extract from a novel about a woman who has travelled to a tropical island. The first two annotations highlight possible themes. What themes might be indicated by the other two highlighted sections?

Meryl stepped out of the plane and breathed in slowly; the air was humid but she could not have been happier to have left the grey skies [1] of London behind her. Navigating the steep airline steps, she glanced down at her phone; the screen was blank and for a moment her body went cold and her stomach clenched [2]...but then she remembered; she had switched it off. She was not going to turn it back on! She was free. For the first time in what felt like forever her time was her own. [3] Her back straightened and a smile spread across her face, softening her gaze [4] as she took in the small airstrip and the tiny terminal building ahead.

[1] Escape?

[2] Destructive effect of technology/work?

[3] ?

[4] ?

2 Note down your predictions of what might happen in the rest of the novel.

Considering the techniques used to build themes

Events in the text can be a quick indicator of the theme. You can also look at the emotions shown by the characters or figures in the text. Also consider the narrator. Are they are independent of the action? If so, do they add any comment or emotion to the text? As you read, look out for repetition of events or emotions that may build up.

Read the extract below, which is from an online biography of Michael Jordan.

Michael Jordan was born in Brooklyn on 17 February 1963. His parents, James (a mechanic) and Deloris (a bank teller), already had two sons and a daughter. They had another daughter after Michael, completing the family. Feeling that the city was not a safe place to raise their children, James and Deloris relocated to Wilmington, North Carolina, while Michael was just a toddler.

James was a baseball fan, and as a child Michael loved to play catch with his dad. However, when his older brother Larry started playing basketball, young Michael also began taking an interest in the sport.

He tried out for the varsity team as a high-school sophomore. However, at a skinny 5' 11", it was felt he wasn't ready to play at this level. This all changed in his junior year, by which time he had shot up another four inches. He had also been practising hard and his game was hugely improved. Finally accepted as a varsity player, he racked up a 20-point average per game in his last two high-school seasons and made the McDonald's All-American team in his senior year.

3 List the events that occur in the text. Do they have anything in common?

4 **a)** How do Jordan's parents behave in the text?

   b) How does Jordan behave?

   c) Do these reactions have anything in common?

5 Which of the following themes is the best fit for the extract?

    a)   triumph over adversity   **c)**   never give up

    b)   effort brings rewards   **d)**   practice makes perfect

Linking theme and purpose

Authors write for many different reasons and ultimately, only they will know why they put pen to paper. However, it is possible to suggest the purpose of a text. Below is a list of possible reasons for writing prose:

- to express emotions
- to express opinions
- to share experiences
- to share emotions
- to educate/inform
- to show that 'we are not alone'
- to provoke debate.

6 Think of some texts you have read recently and work out their purpose(s).

Apply the skills

Read the following extracts, taken from an imaginary diary set in the lands that became Haiti in the time of Columbus.

First Quarter Moon, Day 3

There have been several births in the villages, the most notable being the child of Cuybio's younger sister, Yeybona. Yeybona was born only a few moons before me. I heard many of those who gathered in front of my uncle's house to speak of the birth of Yeybona's son whisper that it will soon be the turn of Matunherí's niece and likely successor, me, to bear children.

Of course I will do this, but my time has yet to come. I have not blossomed as quickly as Yeybona has. She is a flower. I am a sea grape, still clinging to the branch.

Because Yeybona is like a sister to me, I went to see the baby immediately. He is a marvel. His skin is smooth and nut brown. Already his eyes are wide open and he looks up at the thatch canopy above his hammock.

First Quarter Moon, Day 4

Many of the new babies were brought to Matunherí's house so he could see and bless them. In his role as the supreme chief, my uncle is considered the father of all who live in Xaraguá. Our birthright – inherited through my uncle's and my mother's mother – dictates that either Behechio or I are to one day rule Xaraguá, so Behechio and I assist Matunherí in such tasks as greeting the new babies and their parents. It is always a joy to welcome new life to Xaraguá, a pleasure we enjoy almost every moon.

Edwidge Danticat

Practice task

7 After reading the first diary entry, which of the following themes seems most likely to feature in the rest of this text?

    a)   growing up   **c)**   rivalry

    b)   motherhood   **d)**   expectations

8 After reading the second diary entry, which of the following themes seems most likely to feature in the rest of this text?

a) growing up

b) motherhood

c) rivalry

d) expectations

9 What do you think is the main purpose of this text?

a) to inform/educate

b) to share experiences

c) to entertain and intrigue

d) to provoke debate

Test yourself

Read the following extract from a short story.

On an island nobody ever really, truly disappears without a trace. No, what we have here are bodies: a woman found in the bushes at All Saints, a tourist slain at Darkwood, a girl washed up at Devil's Bridge…

They're few and far between. That's why they make the news, because it always kind of
5 shakes us up that there might be someone among us who could do such a thing.

But there are no places to hide bodies, nowhere they won't eventually reveal themselves.

A thin girl crouches behind the cover of a cassi tree when she hears cars, more than one, coming up the path. She is naked and old enough now, at thirteen, to be embarrassed
10 *by that. Her mind is a fog and she is wet, as if she's been in the water.*

Only that isn't possible, is it?

Somehow, she's at Devil's Bridge where the rocks are sharper than a coconut vendor's cutlass, and the waters lash with a vengeance. Nobody swims at Devil's Bridge.

None of that explains why she is wet and why, when she licks her lips, it tastes like salt,
15 *and why, when the water trickles down her back, it burns, as if there are cuts there she can't see. She'd done a little dance earlier, like a dog chasing its tail, trying to see, and aching for the burning to stop.*

It was like the burn of a good beating, the kind she got the first time she'd run away. She thought Mammy was trying to strip the skin off her back that time; the way she sweated
20 *and screamed, her face ugly, arms flapping, as the belt wailed. Then Mammy had called out to everybody she knew: 'You all talk to that gyal dey, you nuh, ca me'll kill she.'*

After the fourth or fifth time, the social worker told Mammy not to hit her anymore; that when she ran away again, Mammy was just to call them and let them handle it. Only they were short-staffed, and the police was 'don' care ah damn'—Mammy's words—and
25 *with everybody looking the other way and her Mammy's hands tied, the girl knew she could stay gone for weeks if she set her mind to it.*

But she didn't plan on ending up here at Devil's Bridge, which she only recognised because of a long-ago school trip.

From 'Amelia at Devil's Bridge' by Joanne C. Hillhouse

1 What is the effect of the phrase 'Her mind is a fog...'?
   a)   It tells the reader that it is misty.
   b)   It creates pathetic fallacy.
   c)   It implies the girl is stupid.
   d)   It suggests that she is confused.

2 What is the effect of the brief paragraph 'Only that isn't possible, is it?'
   a)   It shows us that the girl is speaking.
   b)   It introduces a new type of information.
   c)   It suggests that her thoughts are darting around.
   d)   It presents the narrator's thoughts.

3 What is 'rocks are sharper than a coconut vendors cutlass' in lines 12–13 an example of?
   a)   simile
   b)   personification
   c)   metaphor
   d)   onomatopoeia

4 The overall structure includes an example of flashback. Why does the writer use this technique?
   a)   to warn the reader of something to come
   b)   to give the reader background information
   c)   to create a cliffhanger
   d)   to keep the writing varied

5 What do you think was the writer's intention when she wrote this story?
   a)   to entertain
   b)   to scare
   c)   to make a social comment
   d)   to inform

6 What would you say is the overall theme of this extract?
   a)   violence
   b)   domestic abuse
   c)   the supernatural
   d)   murder

Where might you have gone wrong?

Item 1

d) is correct.

You may have remembered that writers of literary prose often use the weather to reflect mood and so selected b), but in this case the writer clearly links the weather to the girl's mind, so we know that she is saying something directly about the girl's thought processes. You may have selected c), as the girl seems to be having trouble understanding why she is where she is, but actually she is not unintelligent (she works out where she is even after only one visit). However, it is clear that she struggles to connect events, suggesting that her thinking is unclear, just as fog makes things unclear.

Item 2

c) is correct.

You may have thought these were her words spoken out loud and chosen a), but there are no speech marks to suggest this. Equally, it is possible to think this is the narrator, choosing d), but this does not seem to be a new voice from the one that we 'hear' in the surrounding paragraphs. It is not offering new information either, as the paragraphs either side are about where she is and asking why she is wet. Option c) makes sense, as we know that writers can use contrastingly brief sentences and paragraphs to create a sense of movement or change, and this fits with the girl's confusion and rapid search for solutions.

Item 3

c) is correct.

You may have realised that this is a comparison and thought that it was a simile, so choosing a). However, there is no 'as' or 'like' to make the comparison explicit, which means that this is a metaphor.

Item 4

b) is correct.

You may have confused a flashback with other techniques, but the clue is in the word as 'back' suggests previous events, which normally give background information. It is true that knowing this background may create suspense as you read on, or even result in a cliffhanger, if for example her mother appeared at the bridge, but here the flashback gives us useful context about why she may be there.

Item 5

c) is correct.

You may have considered that, as this extract is from a short story, it was written to entertain and have chosen a). You could also have thought that this story might link to a real crime because of the prologue and so connected this with d). However, the mention of abuse at home, social workers and running away suggest that so far the story is making a social commentary on these things.

Item 6

d) is correct.

You may have tried to think about how the story would progress from here – and thought that it was going to turn into a ghost story c), or continue with the theme of domestic abuse, b). However, at this point the only firm conclusion we can draw is that the extract is about murder, as the prologue expands on this topic.

Chapter 6 Recognising and evaluating opinion

6.1 Recognising implicit meaning

Learn how to:

• *recognise implicit information to understand point of view in an argument.*

Why is being able to work out what is implied important?

Specific questions about an argument text will test your understanding of the writer's purpose and overall **attitude** towards a topic. This may be stated explicitly, but it is often implicit so you will need to determine what it is. (For more on **implicit meaning**, see Paper 1, Topic 1.2.)

> **Key terms**
>
> **attitude:** *a writer's feelings and point of view towards their subject or topic*
>
> **implicit meaning:** *meaning that has to be inferred or deduced; implicit meaning often reveals opinions or feelings or can lead you to draw a conclusion about an author's intention or viewpoint*

Building skills

Identifying attitude by looking at content

The easiest way to identify a writer's attitude is to look at the main points made and see if these relate to a particular viewpoint. Look at these topic sentences from a feature article about dangerous sports.

> *Sporting activities such as cliff jumping put lives at risk and waste the time and resources of emergency services.*
>
> *Supposedly, divers gain a thrill from their jumps.*
>
> *Horrifying statistics reveal that over 10 per cent of extreme sporting activities end in fatality.*

1 For each of these topic sentences, write down what you think is the writer's point of view.

2 Rewrite each of the topic sentences to suggest a different viewpoint.

You can use the same approach when looking at visual texts such as the following cartoon. (Tom Brady is a well-known American football player.)

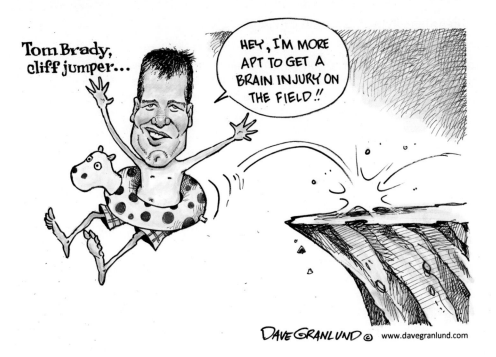

Tom Brady, cliff jumper...

HEY, I'M MORE APT TO GET A BRAIN INJURY ON THE FIELD !!

DAVE GRANLUND © www.davegranlund.com

3 Quickly scan this image and jot down answers to the following items.

   a) What is happening in the cartoon?

   b) Who is in the cartoon? How are they portrayed?

   c) What is the character saying?

4 From this quick scan, do you think that the cartoonist is 'for' or 'against' cliff jumping?

Identifying attitude by looking at connotations

Another way to infer a writer's attitude is to look at the words they have chosen and ask yourself whether they have positive or negative connotations. If most of the words suggest the same type of connotation, this suggests a particular point of view. (For more on connotations see Paper 1, Topic 1.3.)

5 Draw a table with three columns labelled 'Negative', 'Neutral' and 'Positive'. Look at the words in the box below, which could be used to describe a holiday destination. Write each word in the correct column of your table.

dry	humid	bright	dull	well-maintained	pristine	unkempt	
rainy	light	ramshackle	immaculate	neat	moist	tense	
relaxing	littered	unsound	sunny	rustic	carefree	dank	

Identifying attitude by looking at intensifiers

A writer's use of **intensifiers** can also reveal their attitude. Intensifiers are used to strengthen adjectives, so if you see phrases such 'really' good or 'extremely' beautiful, you can infer that the writer is positive about the topic. Other intensifiers, such as 'absolutely', 'completely', 'particularly' and 'exceptionally', can build up an overall sense of a writer's attitude.

Key term

intensifiers: words that are not strictly necessary in a sentence, but which add emotion to the word they modify (e.g. 'He <u>really</u> wanted that ice cream.')

6 List the intensifiers in this text about cliff jumping at Playa Forti.

> At 40ft above sea level it's an exceptionally good place for a really panoramic view of the Caribbean Sea and also an excellent spot for an extremely daredevil jump. Follow the narrow path along the coastline to a platform strategically placed to make the big leap that much easier and take the terrifically terrifying plunge into the crystal clear water below.
>
> From http://blog.f1rst.com

Apply the skills

Read the following article about cliff jumping, then answer the items that follow.

Even the best Olympic divers face dangers when practising diving from platforms into pools, but it is high diving in uncontrolled conditions, such as off cliffs into the sea that carries the greatest risks. You might think that water provides a soft cushion in which to land, but from cliff-top heights it can feel like you're slamming into a solid rather than
5   a liquid.

The problem of speed

The biggest issue is speed. From lower down, you don't gain enough momentum to do major damage. Higher up it is another matter. You might only be in the air for a few seconds, but in that time you can gather some serious speed. From a height of 6 metres you can fall at 40 km/h. At 18 metres you could be approaching 100 km/h! At these speeds, hitting the
10   water at the wrong angle can cause all sorts of damage, from concussion to spinal injuries.

Hidden risks

Even if you break the water safely, there are still risks. In a pool you know there's nothing nasty lurking beneath the surface, but a river or the sea could be hiding rocks, logs and all sorts of other dangers. You'll slow down once you're in the water, but you'll still be travelling fast enough to cause serious injury. Hitting the water wrong could be disastrous, but hitting
15   something solid underwater might be fatal. It is also easy to mistake the depth of the water. This can be changeable, especially in the sea, and an area you might think is safe to dive in might actually be far too shallow.

Drowning danger

You might enter the water without hurting yourself and avoid any hidden dangers below the surface, but you're still not safe. From great heights you plunge to great depths. This
20   can cause confusion – disorientation or fear of how far it is to the surface may cause you to panic, which in turn can lead to drowning. You're even more likely to drown if you've injured yourself in the dive. Just being slightly winded by hitting the water at the wrong angle might make you gasp for breath, which is obviously not advisable underwater. If you've done yourself more harm – broken a bone or knocked yourself unconscious for example – your
25   chances of survival are slim.

7 Look at the subheadings in the article. What can you infer about the writer's attitude towards cliff jumping? It is…

   a) neutral

   b) critical

   c) concerned

   d) against

8 The word 'greatest' in line 3 is an example of which technique?

   a) hyperbole

   b) simile

   c) intensifier

   d) sarcasm

9 Why does the writer use the word 'disastrous' in line 14? You can choose more than one answer.

   a) to upset people

   b) to suggest dramatic injuries

   c) to emphasise the danger

   d) to build his stance against cliff jumping

6.2 Understanding assertion and bias

Learn how to:

• *recognise assertion and bias in an argument.*

Why is being able to recognise and understand bias and assertion important?

Specific questions about an argument text will test your understanding of the writer's purpose and overall attitude towards a topic. You may also be asked to identify examples of **assertion** or **bias**. To do this, you will need to deduce implied meanings in the text.

> **Key terms**
>
> **assertion:** *a strong statement of a view or belief, often without evidence to support it*
>
> **bias:** *a strong favouring of one side of an argument or debate, often without representing the other side of it*

> **Remember**
>
> Assertion and bias are powerful aspects of writing, advertising and promotional materials, or editorials which are, by their very nature, biased. News articles sometimes show bias, but information texts and reports usually try to take an unbiased stance.

Building skills

Identifying assertion

Assertions are usually short, confident statements that offer no supporting evidence. They are not factual. For example:

The Aruba Tropical Hotel is the best in the world!

This assertion is clearly an opinion, and it would be difficult to back up the comment objectively. Notice also how there is no supporting evidence – even of the opinion.

1   Which of the following statements are factual and which are assertions?

   a)   Bananas contain potassium.

   b)   Bananas are delicious.

   c)   Bananas are good for you!

   d)   Over 100 million bananas are consumed worldwide every year.

   e)   Uganda has the highest per person consumption of bananas in the world.

Assertions can be used to sum up a viewpoint, so they are often a useful opening to an argumentative paragraph or essay. However, if they are not accompanied by evidence, assertions can weaken an argument because this suggests that the writer cannot back up their point, which indicates bias.

Read the following extracts from a hotel review site.

> **A**
>
> *The Aruba Tropical Hotel is the best in the world! I should know – I travel weekly for my job and have been doing so for ten years now. There are reasons for my view. The first is to do with the simply amazing location, the second, the quality of accommodation. Parallel in my rankings are the facilities and service provided and lastly, the catering. Let me tell you more. Well, the location is perfect! Just 15 minutes from the airport and yet an unspoilt beach awaits the traveller and there's not a bit of traffic noise.*
>
> **B**
>
> *The Aruba Tropical Hotel is the best in the world! Wow what a great location! It's so good! I can't fault it in any way. It suits me down to the ground. The Aruba has great food and drink and the rooms are fabulous.*

2 Which review uses assertion most effectively? Explain your choice in a few sentences.

Identifying bias

Bias is created in a number of ways. A clear sign of bias is when a writer only considers one side of an issue – for example, if a review only mentions positive aspects. However, bias can also be more subtle – for example, if a writer has only selected certain aspects of a topic, avoiding any that do not 'fit' their bias.

Read the following fact about how hurricanes and extreme weather have been reported over the past ten years.

> *With hurricane season set to start next week, Tuesday marks a record 127 months since a major hurricane has made landfall in the continental United States (National Oceanic and Atmospheric Administration's (NOAA) Hurricane Research Division statistics).*
>
> From an article by Barbara Hollingsworth, CNS News

Despite this well-authorized fact, many media sources announced the start of the hurricane season in an overly dramatic way. Look at the following headlines.

Storm clouds gather   Prepare for meltdown!
Killer storms in the wings   Nightmare season begins.

3 Why do you think the headlines ignored the facts and chose to highlight the potential weather risks?

You can also spot bias by examining content closely. For example, when a writer includes more points in favour of an issue than against it, it is likely that they are biased towards it. However, if the balance of points is equal, then the writer is probably writing neutrally and so without bias.

Another sign of bias is when the connotations of words used are clearly positive or negative. Consider the following headlines, which each sum up a 4–5 losing match result for the Troopers:

Close result for the Troopers
Tragic blow for the Troopers
Shame on you Troopers

4 How do the connotations of the language used in each headline reveal the writer's attitude towards the team?

Apply the skills

Read the following speech, designed to open a public meeting about the development of a coastal area as a cruise ship dock. Then answer the items below.

> Ladies and gentlemen welcome to this vitally important and somewhat distressing meeting, where we must discuss the future of our poor town and protect it from those who seek to plunder it for their own purposes. We must save our town!
>
> 5 This evening we need to consider the issues surrounding this development plan and the many discussion points raised by this scheme. Firstly, the loss of mangroves and sea grass meadows by some 75 per cent, caused by dredging and building processes. Secondly, the disturbance to marine animals caused by the horrific growth in numbers of vessels coming into shore. We will consider the lack of facilities for waste disposal on our island and the possibility of polluting 'tar balls' on our beaches. Lastly, we will debate the dangers caused
> 10 by large invasions of tourists in short periods of time. A disaster is looming!

6.2 Understanding assertion and bias

5 What is the effect of 'somewhat distressing' in line 1?

   a)   to make it seem a small problem

   b)   to casually criticize the plan

   c)   to express how upset people are

   d)   to exaggerate the distress

6 Which sentence in paragraph 2 identifies the purpose of the meeting?

   a)   the last sentence

   b)   the third sentence

   c)   the first sentence

   d)   the fourth sentence

7 Which statement most accurately describes the content of this speech?

   a)   a balance of positive and negative aspects of the scheme

   b)   a range of content slightly biased towards the negative

   c)   a list of negatives

   d)   a range of content biased toward the positive

8 How could the speech be reworked to encourage an open debate in which both sides of the argument are addressed?

   a)   offer evidence

   b)   make the content even-handed and the language neutral

   c)   include all the benefits of the scheme

   d)   include some disadvantages of the scheme

9 Identify any line in which there is an unsupported assertion.

   a)   line 4

   b)   line 3

   c)   line 7

   d)   line 10

6.3 Understanding persuasive techniques

Learn how to:

- *recognise persuasive techniques*
- *analyse the effect of persuasive techniques.*

Why is being able to recognise and analyse persuasive techniques important?

Specific questions about an opinion text will test your understanding of the writer's purpose and overall attitude towards a topic. You may also be asked to identify examples of **persuasive techniques** and/or their effects.

> **Key term**
>
> **persuasive techniques:** *language effects that help a speaker or writer state a point of view strongly in order to change their listener's or reader's opinion or influence their actions*

> **Revision tip**
>
> In an argument text, both sides of an issue will usually be addressed – if only to undercut one side. In persuasive writing, there is no need to consider alternative viewpoints, although it can be effective to do so.

Building skills

Recognising persuasive techniques

Writers use many techniques in persuasive writing. You can remember some of the key persuasive techniques by using the PERSUADER mnemonic:

	Technique	Example
P	**Personal address** (also called direct address)	*You need to listen. We need to act.*
E	Emotive images	*Picture the land, scarred and barren after the mining is finished.*
R	**Rhetorical questions**	*Do you want to be the one to take the blame?*
S	So what?	*If you don't…then…* *If you do…then…*
U	Undercut your opposition	*Some might say that…but…*
A	**Anecdotes**	*Years ago I was standing just where you are now and…*
D	Devices	For example: the rule of three: *We do this for the environment, the animals and the people!* hyperbole: *Whilst you ponder, millions of lives are lost!*

	Technique	Example
E	Evidence	*70 per cent of indigenous animals are already extinct.*
R	**Repetition**	*Please, please help me to save them.*
		We must, must, must vote now!

Read the following letter of complaint.

Dear Sir,

I am writing to complain about the slow internet service currently available to me and to demand that the installation of fibre to my district is brought forward. Unbelievably, internet speed here is currently averaging 256 kbps, which is about as fast as a snail goes! Honestly, could you cope with this kind of service?

In order for my island to be able to compete in the modern world of business we need to be quick, efficient and effective. We cannot do this when an email takes two weeks to load!

Picture the scene: I am sitting in my home office, fingers poised above the keys. An order comes in for my Mam's Original Bammy, which she makes fresh every day. I reply to the enquiry, offer to ship that afternoon. And then I wait…and wait…and wait. The bread would be mouldy before they received my reply! This is not good enough! It is a disgrace!

If I could reply swiftly, I could employ more people like my Mum – honest, good people who want to work and have unique skills to offer. I could build my business and start giving something back to my community.

I know you will say that you've been working on this. I know that my cousin on the Caymans has a full 10 mps. Well is that any use to me? When is fibre coming to my town? When will I be allowed to join the twenty-first century? When?

1 List the persuasive techniques in the letter, using the PERSUADER mnemonic.

(For more on the structure of persuasive texts see Paper 2, Topic 4.4.)

Identifying the effect of persuasive techniques

Writers use persuasive techniques for three main reasons:

- **impact**
- sensory appeal
- conveying emotion.

Look at this advert for Burchell's Hot Sauce.

Ride the storm with
BURCHELL'S HOT SAUCE!
Warning: For thrill seekers only!

2 Draw a table like the one below and make notes on each of the three ways that the Hot Sauce advert persuades you to buy the sauce.

Effect	Analysis
impact	*Personal address: The advert seems to be sending out a dare, which gets the reader's attention.*
sensory appeal	
conveying emotion	

3 Look back at the letter of complaint and draw up a table to analyse the effect of each of the techniques you identified.

Apply the skills

Read the following humorous article about the national holidays of various Caribbean islands and the jealousy this causes. Then answer the items below.

We need a holiday!

Why is it that citizens of Montserrat will be lounging around in the shade, drinking rum punch next Tuesday while the rest of us are toiling away as usual in the heat? Of course we all know the answer: the 'Emerald Isle of the Caribbean' has a national holiday to celebrate St Patrick's Day. 'What?' I hear you cry. 'Why on earth should they have a day off when I
5 *haven't?' Good question – and one that I will try to answer.*

Fans of the holiday will tell you that Montserrat has long held links with Ireland. The island's first generations of European settlers were mostly of Gaelic Irish. The first Leeward Islands census, collected in 1678 by Governor William Stapleton (himself described as Irish), indicates that Montserrat had by far the largest concentration of Irish inhabitants in the
10 *Lesser Antilles.*

They will also tell you that the flag and national dress of the island reveal their deep Irish roots. Well, they go as deep as 1909 when 'the lady with the harp' was added and 1988 when the green white and orange tartan was 'designed'. In fact, if we probe a little more deeply we find that the rules for the competition emphasised that the 'African–Irish/European–
15 *Arawak' origins of the population should be included. I actually have an aunt who submitted a dress covered in shamrocks as her entry!*

The truth is that celebrating St Patrick's Day and all things Irish makes sound financial sense for Montserrat.

My advice is that instead of moaning, you start looking closely at the history of your home
20 *town. Surely there is someone or something you can seize upon and cynically exploit? Let's find a now infamous celebrity with family here and get the bandwagon rolling! We can have a new flag and national dress designed in seconds! After all, we all know that everyone loves a party! Sign up to join our campaign 'Nevis needs a Holiday!' at NNaH@Nevis.org.*

Practice task

4   Why does the writer use sensory imagery in lines 1–2?

   a)   to help us understand the issue

   b)   to make the article fun

   c)   to engage our senses and get our attention

   d)   to make it personal

5   Which word or phrase from the first sentence suggests bias?

   a)   'lounging'

   b)   'rum punch'

   c)   'Why'

   d)   'as usual'

6   'I hear you cry' is an example of:

   a)   alliteration

   b)   personal address

   c)   repetition

   d)   the writer being down to earth

7   Line 17 contains an example of:

   a)   imagery

   b)   simile

   c)   factual evidence

   d)   anecdote

8   In line 22, 'designed in seconds!' is an example of:

   a)   evidence

   b)   exaggeration

   c)   anecdote

   d)   rhetorical question

6.4 Understanding presentation in adverts

Learn how to:

- *recognise the presentation and language techniques used in advertising*
- *analyse the effect of persuasive techniques.*

> **Remember**
>
> Adverts are almost always trying to persuade you to buy something or change your behaviour in some way. Because they have little space to do this through reasoning or evidence, adverts tend to use visual methods which are instantly powerful.

Why is being able to analyse adverts important?

You may be asked specific questions about an advertisement which rely on you having understood its overall purpose. You may also be asked to identify examples of persuasive techniques and/or their effects.

Building skills

Recognising persuasive techniques

There are many presentational techniques used in advertising. Some examples are shown on the advert below.

[1] Header: a memorable statement usually placed at the top of the page to catch the reader's eye

[2] Body text: expands on the main qualities and appeal of the product

[3] Image: must be attention-grabbing and link to the product or its effect; often images will seem to be moving or will be placed diagonally to suggest dynamism

[4] Call to action: an instruction or incentive that encourages immediate action, such as a phone call or shopping trip so as not to miss out on the deal/a product

[5] Contact details: shows the reader where and how to purchase or contact the seller

The **fonts** that designers choose can also convey a **mood** or approach that the reader transfers to the product or its promised effect. Font size can also suggest the importance of the words represented.

1 How would you describe the font in the advert? Does it match what the header and body text say?

Colour can also convey mood. Bright colours might represent energy and happiness. Other colours might suggest calmness or create a more serious **tone**.

> **Key terms**
>
> **font:** a particular design or size of lettering used in print text
>
> **mood:** the atmosphere or 'feel' in a story – for example, tense, joyful, peaceful, etc.
>
> **tone:** a writer's attitude or their 'voice' in a piece of writing, for example the tone of writing could be negative, sour or jovial

2 How would you describe the use of colour in the advert?

Advertising also uses language to persuade. Powerful language often appeals to a basic human need or desire such as:

- doing our best
- fitting in or being loved or admired
- getting a good deal
- being healthier/happier/prettier/wealthier.

Another way that adverts often catch our attention through language is by using wordplay or puns, and also by making the reader feel valued by using words such as 'we' and 'you'.

3 Which of the appeals listed above does the advert use?

4 How does the advert use techniques such as wordplay and inclusive language?

Identifying the effect of persuasive techniques in advertising

Writers use persuasive techniques for impact, sensory appeal and to convey emotions. If they are successful in making you remember their words, believe in their words and perhaps care about them, then you are more likely to take the action they are aiming for.

5 Copy and complete this table, answering the questions to summarize the ways in which the advert persuades you to book this resort.

Effect	Questions to ask yourself
impact	What draws your eye?
	What makes you remember this text?
sensory appeal	Can you picture this scene?
	Can you imagine any sounds/smells/tastes/textures?
conveying emotion	Does this text evoke any emotions in you?

Apply the skills

Look again at the advert, then answer the following items.

Practice task

6 Which of the following appeals is/are used in this advertisement?

   a) competitiveness

   b) being a 'better' tourist

   c) being loved more

   d) improved health

7 The size of font in this advert:

   a) suggests that booking is not a priority

   b) emphasises the type of tourist that will like this holiday

   c) hides the costs

   d) promotes the brand above all else

8 The body text (above the header)…

   a) suggests that the company is very informal

   b) makes the reader feel relaxed

   c) develops the key appeal of the resort

   d) gives booking details

Test yourself

Read the following letter to the Editor of the *Jamaica Observer*. Then answer the items that follow.

> **Dear Editor,**
>
> I write this in firm opposition to the proposal of a name change now before the Ministry of Education for Denbigh High School to be renamed the Michael Henry High School, not only as a Denbigh alumnus but a resident of the parish of Clarendon.
>
> 5   In situations such as this, a name is not just a pronoun for a physical location with a set of buildings, desk and chairs, but a link to a common heritage that invokes 'aqua' pride among those who were lucky enough to be embraced by Denbigh's style of nurturing calling into a career — as the motto states, 'Learning for Living'.
>
> This pride is cemented in its elder alumni, who understand the stigma formerly attached
> 10   to the school's name and its jagged past as Denbigh Comprehensive. At the time of my acceptance into Denbigh — as a transfer student who had been placed at Jamaica College — like most non-traditional high schools, Denbigh was associated with the negative societal stereotypes. I was upset at the thought of attending such a school after graduating from an established preparatory in the parish. Now I have no regrets. And
> 15   this is not just my story, it has been replicated more than a thousand times over.
>
> No school is perfect. Denbigh has its share of imperfections and will have its black sheep among those it shepherds. But it has come a mighty long way under the

supervision of stalwarts from former Principal Joan Wint to custodian emeritus Moses and all the staff, from administrative to ancillary.

20 *Denbigh has reached its rightful place at the top, surpassing many traditional high schools in Caribbean Secondary Education Certificate and Caribbean Advanced Proficiency Examination passes without cutting corners by refusing to have students sit exams.*

We are at a flashpoint in the school's history, and abandoning the name at such point
25 *will only serve to disenfranchise many who felt they have a hand in building the school at the foot of the hill.*

Mike Henry deserves more.

On behalf of the Denbigh alumni, we are ever grateful for the exceptional contributions of the long-serving Member of Parliament for Clarendon Central Mike Henry to
30 *Denbigh High, the township of May Pen and the wider Parish of Clarendon. However, a more fitting award is advisable, as there are many unnamed structures in the immediate township, including the square and the bridge. One would think that placing Mike Henry's name on road infrastructure would be more appropriate for a visionary advocate for Jamaica's transportation sector.*

Mario Boothe

From www.jamaicaobserver.com

Revision tip

When answering multiple-choice items, always read each item twice before making your choice.

1 How does the writer feel about the proposed change of name for the school?
   a) pleased
   b) resigned
   c) angry
   d) opposed

2 The word 'firm' in paragraph 1 is an example of:
   a) a noun
   b) an intensifier
   c) an adverb
   d) a pronoun

3 'Mike Henry deserves more' is an example of:
   a) a complex sentence
   b) an assertion
   c) a fact
   d) a metaphor

4 What persuasive technique does the writer use in paragraph 3?

    a) an anecdote

    b) exaggeration

    c) rhetorical questions

    d) repetition

5 In lines 16 and 17, the phrase 'black sheep among those it shepherds' is an example of which type of figurative language?

    a) simile

    b) personification

    c) metaphor

    d) hyperbole

Where might you have gone wrong?

Item 1

d) is correct.

You may have concluded that the writer was against the name change and therefore assumed that they were angry about it. However, the letter gives a reasoned argument and is not personal in tone or irrational at all, suggesting that the writer is calm but firm in their disapproval.

Item 2

b) is correct.

You may have thought that this was the noun 'firm', as in a company. However, this is clearly not the case if you consider the word in context. It is not being used as an adverb in this sentence. In this case the word is being used to show just how strongly the writer is in opposition. When a word takes this role, it is called an intensifier and is a common feature of argument/opinion writing.

Item 3

b) is correct.

You may have thought that this was a fact, but there is evidence to support it. It is meant literally, so is not a metaphor, and it is not a complex sentence as it only has one clause. It also fits the definition of an assertion perfectly, as it is an emotional opinion stated confidently and emphatically, as if it is true.

Item 4

a) is correct.

You may have forgotten what an anecdote is, but it is the only technique that is used in the paragraph. The other three persuasive techniques are not in evidence. You can spot it by the regular use of 'I' and the fact that a short account or story is told. In this case, it is one of the writer's memories of, or reflections on, when he started at the school.

Item 5

c) is correct.

You may have recognised that a comparison was being drawn between the teachers and students as shepherds and a flock of sheep, but mistakenly thought this was a simile. Remember that similes use 'as' or 'like' to make the comparison obvious. The students are being likened to sheep who need guidance and teaching, so there is no personification!

Chapter 7 Practice questions for Paper 1

Introduction

In this section you will find a complete set of Paper 1 questions. The paper consists of TWO sections which we will call A and B. All the questions in this paper are compulsory.

Section A consists of **25 multiple-choice language-based questions**. You MUST answer all of these questions.

Section B consists of **35 reading comprehension questions** based on five stimuli as follows: one poem, one literary extract, one expository extract, one argumentative extract, one visual extract. You MUST answer all of these questions.

Paper 1 Section A guidance

All 25 of the questions in this section test your ability to understand meaning conveyed through:

- word choice
- grammar
- syntax
- sentence structure
- punctuation and paragraphing.

It is not possible to predict which of these focus areas will be featured in the exam each year. In one year, antonyms could be tested as part of your understanding of word choice, in another year it might be synonyms. Alternatively, this area may not be tested at all.

The 25 questions are divided up into sets of five questions at a time. Each set of five uses a specific question type, such as sentence completion, sentence combination or error spotting. It is therefore vital that you read the instructions carefully before you begin each set of questions.

Each question is multiple choice and you will be offered four possible answers. Some question types offer the option of 'no change' or making a classification of 'no error'. Think carefully when this is a possibility.

Each question is worth 1 mark.

> **Remember**
>
> It is very important to consider each of the four answers before making your selection. Often there will be several answers that may seem possible at first. Look at each one carefully, referring to the precise meanings of words, the nuances and connotations that they carry and the tone and purpose required.

Time management

As you will see, it is suggested that you take 35 minutes to answer Section A.

- As there are five sets of questions, this means you should spend **6–7 minutes** on **each set of five** questions.
- Ideally, aim for about 6 minutes per set – this will leave you five minutes to check or go back to any questions you struggled with.
- If you can't answer a question don't spend ages on it – move on, and return at the end.
- Make sure you answer every question.

Paper 1 Section A questions

(Suggested time: 35 minutes)

The items in this section will test your understanding of **word meanings** and **nuances in meaning**, by asking you to select synonyms.

Remember

You can work out literal meanings using the steps outlined in Chapter 1:

1 Fill in the blank.

2 Read around the gap.

3 Look at the sentence structure.

4 Think about similar words that you know.

However, you also need to consider the register of the original sentences and match your chosen word to the correct register.

Items 1–5

Practice task

Instructions: Each sentence in this section has ONE underlined word. Choose from the four options, the word which is the closest synonym (NEAREST IN MEANING) to the underlined word.

1 The teacher was an <u>incomparable</u> communicator when presenting to a mixed-ability class.

  a) excellent   **c)** unskilled

  b) unmatched   **d)** inspirational

2 The poverty that was <u>evident</u> in the area was distressing and showed that far more help was needed.

  a) hidden   **c)** obvious

  b) noticeable   **d)** glaring

3 Effective landscaping can create a <u>variety</u> of garden areas even in a confined space.

  a) range   **c)** pattern

  b) collection   **d)** number

4 Numerous <u>indigenous</u> creatures have populated the island since it was evacuated 20 years ago.

  a) popular   **c)** new

  b) wild   **d)** native

5 Sadly, it was impossible to receive a refund as the goods were not <u>pristine</u>.

  a) new   **c)** faulty

  b) immaculate   **d)** guaranteed

To revise synonyms and antonyms turn to Topic 1.5.

The items in the next section test your understanding of **spelling**.

Remember

Words can be quite similar in meaning, so think about how positive or negative, strong or weak each one is so that you are aware of the **nuances** of meaning. Check the context around the word carefully: does it link or fit with a specific element of the information provided? Think about similar words you know to the ones given (for example, try changing the form from noun to verb to see if that helps you work out its meaning, e.g. change 'implication' to 'imply').

Items 6–10

Practice task

Instructions: In the following sentences ONE of the underlined words may be misspelled.

Select the ONE underlined word, A, B or C, that you feel is misspelled. If no word is misspelled, choose D No error.

6   Even though he spilled the paint <u>accidentally</u>, he could not in all <u>consience</u> say that he had
            A   B

     been heeding the teacher's <u>advice</u>. <u>No error</u>
             C   D

7   First year university students are <u>privileged</u> to be offered <u>accommodation</u> on campus; which
                A   B

     I would wholeheartedly <u>recomend</u> to you. <u>No error</u>
             C   D

8   <u>Perseverence</u> is a quality which can, at the very least, help you to avoid <u>embarrassment</u> when
      A   B

     in <u>competition</u> against others. <u>No error</u>
       C   D

9   <u>Occasionally</u>, I long for weather which is less <u>changable</u> and does not leave one in a <u>vacuum</u>
      A   B   C

     quite so regularly. <u>No error</u>
            D

10 I <u>guarantee</u> that the average twenty year old spends more on <u>leisure</u> <u>equiptment</u> than
       A   B   C

     I do. <u>No error</u>
         D

To revise spelling, turn to Topic 2.5.

The items in the next section test your **understanding of meaning and register within sentences**.

Remember

Words can be quite similar in meaning, so think about how positive or negative, strong or weak each one is so that you are aware of the **nuances** of meaning. Check the context around the word carefully: does it link or fit with a specific element of the information provided? Think about similar words you know to the ones given (for example, try changing the form from noun to verb to see if that helps you work out its meaning, e.g. change 'implication' to 'imply').

Practice task

Instructions: Each sentence in this section has ONE word or phrase missing. Choose from the four options the word or pair of words which BEST completes the meaning of the sentence.

11 The recovery _____ after major surgery can be up to six months depending on the age and general fitness level of the patient.

    a) limit   **c)** period

    b) zone   **d)** allowance

12 Precise arrangements for the wedding were left to the _____ mercies of the Groom.

    a) gentle

    b) tender

    c) average

    d) delicate

13 Everyone was in awe of the _____ performance of the rally car drivers at the event.

    a) speedy

    b) awesome

    c) risky

    d) skilful

14 The graduating students celebrated with _____, savouring their new freedom.

    a) relish

    b) happiness

    c) keenness

    d) joy

15 The _____ of on-line shopping means that the disabled or housebound can enjoy the benefits of consumerism on a daily basis.

    a) growth

    b) invention

    c) advent

    d) popularity

To revise literal meaning turn to Topic 1.1 and for register, go to Topic 1.4.

The items in the next section test your **understanding of sentence structure** with sentence-combination type questions. Make sure that the combination that you choose does not alter the meaning of the original sentences by removing a sense of time sequence or an intended emphasis.

Remember

When looking for 'correct' sentences, try to work out what the core information is in terms of time, place, subject, action, and so on.
Think about how punctuation is often used to add detail around this core information.

Practice task

Instructions: Decide the BEST option, a), b) or c), to combine each pair of sentences and choose the correct answer. If it needs no change, choose option d).

16 Kayla cycled home after school today. Kayla wore her cycle helmet.

   a)   Kayla wore her cycle helmet today and cycled home after school.

   b)   After school, Kayla wore her cycle helmet and cycled home.

   c)   Cycling home after school today, Kayla wore her helmet.

   d)   No change.

17 Reading *Pride and Prejudice* is great! *Pride and Prejudice* is one of the classics.

   a)   Reading *Pride and Prejudice*, one of the classics, is great.

   b)   One of the classics, *Pride and Prejudice*, reading is great.

   c)   Reading the classics is great, especially *Pride and Prejudice*.

   d)   No change.

18 Who wants to come to the beach? We will need to bring swimsuits, goggles, masks, flippers and towels plus a packed lunch and something to shade us.

   a)   You'll need to bring swimsuits, goggles, masks, flippers and towels plus a packed lunch and something to shade us, because we are going to the beach.

   b)   Who wants to come to the beach and bring swimsuits, goggles, masks, flippers and towels plus a packed lunch and something to shade us.

   c)   Bring swimsuits, goggles, masks, flippers and towels plus a packed lunch and something to shade us: who wants to come?

   d)   No change.

19 I'm receiving a prize. There will be a prize-giving ceremony at my school today.

   a)   Today is my school's prize-giving and I'm receiving a prize.

   b)   Today is my school's prize-giving; I'm receiving a prize.

   c)   I will be receiving a prize at my school's prize-giving ceremony today.

   d)   No change.

20 The emergency services dealt with a large number of distressing callouts today. There was a pile-up on the motorway and two people died.

   a)   There was a pile-up on the motorway today and two people died, so the emergency services dealt with a large number of distressing callouts today.

   b)   The emergency services dealt with a large number of distressing callouts today as there was a pile up on the motorway in which two people died.

   c)   There was a pile-up on the motorway today and the emergency services dealt with a large number of distressing callouts including two deaths.

   d)   No change.

To revise sentence combination turn to Topic 2.2 and the section on Structure and mechanics.

The items in the next section test your knowledge of **vocabulary, grammar and idiom**.

> ### Remember
>
> Subject-verb agreement (e.g. 'He goes' not 'He go').
>
> Check tenses match, so that the order of time (when things happened, and in what sequence) makes sense.
>
> Look out for information that is repeated unnecessarily.

Items 21–25

Instructions: Some of the following sentences are unacceptable because of overused idioms, inappropriate grammar or redundancies. Some sentences may be acceptable as they stand. No sentence contains more than ONE error.

Select the underlined part that you feel is inappropriate – A, B or C. If the sentence is acceptable as it stands, choose D, No error.

Practice task

21 The road is <u>litter</u> with potholes which <u>have</u> caused numerous accidents and <u>damage</u> to
     A   B   C

  vehicles. <u>No error</u>
         D

22 The operation <u>is</u> scheduled for tomorrow but <u>has</u> now been <u>cancelled</u> yet again. <u>No error</u>
      A   B   C   D

23 Recycling is a <u>valuable</u> venture which will benefit <u>future</u> generations <u>in the next century</u>
       A   B   C

  and make life more pleasant for us in the present day. <u>No error</u>
                        D

24 The dogs <u>could</u> be <u>unsettled</u> by the storm so we should probably bring them in before
      A   B

  <u>she</u> starts. <u>No error</u>
  C   D

25 The bindweed is <u>taking over</u> the garden <u>thanks to</u> the fact that
        A   B

  <u>it has been raining cats and dogs.</u> <u>No error</u>
        C   D

To revise idioms turn to Topic 1.7 and for redundancies, turn to Topic 1.8. Relevant grammar points can be found in Topics 2.4 and 2.5.

Paper 1 Section B guidance

In this section, marks are awarded when you:

- obtain information accurately
- grasp insights from reading literature
- recognise and evaluate opinions expressed in various forms.

The 35 questions are divided into groups. Each set of questions will be preceded by a short text which you must read closely. There will be: one poem, one literary extract, one expository extract, one argumentative extract and one visual extract.

Each question is multiple choice and you will be offered four possible answers to each question.

Each question is worth 1 mark.

Time management

The sets of questions will vary in number. This means that you must allow yourself reading time for the extracts as well as making sure you allow more time for the sections with more questions.

For example, although you could spend 6–7 minutes on each section, it might be advisable to spend slightly less time, for example 4–5 minutes, on the shorter texts (e.g. the poem) and items 26–31. Then give more time (perhaps 8–9 minutes) for the longer prose extract and items 32–39. However, make sure you still have time to answer all the questions!

Remember

It is very important to consider each of the four answers before making your selection. Often there will be several answers that may seem possible at first. Look at each one carefully, referring to the precise meanings of words, the nuances and connotations that they carry and the tone and purpose required.

Paper 1 Section B questions

(Suggested time 55 minutes)

The first set of items in the following section is based on a **poem**. You may wish to revisit Chapter 4 and look again at the tips there to help you explore, understand and analyse poetry.

Remember

- Consider where language is used to imply ideas.
- Remind yourself of what you have learned about figurative language.
- Recall what you know about sound effects such as rhythm and rhyme.

Instructions: Read the following poem carefully and then answer Items 26–31 on the basis of what is stated or implied.

The Dawn's Awake

The Dawn's awake!
  A flash of smouldering flame and fire
Ignites the East. Then, higher, higher,
  O'er all the sky so grey, **forlorn**,
5   The torch of gold is borne.

The Dawn's awake!
  The dawn of a thousand dreams and thrills.
And music singing in the hills
  A **paean** of eternal spring
10   Voices the new awakening.

The Dawn's awake!
  Whispers of pent-up harmonies,
With the mingled fragrance of the trees;
  Faint snatches of half-forgotten song —
15   Fathers! torn and numb, —
  The boon of light we craved, awaited long,
  Has come, has come!

Otto Leland Bohanan

forlorn: sad and lonely

paean: a song in praise or thanksgiving of someone or something

26 The dawn is often used as a symbol of:

    a)   joy

    b)   light

    c)   hope

    d)   a second chance

27 What literary technique is being used in line 1?

    a)   apostrophe

    b)   personification

    c)   metaphor

    d)   simile

28 The second sentence of the poem is an example of:

    a)   simile

    b)   repetition

    c)   onomatopoeia

    d)   imagery

29 The words 'whispers' (line 12) and 'faint snatches' (line 14) are examples of:

    a)   simile

    b)   alliteration

    c)   onomatopoeia

    d)   hyperbole

30 The poet implies that the men awaiting dawn are:

    a)   desperate

    b)   happy

    c)   oblivious

    d)   hungry

31 The repetition of 'has come' in stanza 3 is used to:

    a)   describe the dawn

    b)   express their enthusiasm

    c)   create a rhythm

    d)   suggest they are delirious with happiness

To revise reading and understanding poetry turn to Chapter 4.

The items in the next section are based on a **novel extract**. You may wish to revisit Chapter 5 and look again at the tips there to help you explore, understand and analyse literary prose.

Read the following extract carefully and then answer the questions that follow it.

'However,' Jill continued, 'Jade's social worker is asking if you can look after Jade until they find a mother-and-baby placement: four weeks at the most. She'll be moved before she has the baby. Jade won't be going to school any more but they're hoping to arrange some home tutoring. I said I'd ask you, but clearly it is your decision, Cathy. Feel free to say no.'

5 'I see,' I said thoughtfully. 'Just a month?'

'Yes.'

'Can I think about it?'

'Unfortunately no. They need a decision straightaway. Jade's mother has thrown her out and Jade spent last night in Meryl's bed while Meryl slept on the sofa. But Meryl's husband is
10 back tonight from a business trip and they don't have a spare bedroom.'

'I see,' I said again. I felt sorry for Jade: it was bad enough to be pregnant at seventeen but to have no family support must be devastating. 'And the social services will have found her a mother-and-baby carer before the baby is born?'

'Yes. Absolutely.'

15 'All right then, Jill,' I said with a small flush of relief. 'I'll do what I can to help her. I'll be pleased to.'

'Great. I'll tell Rachel, her social worker.'

'I thought Meryl said Jade wasn't having anything to do with the social services?' I queried.

'To be honest, Jade hasn't got much choice,' Jill said. 'Rachel is already involved with the
20 family and although Jade is adamant she wants to keep the baby, she's going to have to prove she can look after it properly. Otherwise it will be taken into care.'

While this seemed harsh, it was in the best interest of the baby; babies are fragile, vulnerable little beings and if parenting goes badly wrong there is often no second chance.

'Jade needs to start cooperating with the social services,' Jill added. 'She also needs their
25 help. I think she's starting to realise that.'

'Good. So when do I meet Jade?'

'I'll phone Rachel now and tell her you've agreed to look after her, and then I'll get back to you with more details. I think we'll probably move Jade in late this afternoon or early evening. I want to be there and obviously Rachel will need to be there too. Are you in today,
30 apart from the school run?'

'Yes. I can be.'

'I'll phone you as soon as I've spoken to Rachel, then. Thanks Cathy.'

We said goodbye and as I replaced the receiver I felt a frisson of excitement. A new child and a new challenge. Although Jade wasn't exactly a child, and she would be only be
35 staying with me for a short while, I would do all I could to help her. I felt sure she would benefit from some stability in her life and my TLC (tender loving care), which I prided myself on offering to all the children I looked after, wouldn't go amiss even with a teenager. A wiser, more experienced teen carer might have asked some appropriate questions – for example, about Jade's boyfriend, the father of her unborn baby, and what involvement if
40 any he would be having in Jade's life. But for me at that moment, elated by the prospect of doing all I could to help Jade, such questions never crossed my mind.

Leaving the hall, I jogged up the stairs and to the spare bedroom to make some last-minute changes so that it was suitable for when Jade arrived and she felt comfortable. I didn't think she'd mind the soft toys dotted around the room, but I removed the toy box.

45 *Then I changed the duvet cover and pillowcase, replacing the pictures of Batman with plain pale yellow. Satisfied the room was clean and welcoming, I returned downstairs. As a foster carer and an individual I try not to be judgemental, and if I thought Jade was far too young to be having a baby and that she should have been more careful I didn't dwell on it. Who knew what past experience had brought Jade to this point in her life and self-righteous*

50 *recrimination is never helpful. My role was to look after Jade and her unborn baby, which I intended to do to the best of my ability, and if she left me feeling less alone and better able to face the world then I would be delighted.*

From http://cathyglass.co.uk/

Practice task

Instructions: Read the passage carefully and then answer Items 32–39 on the basis of what is stated or implied.

32 The writer uses the words 'must be devastating' (line 12) to show that she:
  a) wants to help Jade
  b) has empathy with Jade
  c) is upset
  d) knows what it is like to be homeless

33 'Yes. Absolutely.' (line 14) is effective because it:
  a) makes Cathy sound angry
  b) makes it stand out
  c) adds emphasis
  d) creates a tone of some certainty

34 The phrase 'a small flush of relief' (line 15) suggests that upon deciding to accept the new placement, Cathy:
  a) blushes
  b) is overcome with emotions for a while
  c) is happy
  d) is pleased that it is only temporary

35 The word 'frisson' (line 33) means a:
  a) cold feeling
  b) thrilling feeling
  c) shiver
  d) shudder

36 The sentence 'A wiser…in mind' (lines 38–41) is effective because it:
  a) shows that time is passing
  b) suggests that Cathy is confused
  c) shows the large scale of Jade's problems
  d) suggests that Cathy is moving around

37 The writer uses the word 'jogged' (line 42) to:

   a) show that Cathy is fit

   b) make the reader think Cathy is in a rush

   c) show that Cathy has lots to do

   d) suggest that Cathy is keen

38 The narrator's actions after she gets the phone call suggest that she:

   a) is busy

   b) is thoughtful

   c) doesn't care about Jade

   d) is untidy

39 The last sentence of the extract gives the impression that the narrator:

   a) is weak

   b) will put Jade's care first

   c) will gain less than Jade from the placement

   d) has personal problems

To revise reading and understanding prose turn to Chapter 5.

The items in the following section are based on a piece of **expository writing**. You may wish to revisit Chapters 1 and 3 and look again at the tips there to help you understand and analyse this type of writing.

Items 40–46

Practice task
....

Instructions: Read the following carefully, then answer Items 40–46 on the basis of what is stated or implied.

Remember

- Look for key words from the question to help you locate the information you need.
- Make sure you recognise the type of question you are being asked (e.g. identifying reasons or evidence, checking factual information, understanding vocabulary).
- Use the order of the questions (which is likely to follow the sequence of the extract) to help you locate information.

> *A spectrum of change*
>
> *Research using many different approaches is showing that more than grey matter is changing:*
>
> - *Connections between different parts of the brain increase throughout childhood and well into adulthood. As the brain develops, the fibres connecting nerve cells*
> 5   *are wrapped in a protein that greatly increases the speed with which they can transmit impulses from cell to cell. The resulting increase in connectivity – a little like providing a growing city with a fast, integrated communication system – shapes how well different parts of the brain work in tandem. Research is finding that the extent*

10   *of connectivity is related to growth in intellectual capacities such as memory and reading ability.*

- *Several lines of evidence suggest that the brain circuitry involved in emotional responses is changing during the teen years. Functional brain imaging studies, for example, suggest that the responses of teens to emotionally loaded images and situations are heightened relative to younger children and adults. The brain changes*
15   *underlying these patterns involve brain centres and signalling molecules that are part of the reward system with which the brain motivates behaviour. These age-related changes shape how much different parts of the brain are activated in response to experience and, in terms of behaviour, the urgency and intensity of emotional reactions.*

- *Enormous hormonal changes take place during adolescence. Reproductive hormones*
20   *shape not only sex-related growth and behaviour, but also overall social behaviour. Hormone systems involved in the brain's response to stress are also changing during the teen years. As with reproductive hormones, stress hormones can have complex effects on the brain and, as a result, behaviour.*

- *In terms of sheer intellectual power, the brain of an adolescent is a match for an adult's.*
25   *The capacity of a person to learn will never be greater than during adolescence. At the same time, behavioural tests, sometimes combined with functional brain imaging, suggest differences in how adolescents and adults carry out mental tasks. Adolescents and adults seem to engage different parts of the brain to different extents during tests requiring calculation and impulse control, or in reaction to emotional content.*

30 - *Research suggests that adolescence brings with it brain-based changes in the regulation of sleep that may contribute to teens' tendency to stay up late at night. Along with the obvious effects of sleep deprivation, such as fatigue and difficulty maintaining attention, inadequate sleep is a powerful contributor to irritability and depression. Studies of children and adolescents have found that sleep deprivation*
35   *can increase impulsive behaviour; some researchers report finding that it is a factor in delinquency. Adequate sleep is central to physical and emotional health.*

From www.nimh.nih.gov

40 The first bullet point states that connections in the brain:

  a) increase slightly during childhood

  b) decrease during childhood

  c) work faster during childhood

  d) decrease with age

41 The word 'circuitry' (line 11) means:

  a) a loop of actions

  b) the electronic system used by the brain

  c) the system of connections used by the brain

  d) the fibres that join nerve cells

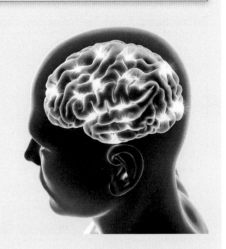

42 Hormonal changes can affect:

  a) behaviour

  b) sexual behaviour

  c) emotional reactions

  d) growth, behaviour and emotional reactions

43 The fact that teenagers react more strongly to emotive pictures than young children shows that:

    a)   they care more than children do

    b)   their brains are different from children's

    c)   they are not sensitive to shocking images

    d)   the brain controls emotional reactions

44 The word 'capacity' (line 25) means the:

    a)   the full extent of

    b)   the size of

    c)   the volume of

    d)   the maximum number of connections

45 According to the passage, teenagers' sleeping patterns:

    a)   have nothing to do with their brains

    b)   are due to personality defects

    c)   are the result of brain changes

    d)   cause depression

46 From the extract, it is evident that:

    a)   teenagers face many challenges

    b)   parents of teenagers face many challenges

    c)   the brain is developing rapidly during teen years

    d)   teenagers cannot be blamed for their behaviour

To revise reading and understanding expository texts turn to Chapters 1 and 3.

The items in the next section are based on a piece of **persuasive text**. You may wish to revisit Chapter 6 and look again at the tips there to help you approach understanding and analysing this type of writing.

Items 47–53

Remember

- Use the key words from the question to identify the part of the text you need to check.

- Texts such as these use a range of persuasive techniques (such as assertion and emotional appeal). Think hard about other examples of persuasive writing you have come across to remind yourself of how they work.

- The structure of persuasive texts is important: different sections may seek to persuade you in different ways.

Instructions: Read the following leaflet carefully and then answer Items 47–53 on the basis of what is stated or implied.

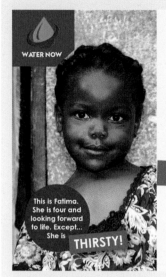

This is Fatima. She is four and looking forward to life. Except... She is **THIRSTY!**

WHEN FATIMA IS THIRSTY THE ONLY WATER AVAILABLE TO HER IS DEADLY! FOR FATIMA'S SAKE, DON'T LET IT HAPPEN!

Fatima loves playing with her friends, and laughing. She loves cuddling her mum, and has the biggest smile. Just like every four-year-old in the world.

But children like Fatima have a different life than most, while most can go to a tap, Fatima has to walk miles every just to get water. While your water will be clean, hers is filled with parasites and dangerous bacteria. Drinking it regularly could put her in hospital, or worse.

Celeste, Fatima's mum fears for Fatima's life constantly. As not too long ago, Fatima had a sister, who also drank that same water. Until one day, after drinking the dirty water for too long, killed her.

CELESTE WOULD DO ANYTHING TO PROVIDE CLEAN WATER FOR FATIMA. AND YOU CAN HELP SAVE HER.

Every day 1000 children die needlessly from drinking dirty water. Children will be dying while you read this article.

By working together with your donations and time, we will build wells, pumps and taps in the most vulnerable communities. Every day in 2019 we built ten points of safe water. Every hour we gave over 300 people access to safe water for the first time in their lives. This is still not enough.

Celeste wiped away her tears as she spoke about losing more children to dirty water.

DONATE £5 PER MONTH AND SAVE A LIFE.

Together, we can make sure that Fatima and children like her, keep laughing. With this small donation alone you will be transforming a child's entire future.

Please donate now. Just £5 a month. With your support every child could be drinking clean water in your lifetime. **Thank you.**

WATER NOW PROMISE:

1. For every pound that is donated, 90p of that is spent helping provide safe water to people like Fatima and Celeste.

2. We will never share your details with any other organisations.

3. You decide how often you are contacted. If you want to hear less from us call 510 1144 7896

4. Our aim is for long lasting changes, so that generations that follow will never experience the same struggles as Fatima and many other children like her.

5. You will always know who you are helping. We work hard to share the stories of those our work, and your kindness reaches.

6. Our aim is to make sure everyone everywhere has taps and toilets, and we won't stop till we achieve this.

47 The author has chosen to mention Fatima's age in order to:

a) be precise

b) evoke an emotional appeal

c) create a shocking effect

d) highlight that it is children who are most vulnerable

48 In which paragraph does the water company use repetition to emphasise its commitment?

a) 2

b) 5

c) 6

d) 7

49 Featuring Fatima and his family in the leaflet is an example of:

a) exaggeration

b) human-interest appeal

c) a statistic

d) persuasion

50 The charity mentions the number of children who will die needlessly, to:

a) show that their work is needed

b) shock the reader

c) appear to be expert

d) add interest

51 The function of paragraph 5 is to:
   a)   add details
   b)   make the reader feel needed
   c)   show what good work the charity is doing
   d)   show the scale of the problem

52 By describing Celeste as having 'wiped away tears' (caption), the writer is emphasising:
   a)   that she needs help
   b)   that the charity is doing good work
   c)   the human pain caused by the problem
   d)   that she loves Fatima

53 Paragraph 7 ends with the words 'Thank you', to:
   a)   show the charity's gratitude
   b)   appeal to reader's sense of importance
   c)   maintain personal address
   d)   act politely

To revise reading and understanding persuasive texts turn to Chapter 6.

The items in the final section are based on a **visual text**. You may wish to revisit Chapters 1, 3 and 6 and look again at the tips there to help you understand and analyse this type of writing.

Items 54–60

Practice task

Remember

- Check you are clear what the table or grid is showing: what are the functions of the columns and rows?
- Texts with tables and grids will often deal with statistics, so think about using vocabulary related to numbers and comparatives/superlatives, e.g. fewer, more, most, greatest.
- Be aware that you may have to combine or synthesise information from different parts of a table or graph.

Instructions: Read the following carefully and then answer Items 54–60 on the basis of what is stated or implied.

> A school cafeteria conducts a survey to determine which two 'sweet treats' should be added to their lunch menu. They need to consider six factors when making their choices. The results of their findings are below.

	Flapjack	Sponge cake	Chocolate brownie	Oat and raisin cookie	Banana bread	Toffee finger
Cost	5	1	4	6	2	3
Calories	2	6	5	4	3	1
Time to produce (the quicker the better)	5	2	6	4	3	1
Allergens	4	5	3	1	2	6
Popularity	6	5	1	4	3	2
Litter/mess factor	1	5	3	2	4	6
Profit	3	1	6	4	5	2

1 = highest ranking; 6 = lowest ranking

54 What are the MOST positive factors about the sponge cake?

   a) It's the quickest to make and has the most calories.

   b) It has the fewest calories, and is the most profitable.

   c) It ranks highly overall and is profitable.

   d) It is quite popular and inexpensive.

55 Which treat would provide the highest calories?

   a) flapjack

   b) chocolate brownie

   c) sponge cake

   d) toffee finger

56 Which sweet treat is the most popular?

    a)   banana bread

    b)   oat and raisin cookie

    c)   chocolate brownie

    d)   flapjack

57 Which two cakes would take the least time to prepare?

    a)   banana bread and oat and raisin cookie

    b)   banana bread and sponge cake

    c)   sponge cake and chocolate brownie

    d)   sponge cake and toffee finger

58 Which cake would be the best option overall?

    a)   banana bread

    b)   toffee finger

    c)   sponge cake

    d)   chocolate brownie

59 In a school where several students have severe allergies, which two cakes would be the wiser choices?

    a)   banana bread and sponge cake

    b)   toffee finger and sponge cake

    c)   chocolate brownie and oat and raisin cookie

    d)   flapjack and toffee finger

60 If the choices were to be made by the cleaning staff, which cakes would be selected?

    a)   banana bread and oat and raisin cookie

    b)   banana bread and sponge cake

    c)   flapjack and chocolate brownie

    d)   sponge cake and toffee finger

To revise reading information from visual texts turn to Topic 3.4.

Introducing Paper 2

Introducing Paper 2

This part of the coursebook introduces the core skills you will need to demonstrate in your Paper 2 exam. In order to support and develop the required writing skills and competencies, you should practise extended writing as often as possible. As you attempt such activities, you should adopt many styles and forms, for example by creating your own stories or writing blogs on topics that are of interest to you.

The four main chapters tackle four discrete writing forms: summaries, informative texts, stories/narratives and viewpoint/argument writing. These are the forms of writing you will need to demonstrate in your Paper 2 tasks, and the chapters set out the particular conventions or features of each text type. You will practise techniques that help emulate these forms, many of which will draw on approaches you explored in Paper 1.

Each of the four chapters break down the writing forms into distinct areas for you to master, whether that is through sentence construction, developing an appropriate tone or style, conveying emotion through powerful vocabulary or using engaging structures to draw the reader in. The work you do should enable you to improve your writing both at detailed word and sentence level, and at whole text, structural level.

In the four main chapters covering Paper 2, each unit ends with a Check your progress feature that you can use to self-assess your progress with the key skills from that section.

This part ends with two useful sections – a set of practice questions based on Paper 2 writing tasks, and a brief section to help you with basic accuracy in language and grammar.

Chapter 1 Writing a summary

1.1 Identifying the main ideas

Learn how to:

- *look for clues about the subject of a text*
- *select main points from a text.*

What clues help me decide what a text is about?

When you read any text, your mind immediately gets to work finding out what it is about, what its focus is, or what the writer's purpose is. In a summary, you write down the answers to these questions in a clear way.

Here are some titles of articles and texts:

a) *Brian Lara – his greatest hits*

b) *On the hunt with killer whales*

c) *Day in the life of the princess of pop*

d) *Soaring death rate leaves retirement community stunned*

Each of these titles gives strong clues to the content of the article or text that follows.

1 Based on these titles, what do you think each of these texts is about?

2 Which titles leave out key information that you would need to check as you read the text?

You can use titles as a guide to test what you expect to find in a text, but they do not give the whole picture. You need to read the whole text.

Look at this opening paragraph for one of the titles above:

> *A huge increase in the early deaths of pet cats in Sunny Heights retirement village has left the residents shocked and saddened. Since the start of the year, at least 12 of their feline companions have been found dead.*

3 Which title does this match?

4 How is the information different from what you expected after reading the title?

Revision tip

Predicting and retrospecting are useful skills to be used when summarizing. You need to think about what is coming next (predicting), but you should also reconsider what you have just read (retrospecting) – your understanding of a text can sometimes change.

Layout and organisation

You can find other clues to what a text is about by looking at the order of the information and how it is laid out. For example, paragraphs can indicate a change in time, focus on a new aspect of a topic, introduce a new voice or perspective, or suggest a different viewpoint or attitude. Paragraphs can also introduce different types of information, such as statistics or quotations.

Look at this next paragraph from the text about cats.

An inspection by local vet, Snupe Dogg, revealed that at least eight of the poor pussycats had been poisoned with an unexplained substance. The remaining four had died in different circumstances but Mr Dogg refused to say more about how they had met their sorry fate: 'Until I have conducted a full autopsy on each of the deceased cats I will be unable to establish anything further.'

5 What *new information* is revealed in this extract compared with what you were told in the first paragraph?

6 What new *types* of information are included here (for example, statistics)?

7 Decide what is the point of the second paragraph and write it out as a short sentence. For example, the main point of the first paragraph could be described as: 'Cat deaths in Sunny Heights retirement village have grown suddenly.'

> **Revision tip**
> ....
> Look for similar or linked vocabulary in a paragraph. For example: *Snupe Dogg, Mr Dogg; poisoned, died, fate, deceased, autopsy; pussycats, cats*. This signposts the focus and will help you to summarize.

Topic sentences

The topic sentence is the sentence that tells you what the rest of the paragraph is about. Read this paragraph from the middle of a text about ocelots, a type of wild cat. The topic sentence comes at the start.

This endangered species, like so many others, is quite stunning to look at. Twice the size of an average domestic cat, it has sleek, smooth fur, which can vary in colour and pattern from cream to reddish-brown, with highly visible black patches, which often come together to form curved stripes. The face is also striped, lined in black on either side – like a wonderful miniature leopard or panther. Visually, the ocelot is highly attractive to poachers.

> **Remember**
> Topic sentences are usually, but not always, at the start of a paragraph. To find the topic sentence, look for the sentence that tells you what is the focus of the paragraph.

Having identified the topic sentence, you still need to decide which part of it tells you what the rest of the paragraph will be about.

- The first noun phrase is 'This endangered species', which might suggest that the paragraph will focus on threats to the ocelot.
- The rest of the sentence ('…is quite stunning to look at') acts as a general introduction to the details about the ocelot's appearance that follow. There is nothing more about being 'endangered'.

8 Which of these notes best sums up the *main point* of the paragraph?

    a) *Hunters are very keen to capture the ocelot.*

    b) *The visual appeal of the ocelot.*

    c) *How ocelots are like leopards and panthers.*

    d) *The size of the ocelot compared with house cats.*

It might not always be so easy to find the topic sentence. Read this new paragraph.

> *Ocelots hunt a wide range of animals such as rabbits, rodents, fish, frogs and iguanas, and even tree-dwelling monkeys or birds. They are aided in this by keen sight and hearing, but they also swim well, and their pointed fangs are perfect for delivering a killing bite. In short, they are perfectly adapted to hunting a variety of prey.*

The first sentence here suggests this is mostly a paragraph about the types of animals that ocelots prey on. However, while the paragraph is partly about this, there are other types of information, too.

9 What other information is *supported by* the first sentence?

10 Which do you think is the topic sentence in this paragraph? Why?

Apply the skills

Read these two paragraphs from an article about Navassa Island and its coral reefs.

> *Navassa has been underwhelming visitors since 1504, when crewmen sent by Columbus arrived and promptly died from drinking contaminated water. An American sea captain claimed the mesa-shaped islet for the USA in 1857 for its rich deposits of bird excrement, used to make fertilizer and gunpowder. Over the next three decades, African-American workers living in virtual slavery mined over a million tons of fossilized guano by hand (which the Navassa Phosphate Company of Baltimore shipped out on the S.S. Romance). In 1889, the workers rose up and killed five supervisors, sparking a legal battle over possession of the island that went all the way to the US Supreme Court. The island and its animal inhabitants – mostly lizards and feral dogs today – were abandoned in 1898 after the Spanish-American War.*
>
> *Haiti still claims Navassa in its constitution, but the US Fish and Wildlife Service declared it a National Wildlife Refuge in 1999. Only researchers can drop anchor there today, but the interesting part is under water anyway. This March and April, scientists with the Global Reef Expedition, a five-year worldwide coral survey sponsored by the Khaled bin Sultan Living Oceans Foundation, made 212 data-gathering dives on Navassa's reefs. They found a surprisingly rich coral ecosystem that has escaped much of the damage that overfishing, pollution and climate change have wrought on other reefs in the region.*

11 Based on this information, write down the main focus of each paragraph.

Check your progress

Competent

- I can work out the overall focus of a text from its title and supporting paragraphs.
- I understand how topic sentences work.

Superior

- I can work out the overall focus of a text from a range of details and track how it changes from paragraph to paragraph.
- I understand how to use a range of strategies to identify topic sentences and main points.

1.2 Identifying opinions

Learn how to:

- *identify the overall opinion in a text*
- *identify how the opinion may develop or change.*

What is an opinion?

In the exam, you may need to identify when a writer is expressing an opinion rather than stating a fact. An opinion is something that can be argued about – something that cannot be proved conclusively. For example:

Basketball is a very exciting sport to watch.

Opinion: not everyone would find basketball exciting.

Basketball is a game played by two teams of five players on a rectangular court.

Fact: these are the rules – this is what you see each time a match is played.

1 Read the following paragraph. Which of the statements are facts and which are opinions?

> *The Bahamas have traditionally been the strongest team in the men's CBC championship with seven gold medals. They have great coaches and great individual players. In addition, in the 2015 women's tournament final, the Bahamas beat Jamaica 55–51. Every man, woman and child in the Bahamas will be desperate for their teams to continue their dominance.*

It is important to understand the overall opinion in a paragraph or a piece of text because you will need to summarize it.

2   Which of the following is the best summary of the *opinion/s* expressed above?

    a)   *The Bahamas are clearly the best team as they have won the most tournaments.*

    b)   *The Bahamas have been very successful at basketball.*

    c)   *Bahamas basketball teams have been successful for a long time due to their coaches, players and their universal support across the island.*

    d)   *Jamaica is depressed at being beaten by the Bahamas.*

(Think carefully: one of these is simply not stated in the text; two are factual statements but not opinions.)

Implicit opinions

In informative texts, opinions are sometimes less **explicit** than they are in persuasive texts. They are **implied**, rather than stated openly. For example:

I believe Jamaica has the best track athletes in the world.

Explicit: the viewpoint is stated in an obvious way. Even without the words 'I believe', it would be clear what the writer thought.

There have been many, many medals won at championships by Jamaican track athletes in recent years, setting a standard that other countries found difficult to match.

Implicit: the viewpoint is supported by the facts – the medals won – and a more subtle opinion ('…other countries found difficult to match').

Remember, the points you are asked to pick out from a text for a summary might not be specific details such as 'many medals won'. You may need to identify the wider point – here, the success of Jamaican athletes.

> **Key terms**
>
> **explicit:** an idea of viewpoint that is stated directly
>
> **implied:** an idea or viewpoint that is suggested/indicated in an indirect or less obvious way

3   Read this sentence from an article about tourism, then choose which of the statements below best describes the overall opinion.

> *Huge cruise ships, luxury villas that locals can't afford, the decline of languages other than English are all effects of global tourism on the island.*

    a)   Tourism is a very important business for the islands.

    b)   Local people cannot afford to buy houses.

    c)   Global tourism has brought problems to the islands.

    d)   Only English is spoken being spoken on the islands.

4 Read this paragraph from an article about Jamaican music. What is the implied opinion?

> *Recently pop music from Caribbean artists has seen an increasing use of patois in the lyrics, for example in Rihanna's excellent 'Work', which features a Jamaican variety, rather than her usual Bajan-tinted words. But she is not the first to freshen up her music in this way, as Shaggy, Sean Paul – and of course Bob Marley, back in the day – can attest.*

Tracing opinions across longer texts

When reading longer texts, it can be easy to lose track of how a particular perspective changes or develops. Read this opening paragraph from an article about competitive sport in the USA.

> *American children not only participate in myriad afterschool activities, they also compete. In 2013 7.7 million children played on a high-school sports team, according to the National Federation of State High School Associations. At the same time, U.S. Youth Soccer, the national organisation that oversees travel soccer, registers more than three million children between the ages of five and 19 who play at a competitive level (not taking into account the thousands of young children who play recreationally each year). Middle-class kids routinely try out for pay-to-play all-star teams, travel to regional and national tournaments, and clear off bookshelves to hold all of the trophies they have won.*
>
> From www.theatlantic.com

To summarize the key points here, first analyse the facts:

- Is the number of children of children playing competitive sport high or low?
- Which children *in particular* regularly play competitive sports and win trophies?
- Are there any obvious opinions here? Or any hinted at? Use the terms 'explicit' and 'implicit'.

Now read the next two paragraphs. Think about what *new* information is introduced and whether it reveals more of the writer's opinion to the reader.

> *It has not always been this way. About a hundred years ago, it would have been lower-class children competing under non-parental adult supervision while their upper-class counterparts participated in noncompetitive activities like dancing and music lessons, often in their homes. Children's tournaments, especially athletic ones, came first to poor children—often immigrants—living in big cities.*
>
> *Not until after World War II did these competitive endeavors begin to be dominated by children from the middle and upper-middle classes. The forces that have led to increasing inequality in education, the workplace, and other spheres have come to the world of play.*
>
> From www.theatlantic.com

5 What information does this extract tell us about poorer children in the past? What happened after the war? How does this imply the writer's view?

6 Look at the final sentence. What does this imply about the opportunities available to poorer children?

Apply the skills

7 Reread the three paragraphs from *The Atlantic* website. Write down the main point of each paragraph. Next to each point, note whether it represents an opinion or is mostly factual information.

8 Using your three points, write a paragraph of no more than 40 words summing up what the article tells us, including any implied opinion if relevant. Do not worry too much about using words or phrases from the text. Use the prompts below to help you.

- *However…*
- *Nowadays…*

Remember

- Focus on what the overall set of facts reveals in each paragraph rather than selecting isolated facts.
- Think carefully about what is being stated, even if this is done indirectly.

Check your progress

Competent

- I can distinguish between fact and opinion in a text.
- I can make notes on the main ideas from each paragraph in an article.

Superior

- I can distinguish between facts, explicit and implicit viewpoints.
- I can explain clearly the key points, taking implicit and explicit information into account.

1.3 Paraphrasing and using your own words

Learn how to:

- *use synonyms or other alternatives to given words*
- *reduce text to a given size using paraphrasing.*

How do I use synonyms?

When you summarize a text, you will have to use far fewer words than the original. This means paraphrasing the information using your own words.

One way to do this is to use synonyms. You may recall from Paper 1, Topic 1.5 that these are words identical to or very close in meaning to another. For example, synonyms for 'animal' are 'creature', 'beast', and so on.

1 Write down a synonym for each of these common words.

> fur   stripe   paw   fang   scent   prey   habitat

2 Read this passage. Consider the meaning of the underlined words.

*Presents are an essential part of any party.
But they can weigh heavily on us, too.
For example, the cost can be exorbitant;
nowadays, people expect more and more,
and it can be embarrassing if you can't
afford something spectacular or unique.*

Think of synonyms for the underlined words, then rewrite the passage using them. Which words or phrases did you find particularly difficult to replace?

Sometimes sets or categories of specific nouns can be replaced by a more general synonym. For example:

- cat, dog, puma, horse, etc. → animal
- table, chairs, bed, wardrobe, chest of drawers, etc. → furniture
- sadness, anger, joy, triumph, bitterness, etc. → emotion

3 Find collective or 'category' nouns to replace the specific ones underlined in the following paragraph.

> *A huge number of celebrated athletes, footballers and cricketers gathered at the island's annual awards ceremony last night. Champagne, cocktails and every conceivable type of wine was flowing as the speeches carried on into the night. Finally, when it was all done, people spilled out of the hotel and awaited taxis, limousines and even minibuses that carried them off into the night.*

Paraphrasing

When you are given a text to summarize, you are expected to use your own words as far as possible. However, some repetition of words from the text is acceptable, for example:

- facts or figures
- proper names
- the topic of the text (if it is so specific that to try to alter it would sound ungrammatical or change the meaning).

In addition, if you need to reduce the original text, you will have to paraphrase by turning a longer extract into a short summary of the information.

Look at the paragraph about the ocelot from Topic 1.1 again. A student's attempt at paraphrasing is in the second column of the table.

Original version	Gina's version
This endangered species, like so many others, is quite stunning to look at. Twice the size of an average domestic cat, it has sleek, smooth fur, which can vary in colour and pattern from cream to reddish-brown, with highly visible black patches, which often come together to form curved stripes. The face is also striped, lined in black on either side – like a wonderful miniature leopard or panther. Visually, the ocelot is highly attractive to poachers.	*Though under threat, it is an impressive creature. It is double the size of a house cat with soft hair and colourful stripes and notable black spots. Its appearance attracts hunters.*

4 **a)** Find the particular words or phrases that Gina has replaced with her own.

b) What words has she retained from the original (apart from words such as 'it' and 'and')?

c) What information does she leave out? Why do you think she does this (other than to reduce the number of words)?

Changing the grammar

You may find that when summarising, you cannot keep the same sentence structures as the original text. Look at this sentence you read earlier:

But they can <u>weigh heavily</u> on us, too.

There is an obvious alternative to 'weigh' here, so you need to think of words other than verbs. The word 'weigh' might have these **connotations**: burden, weight, load, baggage, pressure, force, mass.

> **Key term**
>
> **connotations:** *links created in the mind*

So the sentence could then be rewritten as:

Yet they <u>can be a great burden</u> as well.

Using the noun phrase 'great burden' means you do not need a verb to replace 'weigh'.

5 For each of the following sentences, note down similar words, links or connotations for the underlined words. Then write an alternative version.

   a) *<u>Feeding</u> animals at the zoo is not advisable unless monitored by staff.*

   b) *'Rewilding' or reintroducing species into places where they have <u>died out</u> is one solution.*

When summarising, try to write shorter, more succinct sentences. Look at these two examples:

Loss of habitat, poaching and invasive intrusion from aggressive new species or natural predators have all contributed to their decline in numbers, and have pushed them to the brink of extinction.	*They are close to dying out due to threats from humans and nature.*

The second version begins with the subject 'They' and replaces all the examples with the general phrase 'close to dying out'. The simple connective 'due to' links cause and effect.

6 Paraphrase the following paragraph by beginning with the subject/topic of the text and using a more general description to sum up what is happening. Connect the ideas with 'because'.

> *However, culling of the most intrusive predators, creations of new habitats and prosecution of poachers is now leading to an upsurge in numbers to a level not seen for a decade.*

Apply the skills

Read this text about the Caiman lizard.

Similar in bodily appearance to crocodiles, they have bright green bodies with some darker bands and a head that is red, and can measure up to four feet long. Their <u>heavy</u> bodies nevertheless have short but powerful limbs while their muscular jaws are well-adapted for devouring snails, crawfish and clams. Swimming and diving is made <u>easier</u> by their extended, flattened tail which is similar to that of the Caiman alligator.

It is <u>incredibly difficult</u> and probably not advisable to keep the Caiman lizard in captivity except as a means of ensuring their survival as a species. In fact, many zoos have given up <u>attempting</u> to keep or raise them. Partly this is because they are very choosy about their diet and refuse to eat much else than the snails that are their <u>favourite</u> food. Despite this, in recent years baby Caiman lizards have found their way into the pet <u>trade</u> and as hatchlings are more willing to <u>accept</u> other food sources. However, in captivity they need a large pool or tank, a place to dig and burrow, other dry surfaces for basking, as well as the high humidity they need to <u>survive</u>.

7 Find synonyms for each of the underlined words or phrases.

8 Decide what is the main point of each paragraph – jot them down as notes.

9 Choose one of the two paragraphs. Rewrite it in your own words, using no more than 20 words.

Remember

- Use synonyms or more general 'category' words where you can.
- Do not worry about changing words such as 'Caiman' or 'lizard'.
- Simplify longer complex sentences by starting with 'They' or 'It'.

Check your progress

Competent

- I understand what synonyms are and can find alternative words or phrases.

Superior

- I can use synonyms, paraphrasing or finding alternative ways of rewording texts.

1.4 Structuring a summary

Learn how to:

- *write concise and clear summary sentences*
- *organise a summary into logical sections.*

How are my notes different from the full summary?

Identifying the main points for a summary is only the first part of your task. The more demanding part is deciding how these points will fit together as a summary.

Remember:

- Your notes can repeat words/phrases from the original text; if possible use your own for the actual summary.
- Your notes need not be in full sentences, but your summary must be.
- You do not need to turn each of the points into paragraphs, but this is one possible way of approaching your task.

1 Read the opening paragraphs below. What is the main subject of the article?

Islands of Song

For hundreds of years along the 700 scattered limestone islands in the Caribbean sea that make up the Bahamas, the human voice has been raised in melodious strains to a rhythmic pulse that is deeply influenced by the African ancestry of most Bahamians. Centuries of colonial domination and the nearness of American and Caribbean cultures have also shaped the character of Bahamian music. As a result of these merging influences, Bahamian music is uniquely rich, reflecting generations of joy, hardship, innovation and artistry.

Bahamians are famous for the art of storytelling and their stories are sung as often as they are spoken. Stories of everyday occurrences become popular songs telling of broken hearts, holidays and the beauty of the Islands' natural environment. Biblical and historical stories are also sung to sometimes issue a warning or inspire courage. Popularized widely by the Beach Boys, the song 'Sloop John B' is about the adventures of sailors in Nassau. It is performed by the Dicey Doh singers in the a cappella four-part barbershop harmony typical throughout the Bahamas.

Here are two notes about the first paragraph:

- *Bahamas music influenced by African ancestry plus colonial domination.*
- *Rich because of influences, like America, also because of hardship and joy.*

Now look at how this could be turned into the first paragraph of a summary:

> The [1] music of the Bahamas has developed due to African roots [2], proximity of the US and [3] the power of empires. It [4] is very varied and [5] shows its past troubles and triumphs.

[1] definite article makes this a full sentence

[2] full paraphrase

[3] conjunction links ideas

[4] pronoun links back to previous sentence; helps create full sentence, too

[5] conjunction links ideas

2 Other than point 2 above, what examples of paraphrasing are there in this paragraph? (What was the original text and how has it been changed?)

3 How accurate is this paragraph as a summary of the original? Is there anything that should have been mentioned?

Revision tip

Always consider using a simple pronoun to link one sentence back to a previous one.

4 Reread the second paragraph and decide whether this can be reduced to one or two points. Jot down your point/s in note form. Do not worry too much about using your own words.

5 Now turn the point/s into a full sentence (or two short sentences if needed) of no more than 35 words. Remember to use your own words and include pronouns and conjunctions.

Remember

In the exam, the task will probably ask for five points for the whole text, not just two paragraphs.

Following the structure

Your summary will probably follow the structure of the original source text, especially if it is sequenced chronologically – for example, explaining the origins or background of the subject.

Verb tenses can help show a logical structure. Look at this summary about 'Black Power':

> 'Black Power' as a concept probably began [1] in the early 60s with the emergence of the Black Panther Party. However, it declined [1] in the 80s and 90s.
>
> [...]
>
> Nowadays [2], the Black Lives Matter movement is bringing [3] the concept back to life.

[1] simple past tense

[2] connective of time signals situation *now*

[3] present continuous verb tense tells us the on-going situation

Connectives of time can be useful in structuring your summary, especially if the text relates to past and present events or experiences. Below are some of the most common connectives of time.

> *At the start, initially, from the beginning, firstly*

> *Secondly, then, later, next, after that, from that time onwards, until, up to*

> *At present, nowadays, in the present day, now, in the future, looking ahead*

6   This paragraph comes between the two above ('Black Power' summary). Copy the paragraph and add appropriate verbs and connectives of time in the spaces.

> ...black power was less prominent, and the election of President Obama...the problems in society. The killing of Trayvon Martin...everything...black people fought to get their voices heard.

Revision tip

Bear in mind that texts can jump around in their use of time, especially when they make references to past events that affected later ones.

Apply the skills

Read this paragraph from the article about Black Power.

> *In years to come, it will be the job of governments around the world, not just in the US, to decide how best to tackle the issue of black equality. The fact that there has been a black president of the US is wonderful, but if the problems facing black people in acquiring jobs, being treated with respect, and moving out of poverty cannot be solved, then what has really been achieved? 'Black Power' may not have been the solution, but it did show the world that black people would not tolerate prejudice and inequality. For them, the fight will go on so that Trayvon Martin, George Floyd and others did not die in vain.*

7　Where in the original article do you think this paragraph came from (for example, the start, middle or end)?

8　Write a summary paragraph of not more than 30 words (one or two sentences).

> **Remember**
>
> - In the paragraph above there is a range of tenses – but what is its main focus? What happened in the past, the present or what will happen in the future?
> - Begin with a connective of time (use one from the list in this topic).
> - Use verb tenses carefully to indicate whether you are referring to past, present or future events.
> - Practise using your own words whenever you can, but maintain a similar style to the original.

Check your progress

Competent

- I can understand the time sequence of a summary and how the ideas are ordered.
- I can write a summary paragraph that uses a consistent verb tense.

Superior

- I understand how ideas are sequenced according to quite subtle uses of verb tenses and connectives.
- I can write a summary paragraph that uses verb tenses appropriately, sometimes mixing them to look back or forward.

1.5 Test yourself

Learn how to:

- *read and respond to a practice summary writing question*
- *evaluate your own work and the responses of others*

Your task

Read the following article on Cape Horn carefully and list FIVE MAIN points discussed. Write a summary of the article in NOT MORE THAN 120 words.

As far as possible, use your own words. Your summary must be in continuous prose. You can jot down a plan or notes if you wish.

In your answer, you will be assessed on how well you:

    a) identify the main ideas and opinions in the extract

    b) organise and express these ideas and opinions in your own words

    c) use appropriate grammar, sentence structure, vocabulary, spelling and punctuation.

Cape Horn

If you want a challenge as a sailor, then you could do worse than sail around Cape Horn, at the southernmost tip of Chile in South America, on Horn Island, part of the Tierra del Fuego archipelago. It is considered especially dangerous due to the regular and ferocious storms, the powerful currents and, of course, icebergs – the Antarctic being a close and dangerous neighbour.

The first sailors to pass through Cape Horn in 1616 were the Dutch navigators Jakob Le Maire and Willem Schouten. In fact it was Schouten who named the point 'Cape Hoorn' after his birthplace in Holland – the town of Hoorn. Others followed them and once gold was discovered in California in 1848, it became a passageway between the Atlantic and Pacific coasts. At that time, there was no other way around – unless you navigated the opposite way around the world, which was equally dangerous.

American shipbuilders soon realised that pacy, extremely well-constructed and weather-proofed vessels were required if people wanted to take advantage of trade from California, and a number of famous square-rigged ships were built, such as the Andrew Jackson, *which made the trip in 89 days, and the* James Baines, *which reached an incredible 21 knots under sail.*

However, by the beginning of the 20th century, trade to other parts of the world and the development of the US Navy, led to the US turning its attention to a new route: the Panama canal, which was built and opened by 1914. This dramatically shortened the journey and reduced the danger, and as a result use of the route around Cape Horn became less and less frequent with the last sailing ship carrying freight the Wanderbird *in 1936.*

Now, the challenge of rounding the Horn is one taken up by daring sailors on solo voyages, or teams competing in races, but so demanding is it that even the prestigious Clipper Round the World Yacht Race currently uses the Panama Canal. But its wild weather, dramatic scenery and historical importance still make it as fascinating a place as it ever was – even if the best way to see it is from dry land!

Approaching the task

1 Begin by reading through the text once without stopping.

2 Read it more slowly, jotting down the key point for each paragraph. Are these the five points you need? If not, see if you can find others.

3 Once you have made notes, decide which five points will be the ones you list as your main ones. Then, write them out concisely and clearly, using these tips:

- Try not to use more than 12–13 words per point.
- If possible, use your own words but more importantly include the key points.
- You will probably only have about 10 minutes on this part of the task.

4 Quickly plan what you will say in each paragraph or section you write. Use about 20 words per paragraph, but bear in mind that some points will need more words and some fewer.

Remember

- Topic sentences in paragraphs can give a clue to the main idea or point.
- Key opinions or beliefs can be inferred from the information given, or suggested by language (e.g. positive or negative adjectives).
- To use your own words, think of common synonyms or try to paraphrase the original by reducing a lot of detail to a more general point.
- You can also find alternative words by changing the part of speech, e.g. heavy (adj) – heaviness (noun) – burden (noun).

Reflecting on your progress

Read one student's plan and response to the practice question, including the student's selected list of five points. Then look at the comments that follow.

Response 1

Plan: *Five key points*

1. *Challenging voyage for sailor is round Cape Horn.*

2. *Two Dutchmen were first navigators.*

3. *Important passage way between Atlantic and Pacific coasts as no alternative route.*

4. *Pacy, well-constructed ships were built in 89 days.*

5. *Eventually the Panama Canal was opened in 1914, dramatically shortening the dangerous journey.*

> The most challenging voyage for a sailor is to go round Cape Horn, because of its position in Chile on the southernmost tip of South America on Horn Island, part of the Tierra del Fuego archipelago. [1]
>
> The first navigators were two Dutchmen who named the place after themselves. [2] Because of gold in California loads of others [3] wanted to do the trip too as it was more challenging than going through the Panama Canal, which was opened in 1914. [4]
>
> The US government built fast vessels to make the most of the trade in California [5] but eventually when the canal was opened, people just didn't bother with Cape Horn any more as it was too dangerous and took so long. Now it is only mad people, like sailors on their own who do the trip. [6] Not even proper races bother any more.

[1] geographical location correct but not enough use of own words
[2] not quite correct – one Dutchman named it after his home town
[3] too informal
[4] correct information, but not used relevantly
[5] good use of own words and paraphrasing
[6] broadly correct, but do not introduce your own ideas ('mad')

Comment on Plan and Response 1

This is a *competent* response. The initial list of five key points has one error (89 days to build a ship) and over-simplifies some of the points. Also, more of the student's own words would have helped. It includes many of the key points, but it mixes them up a little and is longer than the word limit by 20 words. Occasionally, long chunks of the original are copied when the student could have used their own words, and the style is too different from the original.

4 Using the comments above and the list of progress points at the end of this chapter, rewrite this response to improve it.

Now read another student's plan and response to the same practice task, then look at the comments that follow.

Response 2

Plan: *Five key points*

1. *Most challenging voyage for sailor is round stormy Cape Horn in South America.*

2. *Two Dutchmen were first navigators in 1616, even named after one of them.*

3. *Only viable passage between Atlantic and Pacific coasts becoming popular after gold rush.*

4. *By 1900, trade developed elsewhere so Panama Canal opened in 1914 – route safer and shorter.*

5. *Sailors now take Horn on as individual challenge.*

Cape Horn, Chile, at the southernmost point of South America [1] is a challenging route for sailors due to strong storms, currents and icebergs. [2]

It was first navigated by two Dutchmen in 1616, one of whom named it after his home town. Once gold was discovered in California in 1848, [3] it became important as the only viable link [4] between Atlantic and Pacific coasts.

The US then built powerful ships such as the 'Andrew Jackson' and they made the voyage in record time. By the 1900s, trade developed elsewhere so America built the Panama Canal; this made the voyage shorter and safer. [5]

Presently, [6] it is individual sailors who take the Horn on, enjoying the fierce weather and remembering its past influence.

---

[1] basic geographical location and correct use of tense   [4] good paraphrase

[2] weather features

[5] focus on decline after 1900

[3] important historical information included

[6] synonym of 'now' introduces current situation

Comment on Plan and Response 2

The five selected points are concisely worded and form the basis for the summary. The core elements of the original text are retained here, with some relevant details where needed. The writer has generally used their own words, except where synonyms are not readily available. The tone of the text is broadly similar to the original too.

Check your progress

Competent

- I can work out the overall focus of a text from its title and supporting paragraphs.
- I understand how topic sentences work and identify main ideas in paragraphs.
- I can distinguish between fact and opinion in a text.
- I understand what synonyms are and how to find alternative words or phrases.
- I can understand the time sequence of a summary and how the ideas are ordered.

Superior

- I can work out the overall focus of a text and track how it changes from paragraph to paragraph.
- I can use a range of strategies to identify topic sentences or main points.
- I can distinguish between facts, explicit and implicit viewpoints and use this to note key points.
- I can use synonyms, paraphrasing or alternative ways of rewording in order to use my own words.
- I understand how ideas are sequenced using variations of verb tenses and connectives.

Chapter 2 Writing an informative text

2.1 Understanding the conventions of informative texts

Learn how to:

- *draw on your knowledge of informative texts*
- *use the conventions of informative texts correctly.*

What are informative texts?

In your exam, informative texts will generally take the form of news reports or articles, letters, emails or notices. In each case, these will set out the facts of a situation, or explain a process or past event.

Read this letter from a young person to a possible employer.

> *Hey!*
>
> *Well, man, there ain't NO WAY, NO WAY I gonna make it to your interview. You get me? You see – I got stuff to do that day (WAY more important stuff) so I was thinkin'…howzabout we make it another day, like Wednesday or Thursday or mebbe Monday?*
>
> *Soun' good, my man?*
>
> *Freddie*

1 In what way is this giving information? Is its purpose clear?

This is obviously an information text, but it is not very effective. Informative texts should:

- be clear about their *purpose* – what they are informing you about and why?
- follow the accepted *conventions* – is there a specific order for the information in such texts? Is there a recommended layout? Does the style and tone suit the audience/reader?

2 Bearing in mind the points above, make brief notes on any aspects of Freddie's letter that could be improved.

Conventions of a formal letter

What should Freddie's letter have looked like? Read this improved version.

No 88 Acacia Avenue St James [1] **12 May 2017** [2]

DH Greenaway, Director Universal Plastics Ltd Green Hill Barbados [3]

Dear Mrs Greenaway, [4]

Thank you for your letter of 7 May inviting me to come in for an interview for trainee production assistant on Tuesday 20 May at 8 a.m. [5] *Unfortunately, I will be unable to attend for a number of reasons.*

The first [6] *relates to my current job as a lifeguard at West Bay Pool. On that day I am the only person on duty due to my colleagues' annual leave. I have spoken to my manager, but he is unwilling to allow me time off at short notice.*

The second [7] *reason is that, as you may be aware, no buses run from my part of the island until 8.30 a.m. and therefore, even if I were to gain time off, it would prove very difficult to make that time.*

I have explored a variety of solutions but have been unable to resolve the situation: [8] *I cannot afford to lose my job at the pool, and no family or friends are able to drive me to the interview.*

However, I am extremely keen to work for your company. Would it be possible to arrange an alternative time for the interview? I do not work on Wednesdays or Sundays, or I could come in on another Tuesday as I could swap my shift with a colleague. [9]

I hope very much that a solution can be found.

Yours sincerely,

Freddie Asomah [10]

---

[1] home address

[2] date of letter

[3] recipient's address

[4] formal, polite opening; greeting includes name and title of recipient

[5] factual details related to situation

[6] paragraph sets out first reason for non-attendance

[7] paragraph sets out second reason

[8] paragraph sets out actions taken

[9] final paragraph makes a request related to the issue

[10] closing of letter, including formal 'Yours sincerely' and full name of writer

3 In what way is this letter an improvement on the first version?

Newspaper reports

There are some similarities between informative letters and news reports, but also some key differences. Read this opening to an article about a Trinidadian writer.

Young Adult fantasy writer launches novella

By JANELLE DE SOUZA Sunday, May 1 2016

Local author, Khadine Grant, is celebrating the publication of a new young adult fantasy story. The novella, 'Missing' is the first instalment of a planned three-part series. The adventure centres on a young girl who has lost her parents. Finding out she has an amazing special power, she is petrified her secret will be discovered. Events unfold when she is snatched and removed to the mysterious isle of Esmeralda. [1]

'Missing' is not the author's first book. That was her children's story, 'The Little Glow-worm', which published as an Amazon ebook last year. However, this is her first piece of writing for young adults. [2]

Grant revealed that her novella has been influenced by the language and setting of the Caribbean. But she hopes the story will resonate with young adults overseas as well. [3]

She chose to write the first book in her series as a novella as she wanted to get readers hooked without overloading them with information. 'I didn't want this to be the kind of fantasy novel where readers have to grapple with an immense family tree or an incredibly detailed imaginary kingdom', she says. [4]

---

[1] first paragraph tells us *who* the report is about, *what* has happened and *when*

[2] second paragraph fills in background

[3] use of **reported speech** for further information

[4] **direct speech** brings immediacy to the report

Key terms

reported speech: someone else's account of what was said, without speech marks

direct speech: the actual words spoken by someone, indicated by speech marks

---

4 Where does the most important information in the report appear? How is this similar/different to the letter in this topic?

5 What do you find out (if anything) about the *writer of the article*? Is this the same as or different from the letter?

6 Make a note of some other similarities and differences in the content and layout of the letter and the article.

Apply the skills

You have seen how informative texts are often structured in the following way.

Start	The specific situation (the *what*, *who*, *when*, *where* and *why* the text is written). This may be followed by a brief reference to past events.
Middle	A more detailed account of the situation, filling in background or elements needing explanation, offering more facts or evidence.
End	The ongoing situation – sometimes an idea or suggestion about the future or outcomes.

However, particular types of informative texts have slightly different conventions, such as including direct speech or titles.

 7   Consider the situation below, then answer the questions that follow.

> *As a reporter on a local paper, you have visited the site of a new sports centre due to open in less than a week. You noticed that much of the building was unfinished or poorly built, and that there was a lack of facilities for the disabled. You tried to talk to the site manager but you were told to 'keep your nose out'.*

You want to write an article for your newspaper explaining what you saw and expressing your concerns. Think about the following:

    a) What type of informative text is it? What will its purpose be?

    b) From whose perspective will you be writing? Who is your audience?

8   Make a grid like the one above containing brief notes about what you would put in each section of your article (start, middle and end).

Revision tip

Be aware that you may have to invent appropriate details – for example, the kind of facilities for the disabled that were missing.

Check your progress

Competent

- I understand the basic conventions of letters and news reports.
- I can identify the basic information I need to include in a text.

Superior

- I understand the similarities and differences between different types of informative texts.
- I can identify the information I need to include and adjust it to fit the type of text I am writing.

2.2 Understanding content, audience and purpose

Learn how to:

- *decode tasks so that you understand the audience and purpose*
- *select appropriate content from the given information.*

How should I decode an information text task?

Exam tasks asking you to explain will often contain information like this:

> *A new restaurant [1] has just opened in your home town. You are there on the opening night [2] but there were a lot of problems, such as hygiene and general food quality [3]. At the end of the meal, you asked for your money back but the owner was rude and unhelpful. [4]*
>
> *Write a review of your visit for a local newspaper [5], explaining what you thought of the restaurant and what happened that night. [6]*
>
> *Make sure to include all the details that would help in highlighting the matter. Your review should include details of the visit, for example:*
>
> - *date and time of visit*
> - *specific problems with the cleanliness of the environment and the quality of the meal*
> - *response of owner. [7]*

[1] topic

[2] when it happened

[3] issues that arose

[4] what happened as a result

[5] more detail about form and audience

[6] more detail on purpose

[7] particular things you *must* include

1 Which of these statements about the task are correct?

  a) You are the owner of a restaurant who is unhappy about a customer.

  b) You need to write a letter to a newspaper about your experiences.

  c) You must comment on the health aspects of the visit.

  d) You must mention the owner's behaviour when you complained.

  e) Your job is to make judgements about all the restaurants in your area.

  f) You must say what you thought of the particular dishes you ordered.

Audience, tone and content

Once you have read the task carefully, you can decide on the tone and content of your response.

2 Which of the following is likely to be the *tone* of your response? What in the task suggests this?

　　a)　disappointed and cross

　　b)　happy and grateful

　　c)　emotionally upset and aggressive

　　d)　bored and uninterested

The audience for this task is likely to be people who read the local newspaper. This means:

* they would be interested in hearing about the new restaurant
* they will be familiar with the local area
* they will not be experts on food or hygiene.

3 Based on this information, which of the openings below would be most appropriate for this review? What is wrong with the other two options?

　　a)　*Casa Franco on the island of Tobago opened its doors last night. However, it clearly contravened Articles 8-15 of recent FSA statutes as set out by the national government.*

　　b)　*Casa Franco, which opened last night, has questions to answer after its opening night. Situated on Bacolet Street, I was expecting food to be up to the standard of our other local eateries. How wrong I was!*

　　c)　*The sea bass at Casa Franco had been prepared sous-vide and then put under the salamander for three and a half minutes precisely. Clearly it should have been seared first, and not grilled at all.*

4 Write a second paragraph for the review describing the state of the restaurant. Use the same sort of style and tone as option b) above, which uses the first person and makes it clear that the writer knows the local area. You could begin:

> *Compared with the Blue Crab just down the road, the whole place looked…*

Appropriate tone and content

The focus of the restaurant review task is to be *clear, concise* and *accurate* in your account. Look at this part of a student's response to the task, which discusses the food.

> *Casa Franco? You've got to be joking! More like Casa Catastrophe! What were they thinking? All three courses were awful. I've never tasted anything like it and I won't be going back. No chance!*

5 What details are missing from this section on the food?

6 What is wrong with the tone of the response?

Now consider this alternative extract.

> *Unfortunately, it was the main course which really let the meal down [1]. I had ordered Casa Franco's Double Delicious Veggie Burger [2] and French fries, but when it arrived on my plate it did not live up to its title. The mushrooms were chewy and wrinkled, the slice of cheese tasted of plastic and the bun was burnt on the top and soggy inside. [3]*

[1] indicates the problem part of the meal

[2] gives the exact name of the dish

[3] three clear details (evidence) of the poor quality of the meal

This response meets the criteria in the task to write about specific problems with the quality of the meal. This means *factual* detail, not just stating that the meal was horrible. The tone of this response is not angry, but the purpose is still clear – to tell readers that the restaurant was not very good.

7 Write a further paragraph about the dessert course. Remember to:

- mention the particular dish you ordered
- give details of the problems, not just say that it was not very nice
- keep the tone measured so that the factual details are not clouded by emotions.

You could begin:

> *I hoped dessert would be better, but it turned out to be just as bad. I had ordered…*

Apply the skills

Look at this task based on an informative text.

> *You attended a music festival on the beach, run by ex-prisoners whose aim was to raise money for a local charity. You were really impressed with the event and how well it was run, and spoke to the organiser of the festival who was proud about its success.*
>
> *Write a review of the festival for your local paper, expressing your enjoyment of it. Make sure to include all the details that would help in highlighting the experience. Your review should include:*
>
> - *date and time of visit*
> - *specific elements of the festival you enjoyed and what made them so good*
> - *response of the organiser when you spoke to him/her.*

8   Based on this information, make notes on:
- the task's purpose and audience
- what tone you will adopt
- what 'factual' details you will include (you will have to make these up!)
- what features or conventions of the form you are writing in that you need to include (think about the fact that this is a newspaper review).

9   Write the first paragraph of the review.

Check your progress

Competent

- I can decode an exam task on an informative text, deciding what the purpose is, who the audience is and what form the response should take.
- I can set my text out in broadly accurate form.

Superior

- I can decode an exam task on an information text, deciding what the purpose is, who the audience is, what my role as writer is and what form the response should take.
- I can follow the conventions of the form, use an appropriate tone and select suitable content.

2.3 Writing clear and accurate sentences

Learn how to:

- *use tenses consistently and coherently*
- *use different types of sentences when required.*

What sort of sentences work best in an information text?

To write clear explanations, you need to pay close attention to the length, style and content of your sentences.

Simple sentences work well if you want to convey a straightforward piece of information or to make a precise point. Remember that sentences are made up of one clause, usually consisting of a subject and a verb.

> *The 10 a.m. bus [1] arrived [2] late.*

[1] subject

[2] verb

However, a letter of complaint to the bus company would sound strange if it was made up of only simple sentences:

> *The 10 a.m. bus was late. So I was late. The company was angry.*
> *I didn't get the job.*

Compound sentences can show cause and effect or link information. Compound sentences are two equally weighted clauses or sentences, usually linked by 'and', 'so', 'or', 'but' or 'because'.

> *The 7 a.m. bus was late [1] so [2] I missed my interview. [3]*

[1] first clause

[2] conjunction linking clauses

[3] second clause – result of first

Complex or multi-clause sentences can be useful in information texts for adding or expanding detail. These are sentences with a main idea or clause, supported by a number of subordinate clauses:

> *While the peak time bus service in the city is usually excellent [1],*
> *you should address the lack of drivers [2] at other times of*
> *the day. [3]*

[1] subordinate clause (this does not work as a sentence on its own)

[2] main clause (this works as a sentence on its own)

[3] further supporting information/phrase

However, avoid making these sentences too long or they will sound confusing:

> The 10 a.m. bus was late, so I was late too and this made the company angry, so I didn't get the job, which means I think you should address the lack of drivers at this time in the day, even though peak time services are usually excellent.

Selecting sentences

You have seen how choosing when to use different types of sentences is important in writing clearly. Too many of one type of sentence, however, will make your explanations sound dull or lack fluency.

1 Copy and complete this paragraph of compound and complex sentences explaining problems with getting around an island.

> The coastal road is full of potholes and…In addition, it is too narrow so buses…Although there are plenty of 'slow down' signs, drivers…However, the worst spot is the u-bend at the bottom because…

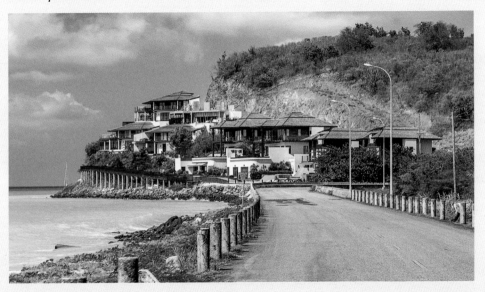

Ending with a simple sentence can be effective in both explanation and argument texts. For example, you could end the paragraph above with 'Something must be done.'

Alternatively, you could end a paragraph, or a whole text, with a sentence beginning with an 'if' clause. This is a clause that suggests what will happen as a result of an action (or inaction):

* *If a faulty tyre bursts*, there will be a serious tragedy.
* *If you fail to make changes to safety*, then the consequences will be fatal.

Read this paragraph from a report about healthy eating.

> We must make changes to school meals so that we can stamp out obesity and eating disorders. [A] When I visited the school I was amazed at what students were eating. [B] Although there were healthy options such as fruit and salads, most students chose French fries or spicy pizzas. [C]

2 Identify the compound and complex sentences in the paragraph.

3 Complete the paragraph with either a simple sentence or an 'if clause' sentence – or both.

Using tenses for clarity

Many explanatory texts use the past tense to explain a series of events that have *already* happened. For example:

> When I arrived [1] at midday at the bike hire shop, the owner told [1] me that all the trail bikes had been rented [2] out. Tourists had been coming in [3] all morning, so there was nothing left for me. I left [1] and tried [1] a number of other hire shops, but I was unable to find anything.

[1] past simple tense verb forms tell reader about single completed actions that have recently occurred

[2] past perfect tense form tells us about an earlier action that came before the actions of the narrator

[3] past perfect progressive tense tells us about a continuous, uncountable sequence of events in the past (if it was one tourist, it would be 'had come in')

These tenses help the reader get the time sequence clear:

Morning: tourists keep coming in to hire bikes.

Midday: narrator arrives and is told there are no bikes left.

Afterwards: narrator tries other hire shops without success.

The present tense is useful for explaining the situation as it is happening. For example:

> I am staring [1] out of the window at the coast road. I love [1] cycling so it is very disappointing that I cannot enjoy [2] your wonderful island. I will return in two months and will visit your shop to try again.

[1] present continuous verb form suggests that the narrator is doing something

[2] simple present tense expresses state or single action now

4 What tense is being used in the highlighted parts of the final sentence?

Apply the skills

Read this extract from one student's response to the 'Apply the skills' task in Topic 2.2.

> I attend the festival on Gold Beach yesterday, which is fantastic. The festival was run by ex-prisoners who now call themselves 'JayBirds' rather than 'Jailbirds' after their founder, Jay Taylor, who does a stretch inside prison until he was released last year. It is his idea to set up the festival.
>
> The festival featured local artists. There was Mama Rag there. Also, there was reggae group, HiFive.
>
> Officially, it is on from 11 in the morning yesterday till 11 at night. In fact, it finished at past three in the morning! Those tunes are still in my head. It was a really wonderful day and night.

I spoke to organiser Jay. It was when the music had finally stopped. He says, 'If we get the funding we'll do it next year.' I say 'Amen to that!'

There are some good ideas here but the tenses are mixed up and the sentences in the last two paragraphs lack fluency.

5 Copy the text, then:
- circle any verbs that are in the wrong tense (for example, where the present tense has been used for a past event)
- underline any sentences that could be combined into one (with the occasional word changed or removed).

6 Rewrite the text, improving the sentences and tenses. If you can, add words or phrases that help to improve the overall standard of the response.

Check your progress

Competent
- I can write in clear sentences and join some together to make them more fluent.
- I can identify where inconsistent tenses have been used.

Superior
- I can improve the sentences in an informative text in several different ways to aid clarity.
- I can identify and replace inconsistent tenses in a text.

2.4 Structuring informative texts

Learn how to:

- *organise information so it is clear*
- *distinguish between the need for clarity and priority.*

What is chronological order?

Chronological order is the recounting of events or a process in the order of time in which events happened. However, you might choose to give information in a different order.

For example, if you were describing an awful holiday, you might *start* with the problems with the hotel room when you arrived, *move on* to the terrible supper you had that evening after you unpacked and the litter on the beach when you went to sunbathe *the next morning*.

If the main problem was the state of the beach, though, you might choose to prioritise that in your account. For example:

> I am writing to complain about our terrible holiday. By far the worst aspect was the dreadful beach, which was strewn with litter and had no running water for refreshment or showers. <u>It ruined our first morning</u>.
>
> However, almost as bad was our experience when we arrived at the hotel <u>the night before</u>.

Look at this task.

> You have been on a solo cycling trip on a nearby island. You discovered the most amazing trail with wonderful wildlife and scenery, and you met a very friendly group of people. When you return you decide to email your parents to tell them about the ride.
>
> Make sure you include details of:
>
> - *the time and location of your visit*
> - *the specific sights you saw and what was enjoyable about them*
> - *your meeting with other people.*

1 Plan to write five paragraphs. In each paragraph, deal with a different time stage in the order it occurred. The first one might be:

    a) *Setting off from Handy Andy's bike hire shop in Bequia by the harbour…*

Paragraphs for points

In an informative text, each paragraph you use should serve a different purpose. The grid below gives some examples.

Purpose	Examples (from different texts)
change of time or location	First paragraph: *I set off along the harbour road…* Second paragraph: *After three hours, I noticed a narrow track in the forest, so I decided to follow it.*
change of idea or point being made	First paragraph: *Rich tourists demolished all the old beachside properties and built huge concrete homes.* Second paragraph: *Another issue is that locals cannot afford the rents or house prices now…*
change of person or perspective	First paragraph: *To me, the new beachside properties are ghastly.* Second paragraph: *However, local resident Jonah tells me, 'I sold my property for 500,000 US dollars. I'm happy as can be!'*

Read this paragraph from an informative text about proposed improvements to a harbour.

> *During my visit to the harbour, the first thing I observed was a complete lack of litter facilities, which meant that there was trash everywhere I looked, not just on the promenade but also floating about between the boats moored nearby.*

2 Write *three* versions of the next paragraph, one based on each of the approaches in the grid above. For example, if you were taking the last approach, you might introduce a local person or tourist who comments on the litter.

Use connectives to move between sentences and paragraphs

Certain connectives are particularly useful when you need to be precise about the information you are conveying.

Type of connective	Example
where things are located	*By the corner of the coast road stands a derelict lighthouse. If you follow the track next to it, you come to a clearing. Between two high banks of trees there is a tremendous view of the sea.* (other examples: 'near', 'under', 'over', 'on top of', 'alongside', 'far from', etc.)
time order or priority	*Firstly, I believe access to the hotel could be improved through constructing ramps to all entrances. Secondly, consider the signage…* (other examples: 'initially', 'next', 'finally', 'ultimately', 'to begin with')
cause and effect	*Because of the money spent on the facilities, the stadium was full of young runners. Membership is cheap so everyone can take part. As a result, I saw families from all parts of town, rich and poor.* (other examples: 'due to', 'thus', 'therefore', 'or')
linking clauses	*The town is now encircled by a new bypass which dominates the view. While this is bad enough, the worst thing is the ugly new hotel on the waterfront.*

3 Identify the connectives in this paragraph that help to make it clear and coherent.

> *Initially I was delighted with the hotel. For a start, the room was spacious and there was an airy balcony running the length of the room. Over the bed were attractive prints of the local area, encouraging me to explore. However, not everything was as it seemed. Under the bed, I could see several large creepy-crawlies, which gave me a shudder. As a result, I rushed to reception and asked to change rooms.*

4 Copy and complete these sentences using appropriate connectives from the examples above, or similar ones.

   a) *…the bridge, there were huge holes in the road which we had to swerve…to avoid.*

   b) *…of lack of spending by the government, minor roads are in a terrible state…accidents are frequent.*

   c) *…we all need to take responsibility to improve our environment…we won't be able to enjoy our own sights and sounds.*

Apply the skills

Read this new informative discourse task.

> *You recently had an interview with a careers officer at your school, who asked you about your ambitions and the sorts of things you would like to do as a job or career and to explain your reasons for these choices.*
>
> *Write your post-interview report about possible careers and your reasons for being interested in them, ready to give to potential employers. Make sure to include all the details that came up in the interview. Your report should include details of the following:*
>
> - *who you spoke to and when*
> - *the role and field/area (i.e. business, sport, etc.) that interests you*
> - *specific elements you think would suit your personality and skills*
> - *response of the interviewer when you discussed this with them.*

5 Based on this, write a plan of your report, dividing it into five or six sections or paragraphs. For example:

Section/ paragraph	Focus
1	*Details of my meeting; who it was with, etc.*
2	
3	
4	
5	
6	

6 Now write the first two paragraphs of your report/account of the interview. Use a range of connectives to make your thinking clear and coherent.

Remember

Remember what you learned about tone and audience in the previous topics – this is for potential employers to read, so it needs to be formal and business-like.

Check your progress

Competent

- I can structure informative texts in different parts.
- I can use some basic connectives to explain ideas and processes.

Superior

- I can divide an informative text in different ways depending on the needs of the task.
- I can choose appropriately from a range of connectives to clarify ideas and processes.

2.5 Test yourself

Learn how to:

- *read and respond to a practice information writing exam question*
- *evaluate your own work and the responses of others.*

Your task

Study the situation presented below and then answer the question that follows.

Your answer will be assessed on how well you:

- format your email
- select relevant and complete information
- organise and express the information in your email
- use appropriate grammar, sentence structure, vocabulary, spelling and punctuation.

Your email must be in continuous prose.

You were walking home from a visit to the shops and were crossing a quiet road near your house when a taxi sped around the corner, missing you only by a couple of centimetres. You noticed that the driver was not paying attention and was talking on a mobile phone. However, when he realised what had happened he stopped suddenly, wound down the window and told you it was your fault.

Write an email to the owner of the taxi company, complaining about the driver's lack of care and the danger caused, as well as his/her response.

Make sure to include all the details that would help in highlighting the matter. Your email should include details of the complaint, for example:

- *date and time of incident*
- *name of the taxi company*
- *specific details of what happened and where*
- *response of driver.*

Approaching the task

1 Begin by spending five minutes reading the question carefully and noting down the key points you will make.

2 Then consider how you will respond in terms of layout, language and tone.

Remember

Informative texts must contain the key information: *what, who, when, where* and *why*. Use these tips:

- Include relevant times, places, names, facts/stats, etc.
- Structure: most important information first; supporting information next; and further information/future situation/outcome last.
- Tone of informative texts must match audience, but is likely to be more formal for unfamiliar audiences.
- Language must be clear and tenses consistent – or used to talk about past, current and future events as appropriate.

Reflecting on your progress

Read the following plan and extract from a response to this practice task by a student, then look at the comments below. Although plans are not always marked in assessments, good ones can help you to structure your response effectively.

Plan 1

Personal details and my anger about things.

What happened and what I want them to do.

End of letter.

Response 1

To: Grab-a-taxi

From: Anita

Subject: complaint [1]

Dear owner, [2]

I was nearly killed by one of your drivers yesterday! Yes, really. I was near my home and as usual I was carefully crossing the road [3] *when out of the blue a madman in a dirty white taxi* [4] *raced around the corner, narrowly missing me. It was a matter of good fortune that I was not thrown into the nearby field.*

Then to make it worse the driver stopped the car and got out. [5] *He blamed me for the incident and said it was my fault. I argued with him of course but it was no good. I was just a silly young person not an adult. According to him.* [6] *I think this sort of behaviour is completely unacceptable. Don't you?*

I think you need to have a stern word with him or the next time it could be a much more tragic outcome. [7]

Yours,

Anita [8]

---

[1] correct layout for email, but lacks detail

[2] in an opening it is better to use the name of recipient

[3] explains the basic incident but a bit vague about time and location

[4] precise detail

[5] new paragraph for next stage in account

[6] attempt at reported speech, but some direct speech might have been more useful here

[7] reasonably effective ending with consequence suggested

[8] style of closing a bit informal

Comment on Plan and Response 1

The plan here is very basic and does not make clear how many paragraphs should be written. Also, by including several points together it is difficult to know which point is most important. This is a *competent* response, which provides the basic detail of the incident, including some additional information about place and time. However, in both cases a more precise indication of the exact spot and what happened would help. The exact words spoken by the driver would also help the owner deal with the matter.

3 Using the comments above and the list of progress points at the end of this chapter, rewrite this response to improve it.

Now read another student's response to the same practice task, then look at the comments that follow.

> **Plan 2**
>
> *Header: clear references to myself and recipient, and incident.*
>
> *Formal introduction: 'Dear...'*
>
> *Body of email:*
>
> *Paragraph 1: What, where and when incident happened.*
>
> *Impact on me.*
>
> *Paragraph 2: Further details about incident, including driver's actions.*
>
> *Paragraph 3: Explanations as to my concern, e.g. local school.*
>
> *Closing paragraph: What I would like recipient to do.*
>
> *Sign-off: formal – 'Yours sincerely'.*

Response 2

> *To: Simeon Ba*
> *From: Danni Tyla*
> *Subject: taxi incident, 16 May 2017, 3 p.m. [1]*
>
> *Dear Mr Ba, [2]*
>
> *As proprietor of Taxi-Go I thought you would like to know about an unfortunate incident concerning one of your drivers which took place at 3 p.m. yesterday. The fact is that as I was about to cross Ocean Crescent, on the corner near the post-box at the southern end, [3] one of your taxis sped around the bend, and narrowly missed hitting me. Needless to say, I was very, very shaken.*
>
> *Although everything happened very quickly, I was able to catch a glimpse of the driver who had his mobile phone to his ear, and was leaning over as if trying to reach something from the passenger seat. [4] Rather surprisingly, he must have seen me, because he applied the brakes hard and reversed up the road. Winding down the window, he let fly a torrent of abuse, calling me 'idiot', 'stupid child' and much, much worse. [5] He raced off in a screech of tyres.*
>
> *Apart from the obvious distress this caused me, I am particularly concerned as the driver showed absolutely no concern for my safety or that of other road users. [6] A lot of children from the local primary school cross at the same point, and I fear that a more serious incident could result in the future.*
>
> *Please would you identify the driver and speak to him about his behaviour. I would also be very grateful if he would have the courtesy to apologize and accept that his driving was dangerous and foolhardy. [7]*
>
> *Yours sincerely,*
>
> *Danni Tyla [8]*

[1] clear, formal details

[2] appropriate formal opening greeting

[3] extremely detailed and precise information

[4] new paragraph moves on to next stage of incident

[5] short, direct quotes add authority to explanation

[6] polite, formal tone but new point made clearly

[7] ends with desired outcome

[8] correct formal closing – same for email as for letter

> ## Comment on Plan and Response 2
>
> This plan is clear but provides far more detail about what to include and where, setting out the number and purpose of each paragraph. This is also a *superior* response, which explains the incident clearly and concisely but with all the relevant information included. The tone and style match the seriousness of the incident, and the structure assists the reader in following what happened.

Check your progress

Competent

- I understand the basic conventions of letters and news reports.
- I can identify the basic information I need to include in a text.
- I can decode an exam task on an informative text, deciding what the purpose is, who the audience is and what form the response should take.
- I can set my text out in broadly accurate form.
- I can write in clear sentences and join some together to make them more fluent.
- I can identify where inconsistent tenses have been used.
- I can structure informative texts in different parts.
- I can use some basic connectives to explain ideas and processes.

Superior

- I understand the similarities and differences between different types of informative texts.
- I can identify the information I need to include and adjust it to fit the type of text I am writing.
- I can decode an exam task on an information text, deciding what the purpose is, who the audience is, what my role as writer is and what form the response should take.
- I can follow the conventions of the form, use an appropriate tone and select suitable content.
- I can improve the sentences in an informative text in several different ways to aid clarity.
- I can identify and replace inconsistent tenses in a text.
- I can divide an informative text in different ways depending on the needs of the task.
- I can choose appropriately from a range of connectives to clarify ideas and processes.

Chapter 3 Writing a narrative

3.1 Structuring and resolving stories effectively

Learn how to:
- *structure a story in an interesting and engaging way*
- *begin and end a story effectively.*

What are the key elements of a good short story?

A short story should have a single, clear storyline. There should be some sort of **narrative hook** to draw the reader in, and it should also end in a way that is satisfying, if not always happy or straightforward.

Most stories depend on the main character facing a problem or challenge. This problem often brings the character into conflict with someone or something. As the story develops, the main character usually faces further **plot reversals**. The issues need not be life-threatening, but they must make the reader want to find out how the character overcomes them.

> **Key terms**
>
> **narrative hook:** *any technique the writer uses at the start of a story to interest the reader*
>
> **plot reversals:** *events that block or create problems for the main character*

1 Read the following summary of a story, then answer the questions below.

> *Leroy is on a first date with a girl he really likes. He has borrowed money from his brother to take the girl for a meal at an expensive restaurant. When paying, he realises his wallet and phone were stolen while he was on the bus.*

    a) What is/are the problem/s Leroy has to face or overcome?

    b) What possible conflicts might result from this situation?

The typical structure of a short story is as follows:

Introduction or exposition	The writer establishes the main character and his/her situation.
Complication or problem	The reader learns that the main character faces a challenge or obstacle. This creates difficulties or conflict with others.
Rising action	The character tries to resolve or tackle the issue, but tension or suspense increases as they struggle.
Climax	The writer describes a key moment or crisis – the highest level of tension – when the problem is faced or the conflict comes to a boiling point.
Resolution	For better or worse, the reader finds out what the outcome was (was the main character successful in overcoming the problem, or were they damaged by it?)

2 Sequence these four elements from the story so that they fit the order above. You already know the first complication. Remember that the introduction will come first.

    a) *Leroy's brother turns up at the restaurant. He has Leroy's wallet and phone, which Leroy dropped while rushing out of the house. Leroy calls the girl, but gets a voicemail, so he leaves a message asking for another chance.*

    b) *Leroy is on the bus with his new girlfriend nervously chatting about the meal. The bus is really crowded.*

    c) *Leroy's girlfriend storms off when he admits he can't pay. The restaurant owner calls his parents.*

    d) *Leroy searches desperately for his wallet, and even tries to sweet-talk the manager, but this just makes things worse.*

3 What other plot reversals might Leroy face as part of this story?

Structuring character

The way you structure and sequence the character's 'journey' over the course of the story is equally important. For example:

- Where, when and what are the choices the character has to make?
- How can uncertainty or indecision about these choices add to our interest in the character? Will you show these (through speech or actions) or keep them as internal thoughts?
- What are the reactions of others to the actions he or she takes?
- What are the consequences of actions taken by the main character?

4 How are the character elements above addressed in the structure of the story about Leroy?

    What elements could you strengthen in the story itself to make it interesting for the reader?

5 Although there is a logical structure to the story, how and where you begin it is up to you. The main thing is that you include a 'hook'.

    Here are some potential hooks for the opening sentence. Discuss with a partner which of these you think is the most likely to capture a reader's interest and why.

    Hook 1: Leroy felt uncomfortable on the bus; he was sweating and nervous about the date ahead of him.

    Hook 2: He reached for his wallet to pay but he couldn't find it!

    Hook 3: Leaving the house, Leroy was worried he'd miss the bus.

    Hook 4: 'Hi bro,' said Leroy, rushing into his brother's room. 'I need a favour.'

Generating ideas

In the exam, you will need to quickly generate ideas for your story based on the stimulus you are given (a choice of a picture or some words that begin, end or are to be included in your piece of writing). You should take about 45 minutes to write your story, so allow at least five minutes to generate ideas and a plan.

6 Look at the photo opposite. Bearing in mind the story structure you have just examined, jot down notes or create a spider diagram to help you generate ideas for a story based on this picture. Think about the following questions:

a) Who is the person?

b) Where and/or when is this happening?

c) What might have happened or be about to happen?

d) What is the overall mood?

You might begin like this:

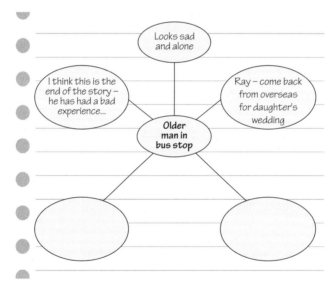

This spider diagram can then be turned into a plan:

- **Introduction:** Ray walking up the path to his daughter's wedding. He was not invited but thought that was just a mistake. He has come back from another country after moving away years before.

- **Complication:** Ray meets a relative outside the house who tells him he is not wanted there.

- **Rising action:** Ray argues, but he is told to leave. Ray searches for a way in and finally finds a back window open. Desperate to get in, he rips his suit and the gift he has brought gets damaged.
- **Climax:** He sees his daughter on the dance floor and gives her the damaged present. She starts crying and tells him to leave. He does so.
- **Resolution:** He waits at the bus stop for the bus to the airport, then…

7 Jot down some ideas for how to hook the reader at the start and an ending. This can be happy, sad – or a bit of both!

8 Note down a plan for your own story idea based on the photo.

Effective ways of telling your story

You have seen that, in a successful story, the main character should face a problem or conflict that must be overcome. The next question is *how* should you tell the story?

The simplest method is to use a straightforward chronological structure in the first person narrative. However, you might want to use a different method. The grid below outlines some alternative story structures.

Technique	Explanation	How it might be written	But remember…
flashback	The story takes the reader back to past events.	*As I sat at the bus stop I remembered getting off the plane…* *'Is this the place I grew up?' I thought as I looked around the modern airport…*	You can use flashback at any point in the story (for example, Ray might remember his daughter as a little girl).
in media res	The story does not 'set the scene' but plunges right into the action.	*I looked at my daughter across the room in her beautiful wedding dress, tears streaming down her face.* *'Get out!' she cried…*	You may need to explain the background at some point otherwise the reader may get confused.
dual narration	The reader hears two sides of the same story.	*There he was, my father, back after all these years, at my wedding!*	You only have 45 minutes – what will dual narration add?

9 Try turning the examples in the third column of the grid into the third person. What effect does this have?

Working from a verbal prompt

You should apply the same planning process when you are given words rather than a picture as a stimulus. However, there are additional things to bear in mind. For example, the text you are given may provide you with some help by including the core elements of the 'character journey'. Ask yourself:

- If I am given words from the story, could they work as an opening hook or as a satisfactory ending?
- What conflicts, choices and consequences are suggested by the given text?
- Who might be other characters in the story who could react in interesting ways to the main character?

Read this verbal prompt.

> Write a story that includes the following words:
> *She saw the lights go up and the murmuring and chattering stopped. This was it.*

Look at how one student has planned ideas with the task above in mind.

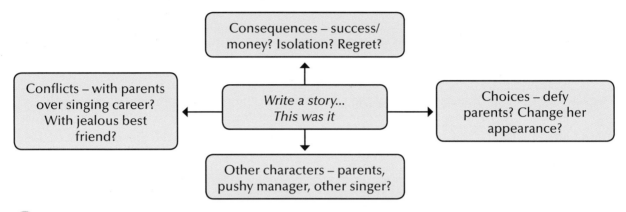

Consequences – success/money? Isolation? Regret?

Conflicts – with parents over singing career? With jealous best friend?

Write a story... *This was it*

Choices – defy parents? Change her appearance?

Other characters – parents, pushy manager, other singer?

10 Add any other examples of your own to the suggestions in the spider diagram. Remember, you will still need a clear structure for your story to hang the character journey on.

11 Jot down a five-point structure based on the given ideas (and your own). Remember, you should think about how the introductory part of the story can hook the reader.

Apply the skills

12 Generate ideas and plan a story based on the following photograph.

13 Write a story based on the following words:

I stood in front of the Principal's desk. Should I tell the truth?

Check your progress

Competent

- I can come up with a main character and setting based on a given verbal or visual prompt.
- I can plan a logical story structure.

Superior

- I can generate a set of interesting ideas including main character, setting and atmosphere.
- I can generate an interesting and engaging way of telling the story.

3.2 Developing vocabulary for characters and settings

Learn how to:

- *use vocabulary economically and appropriately*
- *create convincing characters and settings.*

Writing economically

When you write a short story, you do not need pages of description or lots of adjectives. Make each word and detail count.

Characterization is based on such things as physical appearance (hair, height, facial features, etc.), clothing, gestures and speech. However, you do not need to describe all these things to establish the character in the reader's mind.

1 Which of the following descriptions gives a better idea of a superhero character?

    a) *He was six feet five inches, and weighed 17 stone. He had a 48-inch chest. He had hair that was two feet in length and yellow in colour.*

    b) *He was a huge lion of a man with a golden mane of hair tumbling over his broad, muscular shoulders.*

One of these descriptions gives accurate information, but it does not really convey anything about the character's powerful, proud appearance.

A key method for conveying character is to use **noun phrases**. For example:

> *The old man's <u>hollow eye-sockets</u> with <u>dark shadows</u> underneath followed my every step as I filled my basket with rich juicy fruits and freshly baked loaves.*

The following carefully selected noun phrases relate many details in a few words:

- 'hollow eye-sockets' suggest emptiness in the old man's life.
- 'dark shadows' suggest death or illness.

2 Which other noun phrases from the sentence suggest that the narrator has a happy, healthy life?

> **Key term**
>
> **noun phrase:** *a noun that is modified by additional information, often adjectives*

Using imagery to evoke character

In the first example, the character was described as a 'huge lion of man'. Vivid word pictures are known as imagery. You should only use imagery when it adds something to the story.

Read the following description of a different character.

The tall figure dismounted languidly from the sleek motorbike, and looked over at the group sitting on the bench. The rider was like a coiled spring, muscles flexing through the black leather. Just visible through the visor of the helmet, her eyes were bullet-holes of grey, searching for a target.

Here the imagery *adds* to the suspense by conveying a sense of danger and menace. For example:

- The **simile** 'like a coiled spring' suggests that some sort of sudden, powerful action is about to happen.
- The **metaphor** 'eyes were bullet-holes of grey, searching for a target' continues the theme of danger.

> *Key terms*
>
> *simile: a comparison in which one thing is said to be* like *another.*
>
> *metaphor: a comparison in which one thing is said to actually* be *another.*

3 Read the text below. Select the most appropriate simile from each set of options to develop the same sense of menace.

> *The rider removed her helmet and her black tresses sprang out on all sides like streaks of <u>lightning/water/sunlight</u>. Zigzagging between the parked cars like a <u>slug/bear/snake</u>, she walked towards the group. Finally she stopped and removed her gloves, revealing long fingernails like tiny, pointed <u>spoons/forks/knives</u>.*

4 Copy and complete this opening to a story in which a climber falls down a crevasse while climbing the Blue Mountain in Jamaica. Fill the gaps with similes or metaphors that help explain the character's feelings.

> *Above him, he could see a tiny slit of blue sky like a…in the side of a wall. He called out for help but the walls answered back, …ing at him, mocking him. He should never have tried the climb; he didn't have the skills. Shame burned inside him like…*

Remember

You can use verbs metaphorically – for example: 'She *poisoned* him with her remarks.'

Establishing time, place and mood

In your story, make it clear *where* and *when* the action takes place, and also what the **mood** will be. You can do this by deciding:

- what the weather is like and/or at what time of year the story takes place
- whether the settings are inside or outside (or move between the two)
- how the setting and mood link to the story you are telling.

Read this example from one student's story opening.

> *It was the hurricane season. By the harbour, anxious fishermen trussed up their boats in thick tarpaulins. Jayden hurried home from school, his white shirt billowing in the strengthening wind. He had a worried frown. With his father out at sea it was up to Jayden as 'man of the house' to secure their home in time.*

5 How well has the student established setting and mood? Identify:

    a) words, phrases or other details that tell us *where* the setting is, *what the weather is like* and *when* it takes place

    b) how the setting and weather are *connected to the plot/Jayden*

    c) what mood is created.

Settings and mood/atmosphere often depend on **sensory details**. However, you should not include these for the sake of it; they must contribute to the plot or help develop the mood.

> **Key terms**
>
> **mood:** *the atmosphere or 'feel' of a story – for example, tense, joyful, peaceful, etc.*
>
> **sensory details:** *references to sight, sound, smell, taste or touch*

6 In the extract below, identify the verbs used to convey the impact of the storm.

> *The gale howled and roared as Jayden grappled desperately with the shutters. Each time he rammed them into place they flung open again, rattling against the wall. As he finally forced them into position, he felt the first tiny drops of rain pricking his skin and face. More worryingly his lips sensed salt. The waves must have broken through the storm barrier.*

7 The writer has added one small sensory detail that very effectively signals a new piece of information in the story. Find this detail. What new information does it reveal?

Apply the skills

8 Plan and write the opening two paragraphs of a story that contains these words (they do not have to be in the paragraphs you write):

> *She opened the window and climbed out. That was the easy bit – what came next was far more difficult.*

Remember

Establish a *setting and mood* quickly:

- Where is the girl/woman? What time is it?
- Where has she come from; where is she going?

Convey *character* effectively and *link* it to the plot and setting:

- Who is the girl/woman and what does she look like?
- How does she move or behave?
- What sort of person is she and how will this be shown?

Make sure you use:

- noun phrases and well-chosen verbs that convey sensory information
- imagery in the form of similes or metaphors to convey powerful and vivid ideas.

Revision tip

Observe buildings or natural features (such as lakes, shorelines, etc.) and make notes on their shapes, textures, colours and sounds in order to build a catalogue of vocabulary to use in your writing.

Check your progress

Competent

- I can show the reader what is happening through my choice of vocabulary.
- I can create a basic setting or settings that establish time and place.

Superior

- I can manipulate vocabulary and use imagery to make my writing vivid for the reader.
- I can write or use vocabulary in a lively and economical way to convey setting and character.

3.3 Effective speech and dialogue in stories

Learn how to:

- *set out and punctuate speech accurately*
- *use dialogue to create mood, reveal character or advance the plot.*

Use of speech in stories

The words that a character uses and how characters speak to each other (dialogue) can create dramatic moments, give insight into their personalities and reveal key information about the story.

Here is an example of spoken language from the story structure in Topic 3.1.

> *Ray looked across the room at his daughter. She held a bunch of flowers in her hand but her face was streaked with tears.*
>
> *'I...I wanted to surprise you,[2]'[1] he said, standing on the edge of the dance floor.*
>
> *'Surprise me?' his daughter replied [3], her voice trembling. 'Are you trying to be funny?' [4]*
>
> *Ray took a step into the room.*
>
> *'DON'T come near me!' [5]*

[1] speech marks go around the spoken words

[2] punctuation related to what is being said goes inside the speech marks

[3] start a new line for each 'new' speaker

[4] stay on same line if same speaker continues to speak

[5] if it is obvious, it is not always necessary to say who is speaking

1 Look at the next part of the conversation below. Use the rules above to help you correct the layout of the dialogue.

> *Ray hesitated, clutching the small, broken gift in his hands. He felt ridiculous. I guess you don't want my present then? he asked. The only thing I want from you is for you to leave Linda said, wiping away her tears. You think one present can make up for all those missing years? Ray put the damaged photo frame down on a nearby table. Of course not. I'm sorry I spoiled your big day. He paused for a moment, then turned and walked out.*

Establishing character through dialogue

Dialogue is especially important for telling readers more about characters and their relationships. It can also help advance the plot.

2   Look again at the dialogue in Question 1. What do you learn about:

a) the story (what had happened)?

b) Ray and his daughter (how do they feel)?

Here is another example of the use of speech. It continues the story about the girl on the motorbike in Topic 3.2.

> *'Hey Deon. Where yuh been hidin'?'* [1]
>
> *Deon looked up, and his mouth fell open in surprise.* [2]
>
> *'Shana…we…I…,'* [3] *he stammered* [4]*, beads of sweat breaking out on his brow.* [5]
>
> *'Yuh lost your voice? Seen a ghost? Well, maybe that's right, cos I'm back from the dead.'*

[1] question tells us she has been looking for him

[2] description between the spoken lines adds to the action and mood – Deon is shocked

[3] fragments of speech convey Deon's fear

[4] verb tells us precisely how he speaks

[5] additional description confirms what we know: he is scared

3   What does the final line of speech suggest about what might have happened?

4   Who has the most power – or **status** – in the conversation? How can you tell?

> **Key term**
>
> *status: power or control in a dramatic situation; this can change during a conversation so that the balance shifts from one character to another*

Improving your use of dialogue

Read the next two lines of dialogue from the same story. As you read, think about the ways in which the conversation lacks impact.

> *'I think you thought I'd be driftin' in that boat out in the storm until a big wave came and knocked me overboard which you would have liked wouldn't you I guess?'*
>
> *'No, you don't understand, Shana, that wasn't my intention, honest. I wasn't to know the boat would start sinking with those few things I smuggled and which I meant to tell you about.'*

5 Rewrite the dialogue.

- Remove unnecessary words or phrases, for example shortening Shana's speech so it is more forceful.
- Add detail or description between the two sections of speech, for example describing what Shana does and how Deon reacts.
- Consider interior thoughts – for example, how Deon is feeling, which may not match what he says (for example, frustration and anger that Shana has got the better of him).

Dialect and accent

Dialect and **accent** can make dialogue sound realistic, but you should use them sparingly. They should be used to provide:

- contextual clues about the character (for example, their age, class, etc.)
- detail about the setting (for example, dialect linking someone to a particular town or region)
- shifts between times or social settings (for example, moving between an adult business meeting to a group of teens chatting on the street).

> *Key terms*
>
> *dialect: the different vocabulary and grammar used in particular places or by specific groups of people*
>
> *accent: refers to pronunciation – for example, 'Yuh' rather than 'You' (pronounced 'yoo')*

6   How have dialect and accent been used in the following extract?

> *The grey-haired man in the smart suit stepped gingerly off the boat.*
> *He approached one of the fisherman.*
>
> *'Ah, my good man. Would you be so kind as to tell me the way to the hotel?'*
>
> *The fisherman's face creased into a smile.*
>
> *'Hotel? Hotel? Why, friend, there ain't no hotel here. Yuh gotta get right back*
> *on tha' boat. Is a hundred miles north.'*

7   Write another line of speech for each of the two characters in the dialogue above. Try to retain the same accent and dialect for each.

Apply the skills

8   Write a dialogue that could be part of a story based on the following situation.

> *A mother and her five-year-old child are shopping in the big city. However, the*
> *child wanders off and the mother cannot find her.*

You can choose to write dialogue from any stage of the story – for example:

* before the child disappears (between mother and child)
* when the child goes missing (between the mother and a local person, or the child and other adults).

Once you have drafted your ideas, use the checklist in the Remember box below to ensure that the speech is set out accurately and also advances plot and characterisation.

Remember

* Use speech marks around spoken words.
* Use a new line each time a new person speaks.
* Punctuation related to what is said sits inside the speech marks.
* You do not need to say who is speaking if it is obvious.
* Use descriptive details – for example, what people are doing or how words are spoken – embedded in the dialogue itself.
* Interior thought can add to – or even contradict – what a character says or does.
* Dialogue tells us about character of speaker.
* Dialogue moves the story forward.
* Accent or dialect, if used, adds characterisation (but not too exaggerated).

Check your progress

Competent

* I can generally set out and punctuate speech clearly and correctly.
* I can use dialogue to tell the reader something about the story.

Superior

* I can set out and punctuate speech correctly and appropriately in a story.
* I can use dialogue for a range of functions: advancing the plot, revealing character, establishing mood.

3.4 Writing meaningful sentences and paragraphs

Learn how to:

- *use a variety of sentences*
- *develop and link paragraphs fluently.*

Writing clear and meaningful sentences

If your sentences and paragraphs are properly developed then your story will be easy to follow. In addition, the type of sentences you choose to develop your paragraphs can have an important impact on the reader.

Simple sentences always have a subject and a main verb. They often include additional information such as the object. For example:

> *The girl [1] removed [2] her sparkling engagement ring. [3]*

[1] subject

[2] verb

[3] object

A compound sentence can add equally important information. For example:

> *The girl slyly removed her sparkling engagement ring and [1] put it in her pocket.*

[1] conjunction

1 The second clause in the example above adds information about the girl and the story. What new information has been added? How does it develop the story?

Additional information can come in many forms, including adverbs, adjectives and supplementary clauses or phrases. However, you should only include these if they will advance the story, create mood or aid characterisation.

2 What adverb has been included in the example above? How does it affect the reader's view of the character?

Multi-clause or complex sentences add extra clauses to provide even more detail or change the direction of what is being said. For example:

> *The girl slyly removed her sparkling engagement ring and put it in her pocket, although she had only been given it by Robbie that same evening.*

Here, the last clause adds further information about the ring.

3 **a)** What does this add to our understanding of the girl and the story?

    b) What does it tell us about anyone else?

4 Construct a sentence in the same way. Use the simple sentence below as a starter.

> *Robbie watched Shelley from the shadows.*

Selecting the style and length of sentences

The type of sentence you use can also have a dramatic impact on the mood of your story. Read the following extract.

> *Shelley turned it over and over in her mind, trying to figure it out, trying to make sense of what had happened, but none of it seemed to fit. She had despised him, found him irritating, taken his ring out of pity, but now, as if the fog was clearing she could finally see the light. She loved Robbie. That was the truth.*

5 **a)** What does the text tell us about Shelley?

    b) What do you notice about the lengths of the sentences in this extract?

    c) Why does the writer change from one style of sentence to the other at the end? What effect does this have?

In stories, shorter sentences may be used for many reasons and for many different effects.

For example:

- **To show a character making a decision:** *He would enter the race. He had no choice.* (Simple statements sound decisive and definite.)
- **To convey tension or that a character is under pressure:** *She stopped. Was there someone behind her? A tapping on the ground? No, just an echo. Her own nervous footsteps. On she went, quickly.* (Shorter or minor sentences and questions create a jumpy, staccato effect.)

Linking sentences and paragraphs effectively

You should use new paragraphs for new information or speech, or to indicate a change in time, mood or place. How you link paragraphs is also important. For example:

> *The light grew brighter and brighter until [1] it dominated Deonte's vision. She [2] put her hands to her face but it was no good. Now [3] she was completely blinded. She felt faint, and found herself sinking to the ground.*

[1] conjunction tells us how Deonte came to be blinded

[2] pronoun relates back to Deonte

[3] time marker tells us the present situation Deonte is in

In a story, you may want to indicate a shift in time by using a new paragraph. For example:

> *When Deonte awoke, she was in a dark room lit only by a candle. A shadowy figure sat by her on the bed. It leaned forward and took her hand. After several minutes of silence, the figure stood up and a door opened. Finally she realised where she was. However, before she could act, she felt herself slipping into sleep again.*

6 The adverbial phrase 'When Deonte awoke' signals the shift in time. What other phrases show you that the story is moving along?

7 What other linking word is used at the end of the paragraph? What does it tell us?

8 Choose suitable linking words and phrases to fill the spaces in the paragraph below and make the transitions clear.

> *…, Deonte awoke again, properly this time. She got out of the bed and checked the door…it was locked. …the next few minutes she banged on it again and again, shouting to be released. …no one came.*

It is also important to be able to move back in time through your use of paragraphs. To do this, you can use tenses and demonstrative pronouns. For example:

> *It had been [1] a lovely day when she started the job on the ship. That [2] was before things started going wrong.*

[1] past perfect form tells us about a situation that has ended

[2] demonstrative pronoun stresses the end of the pleasant weather

9 Write a further paragraph going back in time to add to the paragraph above. Begin 'It had…' or 'She had…'.

Apply the skills

Here is a task similar to one you might face in the exam.

> *Write a story that includes the following words:*
>
> *'He emerged from the wreckage and looked around. He was safe, but utterly alone.'*

10 Imagine these are the final words of your story. Write the preceding two paragraphs. You will need to spend a bit of time thinking about the situation and what has happened leading up to this moment.

Remember

- Think about how ideas (in terms of time or of action) relate to each other – for example, what comes first and second, and so on.
- Use a variety of sentence types (simple, compound and complex) for different effects.
- Make sure you construct sentences so that they are clear and grammatically accurate, unless you are using minor sentences for effect.
- Link your sentences and ideas fluently using pronouns and other linking words or phrases.

Check your progress

Competent

- I can write sentences and paragraphs with clear functions and which are usually grammatically correct.
- I can link my ideas in a logical way using connectives of time, for example.

Superior

- I can write fluent sentences and paragraphs that are always grammatically correct.
- I can link ideas seamlessly, using a variety of ways of conveying change in time, ideas or focus.

3.5 Test yourself

Learn how to:

- *understand and respond to a practice narrative writing question*
- *evaluate your own response and that of others.*

Your task

Write a story based on the picture below. You will have the chance to complete a practice task on a verbal prompt on page 215.

Approaching the task

1. Remind yourself of the skills you will need to demonstrate in your writing. These will include:

   - a storyline that is clearly developed, including a problem or conflict that is satisfactorily resolved
   - a narrative 'hook' to capture the reader's attention
   - a clearly established setting
   - believable, developed characters with motives or reasons for acting in the way they do
   - dialogue/speech that has a purpose
   - varied, well-chosen sentences for effect
   - economic and lively use of language/vocabulary to create character, setting and plot
   - smooth links between sentences and paragraphs
   - correct spelling, punctuation, paragraphing and general grammar.

2 Spend about five minutes generating ideas using either a list or spider diagram. Decide what your plot will be. Think about the choices and consequences of the main character's actions and how others react to them. Remember the five-part sequence you learned about.

3 Finally, write your story.

Reflecting on your progress

Read the following sample plan (not assessed) and extract from a response to the practice task by one student, then look at the comments below.

Plan 1

- *Who: student – school sports day.*
- *Where: playing fields and changing room.*
- *When: end of term – big day.*
- *What's happened: someone (main character?) won race.*
- *Mood/tone – exciting.*

Response 1

Everyone was very quiet as we lined up for the race. It was a windy afternoon so I could see everyone else's vests flapping in the wind. [1] *I was the favourite as I had won all the practice races, but today I felt nervous, like something was bashing the inside of my belly.* [2]

I looked down at my new running shoes, which I had bought with the money I saved from my job at the general store. I was very proud of them. They were bright green with a black arrow down the side. [3] *Everyone in the class was jealous of them.*

Suddenly I noticed that one of the laces was undone! [4] *I wanted to bend down to tie it up but our sports teacher looked at me in a warning way.* [5]

'Keep still!' he shouted to us all.

'Mr Braithwaite...' I began to say, but he interrupted me. [6]

'Ready. Set...' He fired the pistol.

I didn't react as quickly as usual as I was worried about my shoe. Ahead of me I could already see my biggest rival, Jem. [7]

---

[1] sets the scene and mood in the opening sentence with good detail

[2] use of simile but not very appropriate

[3] visual detail is appropriate to the situation

[4] introduces problem

[5] tells us how teacher reacts, but vocabulary is rather vague

[6] speech punctuation accurate and dialogue included for a reason

[7] suggests conflict, but lacks detail and could show rather than tell

Now read another student's plan and response to the same practice task, then look at the comments that follow.

Plan 2

- *Who: girl Lisa and her rival, Melody, from another school, and her parents.*
- *Where: start at athletic track but also flashback to row at home.*
- *What's happened: father forcing her to train even when she doesn't want to, wants to hang out with friends.*
- *Mood/tone: tension as Lisa faces choice of what to do.*
- *Consequences: parents begin to realise what they've done.*
- *Plot: end of race, flashback; row with parents, talk with teacher; the race – she thinks about losing – but can't stop herself winning, but tells her parents she's going to take a break from sport for a while.*

Response 2

Lisa lay on her back on the ground, panting for breath, her chest rising and falling. Above her she could see the clear blue sky of the May afternoon. [1] Slowly, a face came into view, the face of her rival, her oldest enemy [2], her sharp, almost black eyes staring down at her.

Lisa thought back to the start of the race [3] – the national trials to represent the country. She remembered her trainer, Ms Saldana, tall and strong like an ash tree standing firm in the breeze, [4] taking her by the shoulders and looking at her closely.

'This is your big, big chance, girl! Don't blow it. Believe in yourself!' [5]

If only she could have told Ms Saldana what she really felt. She wanted to say, 'I hate running. I hate competing. I'm only doing this because you, my parents and the school want me to!' [6]

But she said nothing. [7] Instead, she checked her running spikes, checked the blocks, did her stretches and settled down in her lane, the long curving cinder track snaking ahead of her. [4] Alongside her she was aware of Melody preparing too. Only one would be selected, but Lisa didn't care. She was going to lose – deliberately. [6] Then they would all stop pressurizing her.

[1] atmospheric start that hooks the reader as it introduces character and setting

[2] introduces possible conflict

[3] clever structural choice – flashback to keep us guessing who won

[4] vivid descriptive detail

[5] correct and appropriate use of speech to establish character

[6] possible conflict and problem to overcome

[7] effective short sentence conveys main character's dilemma

Comment on Response 2

The plan is much more helpful in suggesting the conflicts and choices the character will face, and the five-part structure has been considered. This is a *superior* response, demonstrating excellent storytelling. Character and situation are established quickly and vividly, and there is a logical structure to the plot, which engages us and makes us want to know what happened next.

Your task

Write a story that includes the following words:

The figure in the boat cried out to him and reached up.

Approaching the task

1   Remind yourself of the skills you will need to demonstrate in your writing. These will include:

- a storyline that is clearly developed, including a problem or conflict that is satisfactorily resolved
- a narrative 'hook' to capture the reader's attention
- a clearly established setting
- believable, developed characters with motives or reasons for acting in the way they do
- dialogue/speech that has a purpose
- varied, well-chosen sentences for effect
- economic and lively use of language/vocabulary to create character, setting and plot
- smooth links between sentences and paragraphs
- correct spelling, punctuation, paragraphing and general grammar.

2   Spend about five minutes generating ideas using either a list or spider diagram. Decide what your plot will be. Think about the choices and consequences of the main character's actions, and how others might react to them. Remember the five-part sequence you learned about.

3   Finally, write your story.

Reflecting on your progress

Read the following sample plan (not assessed) and extract from a response to the practice task by one student, then look at the comments below.

Plan 1

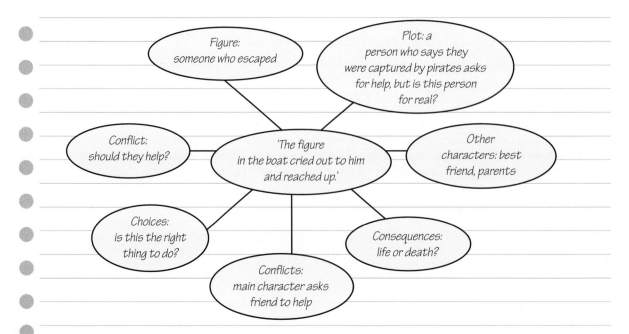

Response 1

Antony was walking by the harbour at night. It was dark and stormy and the sea was rough. [1] *The rain fell like hammers* [2] *on the road and it was hard to see even a few feet in front of you. Suddenly, he heard a voice in the darkness.* [3]

'Hey, you! Help!'

Antony went to the harbour wall and looked down. There was a small boat being smashed up against the rocks. There was someone in the boat swaying about and waving their hands. Antony rushed down the steps. The figure in the boat cried out to him and reached up. Who was this person, he wondered? And how did he get there? [4]

Antony was unsure what to do. [5] *His parents had warned him to keep away from the old harbour because drug smugglers sometimes used it. But it was the quickest way home after going to the club.*

'Wait a minute,' Antony shouted. 'Grab this!' [6]

He threw the figure an old rope that was hanging from the wall, and then pulled hard. The figure grabbed it and jumped from the boat. The person fell into the sea and thrashed around. [7]

[1] details about main character and the atmospheric setting

[2] use of similes

[3] problem or challenge for main character

[4] character's internal thoughts

[5] character indecision adds some depth to story

[6] simple but effective use of dialogue

[7] action advances story but rather lacks in detail

Comment on Plan and Response 1

The plan is basic and rather vague, suggesting the student did not have many different ideas. The response itself is competent and establishes the situation and the challenges the main character faces effectively. However, apart from the warning not to go near the harbour, little information is given about Antony. In addition, more detail about the setting and a wider use of imagery could 'hook' the reader into the story.

4   Using the comments above and the list of progress points at the end of this chapter, rewrite this response to improve it.

Now read another student's plan and response to the same practice task, then look at the comments that follow.

Plan 2

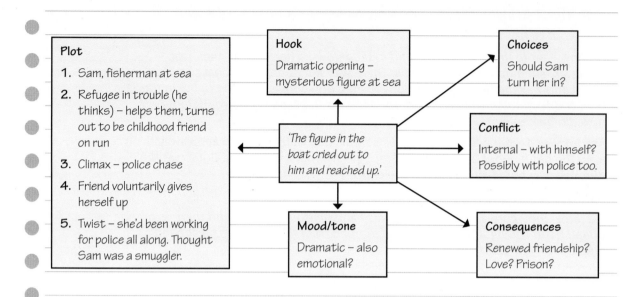

Plot

1. Sam, fisherman at sea
2. Refugee in trouble (he thinks) – helps them, turns out to be childhood friend on run
3. Climax – police chase
4. Friend voluntarily gives herself up
5. Twist – she'd been working for police all along. Thought Sam was a smuggler.

Hook

Dramatic opening – mysterious figure at sea

'The figure in the boat cried out to him and reached up.'

Choices

Should Sam turn her in?

Conflict

Internal – with himself? Possibly with police too.

Mood/tone

Dramatic – also emotional?

Consequences

Renewed friendship? Love? Prison?

Response 2

Yes, there it was again! A faint light bobbing on the moonlit water as the waves rolled and swelled ominously around his fishing boat. [1] *Another fisherman? Possibly, but he'd seen most of the other boats returning before sunset, getting back before the storm.*

He turned the boat around, and headed towards the light. Slowly, like a pale eye in the face of the sea [2]*, it came into view. It was no fisherman. No, all he could see was a tiny dinghy and a hunched figure wrapped in a grey tarpaulin.* [3]

'Ay, what happen? You alright, man?'

The figure turned suddenly and cried out to him and reached up. He couldn't hear what they said, so pulled his boat alongside and threw down a rope ladder. The owner of the dinghy, which was now almost completely full of water due to the rising waves, tried to grab the ladder but failed. Three times, Sam swung his boat around to get closer to the dinghy. It was surely going to sink. [4]

Finally, hands grasped the rope, and the figure wearily, step by step hauled itself up, before collapsing over the side and falling to the ground.

Sam reached down and helped the figure to its feet. The tarpaulin fell off, and Sam gasped.

'You! What in God's name you doing here, girl?' [5]

It was Tasha, a girl he'd known since childhood, a girl he'd hung around with until she'd got in with the wrong crowd. [6]

'You ha' to help me, Sammy!' she sobbed and flung herself into his arms. [7]

[1] very effective hook draws reader in

[2] powerful image

[3] visual details paint picture but also create mystery

[4] effective short sentence creates drama

[5] convincing dialogue expresses character's feelings

[6] hints at/foreshadows consequences

[7] suggests character choices to come

Comment on Plan and Response 2

The plan sets out in detail what the story is, and the possible choices, conflicts and consequences. The response itself is a superior one, capturing the reader's attention with a hook at the start, developing the setting through well-chosen detail and conveying the dramatic mood intended. There is rich vocabulary use, including adapting register to include dialect to establish character and some powerful imagery too.

Check your progress

Competent

- I can come up with a main character and setting based on a given stimulus.
- I can plan a logical story structure.
- I can show the reader what is happening through my choice of vocabulary.
- I can create a basic setting or settings that establish time and place.
- I can generally set out and punctuate speech clearly and correctly.
- I can use dialogue to tell the reader something about the story.
- I can write sentences and paragraphs with clear functions and which are usually grammatically correct.
- I can link my ideas in a logical way using connectives of time, for example.

Superior

- I can generate a set of interesting ideas including main character, setting and atmosphere.
- I can generate an interesting and engaging way of telling the story including how I will 'hook' the reader.
- I can manipulate vocabulary and use imagery to make my writing vivid for the reader.
- I can write or use vocabulary in a lively and economical way to convey setting and character.
- I can set out and punctuate speech correctly and appropriately in a story.
- I can use dialogue for a range of functions: advancing the plot, revealing character, establishing mood.
- I can write fluent sentences and paragraphs that are always grammatically correct.
- I can link ideas seamlessly, using a variety of ways of conveying change in time, ideas or focus.

Chapter 4 Writing an argumentative text

4.1 Effective ways of arguing a point of view

Learn how to:
- *use the key features of point-of-view writing*
- *generate ideas for an essay arguing a particular viewpoint.*

When arguing a particular point of view, you need to be clear and consistent in what you say. You also need to support your arguments effectively and suit your style to your audience – your readers or listeners.

Approaching the question

In the exam you will be given a task in which you have to present your views on a particular proposal or issue. So, how do you decide on the exact requirements? Read the sample task below, then answer the questions that follow.

> *You are a member of a local corporation that wants to improve the health and well-being of young people in your town. One of the proposals being discussed is a ban on all fast-food shops and restaurants within half a kilometre of any school.*
>
> *Write the speech you would make to the council, giving your views on the proposal.*

First of all, it is vital that you understand the main *purpose* of your speech.

1　On what do you have to give your views?

    a)　the health and well-being of young people

    b)　a proposal to ban fast-food outlets in your town

    c)　a proposal to ban fast-food outlets near schools

    d)　whether fast-food can be healthy or not

It is equally important to understand your role. You will be giving your own views, but you may be asked to represent a particular perspective, as an older person or someone in authority.

The role you are asked to take will affect *how* you respond. For example, if you were the owner of a fast-food shop, your views might be different from those of a health adviser.

2 Look at the task again. From whose perspective will you write the response?

    a) town councillor

    b) student

    c) owner of a fast-food shop

    d) health adviser

Finally, you need to know who is your audience. This will affect the tone and style of your response. Imagine how differently you might speak if you were addressing teenagers rather than owners of fast-food outlets.

3 Who is the audience for this task?

    a) owners of fast-food outlets

    b) students

    c) parents

    d) members of the regional corporation

4 Here is a new task. Write down the *purpose*, the *role* and the *audience*.

> *You have been elected as a student councillor. Your principal has asked you to attend a meeting of the school council (with other student councillors) to discuss how to spend a donation of $10,000 made by a local business.*
>
> *Write the speech you would give to the council, offering your views on how the money should be spent.*

What makes argument texts effective?

It is vital to understand these three key requirements – purpose, role and audience – because these things determine *what* you include in your argument and *how* it is expressed.

Look at these notes that a student has made for some key ideas for the argument for the fast-food task.

> *My notes*
>
> a) School students should be able to make their own choices about diet when they leave the school premises.
>
> b) Fast-food chains are businesses that pay taxes, which is good for everyone.
>
> c) It's impractical to ban fast-food outlets: teens love fast food and will go a bit further for their favourite snacks.

5 What point of view is being argued here (for or against the ban)?

6 Note at least two additional points for this argument.

The best arguments also take account of the **counter-arguments**. The following opposing views present examples:

- *Students/teens are basically lazy – if the fast-food outlets are not near the school they won't bother walking kilometres for them.*

- *Banning fast-food chains will encourage other, healthier cafés and shops to set up near schools.*

7 Which point (a, b or c) under 'My notes' do these counter-arguments oppose?

8 Note a counter-argument for the remaining point.

> **Key term**
>
> **counter-argument:** *a point that is opposite to the one you are making*

Having such a list of pros and cons means that when you begin to argue your point of view you can *anticipate* opposing arguments and be ready to 'knock them down'. For example:

> To those who say that teens are inherently lazy, and won't be bothered to walk for kilometres to get their sugar rush or salt fix, [1] I say that they love fast food too much and this will prove more of a magnet than the desire to relax and eat near the school.

[1] counter-argument comes first, so the writer can answer it in the second part of the sentence

Apply the skills

Look again at the task in Question 4. Decide what your view will be – what might the money be spent on? You could use a list or a spider diagram like the one below to work out your ideas.

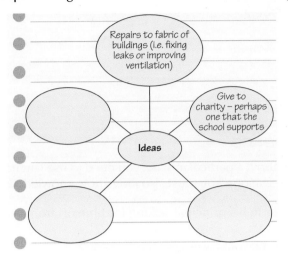

9 In what other ways could the donation be spent?

10 Think of arguments for and against your proposal and quickly jot them down in a table like the one below.

For (spending on charity)	Against
Helping others will make us feel better about ourselves and less selfish.	*The donor might object if the money is not spent on the school itself.*

Remember

- Use a spider diagram or list of notes to generate ideas.
- Choose a viewpoint or idea that you can expand and develop, not one that is too 'narrow' or to which you cannot add information.

Revision tip

You may not have time to plan both lists in the exam, but if you think like this as you write, it will help you structure your argument.

Check your progress

Competent

- I can understand and 'break down' an argument-style task.
- I can generate ideas to support my point of view.

Superior

- I can understand how role, audience and purpose affect my response.
- I can generate arguments and counter-arguments both for and against my point of view.

4.2 Using an appropriate tone and language

Learn how to:

- *judge the audience's needs*
- *use appropriate register and tone.*

Judging your audience

In order to persuade people about a particular issue, you need to use language that is appropriate and matches your audience's expectations. You must also judge how knowledgeable they are about the topic.

1   Read this student's letter to his principal, asking for time off from school to go on an adventure trip.

    a) What is *good* about this opening to the letter?

    b) What *shouldn't* the student have said or mentioned?

> *A principal's job is very busy, as you've got to maintain discipline and keep teachers motivated, so you probably don't have time for anything enjoyable like adventure holidays. Your job is very important to you, but school isn't so important to me as I think I learn better from doing things, which is why I'm asking you for time off for a trip to the Antarctic.*

The student makes the valid point that learning by doing suits some people. However, by including negative comments such as 'school isn't so important to me' and 'you probably don't have time for… adventure holidays', he is unlikely to make himself popular with the principal! In addition, telling the principal what he already knows about his job ('maintaining discipline') could sound insulting.

2   Read the text below. What is better about the student's judgement of his audience here? What does the student say about school that is likely to please the principal? What does the student say about the trip that supports his argument?

> *I recognise the importance of school, and how study can advance my social skills and career prospects. However, the opportunity of a lifetime has emerged that will enable me to expand my horizons and become a wiser, brighter and better member of the school community. What is more, imagine me proudly planting the school flag at the top of an icy peak. Unfortunately, this opportunity will mean I would have to miss some of my schooling, but surely the student who returns will be twice the one who left?*

Persuasive language

When used correctly, persuasive language can help to make an argument more convincing:

- **Patterns of three** can have a strong, almost poetic effect on the rhythm of an argument.
- **Powerful images** help make abstract ideas vivid.
- **Rhetorical questions** (ones that have an expected answer) are also useful.

3 Identify the pattern of three (three adjectives) in the second sentence of the student's letter.

4 Where has the student used powerful images to describe a situation that the principal can picture? Why would this image be effective?

5 Where does the writer use a rhetorical question for effect?

Register and tone

The *register* you use relates to the degree of formality or informality in your language when communicating with particular people or groups. This in turn affects the tone of your writing – the overall 'feel' or style (whether it is authoritative, friendly, polite, etc.).

Formal language...	Informal language...
<ul><li>is sometimes referred to as impersonal, but can present quite personal opinions and feelings in formal ways, as long as your vocabulary is clear and your grammar correct ('I am incredibly disappointed in the outcome...')</li><li>is expressed in Standard English (not dialect or regional forms) and tends to be used between people who do not know each other well</li><li>uses full sentences and avoids abbreviations and 'short-hand' phrases.</li></ul>	<ul><li>may use dialect or local vocabulary and structures; it is more like spoken language, and perhaps reflects the way you might chat with family or friends</li><li>often has shortened or abbreviated forms ('you're', 'they're', LOL), and may use question marks and exclamation marks more frequently</li><li>is sometimes grammatically incorrect ('we was').</li></ul>

6 Which of the two texts below is 'informal'? How do you know?

7 How does the level of formality in both cases affect the tone?

> *I'm tellin' you, you gotta get out there and use your vote, right? Cos if you don't, then you can't expect no one to listen to you when you grouse about your sad life!*

> *It is important that you utilize your vote, because if you don't, then you can't expect anyone to listen to you when you complain about your unpleasant living conditions.*

Revision tip

It is generally better to use formal, Standard English in the exam, as you can lose marks for being too informal or using dialect. If you do need to use a more informal style, use it sparingly.

8 You have a weekend job in a shop. Write the opening paragraph of an email to your manager, explaining why you are leaving to take up an unpaid role working as a drummer in a band touring the Caribbean for six months.

Your manager knows you well, so the tone can be friendly and personal. However, the subject matter is serious so do not make it too informal. You could start:

> *Dear Mr Martinez:*
>
> *As you know, I have always loved music. Well…*

Style and vocabulary

The most effective arguments sound logical and balanced, and when making your argument you should seem reasonable yet authoritative. No one expects you to be an expert, but if you were writing about facilities for the disabled in an exam task, for example, you could use common **abstract nouns** such as 'equality', 'discrimination' and 'respect' in relation to attitudes, and more **concrete nouns** such as 'ramp', 'access', 'hand-rail' and 'elevator' for specific proposals.

9 Here are four topics about which people often disagree. Copy the table, then spend five minutes writing down as many words as you can (which you may use in an argument) that are broadly related to each topic. Some examples have been given to get you started.

Healthy eating	Dangerous dogs	Designer brands	Homelessness
diet, well-being	muzzle, aggression	logo, fashion	shelter, humanity

> **Key terms**
>
> **abstract noun:** a noun that expresses an idea of feeling, not a physical object – for example, 'fear', 'spirit', 'politics'
>
> **concrete noun:** a noun that relates to a physical thing – for example, 'building', 'ladder', 'bucket'

You can also use carefully chosen adjectives and sentences to emphasise your point. For example:

Feature	Example (Homelessness)
powerful, emotive adjectives	*Heartbreaking sight of desperate young people.*
intensifiers (adverbs used with an adjective)	*Totally unacceptable attitude of government.*
rhetorical questions	*Can it be right that so many face a night on the streets?*
short, blunt sentences	*We must act now.*

10 Make your own copy of the table above, listing the features in the left-hand column. Then fill in the right-hand column using one of the topics from Question 9 for your examples.

Apply the skills

Read this situation from an exam-style task.

> *The school board for your region wants to introduce compulsory self-defence classes for all students.*

11 Write the opening two paragraphs for two different speeches.

    a) In the first speech, write from the position of a board member *recommending* that the proposal goes ahead.

    b) In the second speech, write as a student at the school, speaking to your year group advising them to speak out *against* the proposal.

Firstly, jot down the possible arguments for and against. Secondly, consider the tone and style of each speech: which is likely to be the most formal?

Remember

- Write two paragraphs of each speech.
- Think carefully about your audience in each case and their expectations/concerns.
- Choose an appropriate register and tone, but do not make either speech overly informal.
- Select powerful images, rhetorical questions and patterns of three.

Check your progress

Competent progress

- I can identify the audience and the purpose of an argument task.
- I can use an appropriate tone to express my viewpoint.

Superior progress

- I can match the ideas for my argument to the audience and purpose.
- I can adapt and modify tone and style to persuade the reader.

4.3 Explaining, expanding and illustrating an argument

Learn how to:

- *explain and illustrate an argument*
- *expand and develop a particular point of view using different techniques.*

Illustrating an argument with anecdotes and statistics

When arguing a point of view, you cannot simply state your opinion and expect your readers to agree with you. You need to provide evidence and examples to support your case.

One effective way of illustrating an argument is to use an **anecdote**. These are often used at the start of articles to engage the reader's attention.

> *As I was walking back with my partner from a popular beach-side restaurant last night, I noticed a bundle of rags by the side of the road. [1] It turned out that in fact this was no bundle of rags. It was a person – a young homeless woman. What struck me most, however, was the fact that she looked like my own sister, indeed was about her age. [2] And that was when it hit me: homeless people are not statistics – they are real people, individuals with brothers and sisters – with lives and backgrounds.*

[1] this is the 'real-life' moment – the anecdote

[2] the anecdote is used to make a connection between the chance encounter and the writer's own life

> **Key term**
>
> **anecdote:** *a short account of something that happened to you, or which you have heard or read about elsewhere*

1 What point of view about homelessness does the writer use the anecdote to illustrate?

- **a)** Homelessness can be found everywhere, even near nice restaurants.
- **b)** It is easy to mistake real people for rags.
- **c)** Homeless people should be respected as individuals.
- **d)** His sister will probably become homeless.

The writer could have used other techniques for supporting his argument. For example:

> *A recent survey of local people found that of those questioned 94% had seen at least one homeless person while on their way to work. However, only 8% of those questioned had ever asked the homeless person their name or stopped to chat.*

2 What different method is used in the extract above to illustrate the argument that homeless people are often invisible and not seen as 'real' people?

You can use statistics (numerical data) from surveys or 'expert' sources (although you can make up the sources and the statistics).

3 Copy these sentences from an argument text about the rise in the number of fast-food outlets and fill in the gaps with some statistics.

a) *In my school, …told me that they had visited a fast-food outlet in the past week. That is an incredible…increase on last year when I carried out the same survey.*

b) *Fast-food now accounts for…of the average teenager's diet, according to…of the…Institute*

You can also set out your argument by defining or spelling out the issue.

> *Obesity is a huge threat to public health. But what does it actually mean? After all, everyone goes up and down in weight during their life, and has moments when they weigh slightly more than they should. Well, one definition relates to an abnormal accumulation of fat of more than 20% of an individual's recommended body weight (for their height, build, etc.).*

This sort of technical explanation is useful because it does not assume that the reader knows a lot about the topic. Even a topic such as homelessness can be defined:

> *Homelessness is a real problem. Not having a permanent roof over your head, nor a home address to give to banks or employers are obvious signs, but there are others.*

4 How does the explanation in the extract above make it clear that homelessness does not just mean having to sleep outside?

5 Write your own definition of 'healthy eating' to complete the opening paragraph of a point-of-view speech below.

> *I am sure you all agree that healthy eating is a 'good thing', but what exactly is it? Well, my definition is eating food that…*

Using comparison

You can also use comparison to make an impact when illustrating an argument. For example:

> *Imagine, if you can, a major city like New York in the future, under water.*
> *Instead of gleaming skyscrapers and buzzing night-life, there is a ghost town –*
> *shacks and shelters on the odd bit of dry land, but everything else smothered*
> *by the ocean and rivers.*

6 What two contrasting pictures are painted in this extract? What do you the think the article might have been about?

Writing about cause and effect

A key way of illustrating your argument is to demonstrate causes and effects. The *cause* is what led to the problem; the *effect* is what the problem itself leads to.

7 Read this article about disappearing coral reefs. What cause(s) are given, and what is the effect?

> *Sponges are increasing at a rapid pace, killing off other forms of life on coral*
> *reefs. This is because over-fishing has destroyed their natural predators,*
> *such as angel fish. As a result sponges are able to spread and smother their*
> *competition.*

8 Complete these statements by adding a cause or an effect, either positive or negative. (You can make them up!)

    a) *People's busy lives have meant that when it comes to food they are much more likely to…*

    b) *The popularity of basketball is hardly surprising when you consider…*

    c) *The West Indies cricket team's success in the 2016 World 2020 has led to…*

Revision tip

When you read newspaper or magazine articles that argue a particular point of view, try to spot the use of anecdotes, definitions, comparisons or comment on causes and effects.

Apply the skills

Read this exam-style task:

> *Write an article for the school newspaper/website in which you give your views on whether teenagers should have 'mobile phone-free' weekends, when their parents take their phones away from them.*

9 Firstly, note arguments for and against the idea of 'mobile phone-free' weekends. Then, decide your own view on the idea.

10 Write three paragraphs of your article, deciding the order in which they should be arranged.

- In one paragraph use an anecdote that has something to do with using a mobile phone, such as an incident when you lost it and how you felt (or similar).
- In another paragraph, try to describe two contrasting situations of a weekend with a phone and a weekend without one.
- In a third paragraph, try to explain the causes and/or effects of having or not having access to a phone.

Remember

- Use your anecdote to engage the reader's interest at the start, but make sure it is relevant to your viewpoint.
- Keep your main point of view in mind throughout – each technique should add to your argument.
- If possible, weave in some 'factual' information, even if your statistics are made up.

Check your progress

Competent progress

- I can use an anecdote to support my point of view.
- I can sustain my point of view clearly throughout several paragraphs.

Superior progress

- I can use anecdotes and a range of other methods to expand or illustrate my argument.
- I can develop my point of view in a logical way across several paragraphs.

4.4 Structuring an argument

Learn how to:

- *sequence your ideas logically*
- *write an effective conclusion.*

Organising points and counter-points

The best speeches or articles express points of view clearly and logically, so that the reader can follow the argument. However, they should also give a sense that there is a reason why the points have been arranged in this particular way.

Even if your purpose is to persuade the reader of a certain point of view, remember that there are two sides to every argument. You need to include both sides, but also make sure your point of view remains clear. The grid below shows three ways of doing this, based on an essay of eight paragraphs.

Half and half	Ping pong	All together
Intro paragraph: introduce the issue.	Intro paragraph: introduce the issue.	Intro paragraph: introduce the issue.
Paragraphs 2–4 (first half of essay): put forward the arguments *against* your view.	Paragraph 2: first set of points *against* your view	Paragraph 2: first points both *for* and *against* your view.
Paragraphs 5–7 (second half of essay): put your arguments *for* your view.	Paragraph 3: first points *for* your view.	Paragraph 3: second set of points both *for* and *against* your view.
Concluding paragraph: sum up and restate your point of view.	Paragraph 4: second points *against*.	Paragraph 4: third set of points both *for* and *against* your view.
	Paragraph 5: second points *for*.	(Longer paragraphs perhaps as more will be included in each paragraph.)
	Paragraph 6: third points *against*.	Concluding paragraph: sum up and restate your point of view.
	Paragraph 7: third points *for*.	
	Concluding paragraph: sum up and restate your point of view.	

Read this paragraph from a speech about having 'mobile phone-free' weekends.

It is true that there is something attractive about being able to shut yourself away from everyone: no more irritating texts when you're trying to get to sleep, or feeling you have to check what a fantastic time everyone is having on the beach without you. However, what would happen if you missed that all-important call about a job interview, or that smiley emoji from the girl you really like? That would be a disaster. Far better to have your phone on.

1. What point of view is being argued? Are both sides of the argument covered?

2. Which one of the three structures above is this student using?

General to specific

As you have seen, there are several ways to organise your argument, but moving from the general to the specific with your points can help. Read this opening paragraph.

> *Deciding which Caribbean figure deserves a new statue is a complex and emotional subject. [1] For example [2], should the person reflect our history or be someone who is making an impact today [3] – someone like civil rights activist Stokely Carmichael, or pop phenomenon Rihanna [4]?*

[1] topic sentence tells reader what is the general subject and why it is difficult

[2] tells reader the next sentence is going to give more detailed information

[3] a reason for the decision being complicated

[4] even more detail/alternatives – actual possible names

You can use this idea of moving from general to specific information in different types of writing (including describing people or places in stories). It is useful in writing an argumentative text because it allows you to explain the general situation and then provide concrete examples of the points you want to make.

3. Choose one of the following options to complete this paragraph. Remember, the second sentence must be more precise and specific than the first.

> *Shortening the school holidays would cause a lot of anger and resentment.*
> *[topic sentence]*

    a) For others it would create opportunities and new possibilities.

    b) For a start, most parents and children would be alarmed at having less time for relaxation.

    c) Doing this would create bitterness and problems too.

Linking your points

Another key to structuring your argument effectively is to use suitable connecting words and phrases when moving from one idea to the next. Connectives that help contrast or develop ideas are particularly useful in argument texts. The grid below outlines some useful connectives.

For contrast	For development
However	*Furthermore*
On the other hand	*Moreover*
Alternatively	*Also*
Conversely	*In addition*
Whereas	*What is more*
Although	*Similarly*
Yet	*In the same way*
But	*Thus*

4 Copy the extract below and fill in the gaps by selecting appropriate connectives from the grid.

I personally have no objection to having an iconic modern celebrity as a statue in the main square, …I think a statue has to be one that everyone accepts, young or old. …I would select a figure from Caribbean history…it should be someone who has had a real impact on the way we are viewed by the world.

Apply the skills

Read this exam-style task.

You are the member of a local youth group who has been asked to represent the group's views to a regional corporation on a proposal to open a new facility for young people in your area. One proposal is to build a new skateboarding park.

Write the speech you would give to the corporation, outlining your views on the proposal.

5. Write the key words from the task, then decide what your viewpoint will be.

6. Now, jot four or five ideas for and against the proposal.

7. Decide how you will organise these ideas, using one of the three structures set out at the beginning of this topic, or a mixture of them if you think that will work.

8. Now, write your points out in the structure you have selected. For example:
   - *Paragraph 1: introduction*
   - *Paragraph 2: first point for the skate park – it will give young people a focus…*
   - *Paragraph 3:*

9. Finally, write one paragraph from the essay, showing your use of logical sentences and connectives.

Check your progress

Competent progress

- I can put ideas for an argument into a clear structure.
- I can make my ideas clear through my use of connectives and the sequence of my sentences.

Superior progress

- I can select from a range of structures for my argument.
- I can adapt and modify my argument through using a range of connectives and sentences.

4.5 Test yourself

Learn how to:

- *read and respond to a practice argument writing exam question*
- *evaluate your own work and the responses of others.*

Your task

A number of proposals are being discussed by your local government for 'modernizing' education. One proposal is to remove all printed books from classrooms and libraries in schools in your area and move to a completely digital environment.

Write an article for your local newspaper in which you give your views on this proposal.

Approaching the task

1. Remind yourself of the skills you will need to demonstrate in your writing. These will include:

   - deciding what your viewpoint is
   - identifying the audience, form and purpose of your writing from the wording of the task, and how this will affect style and approach
   - planning points for and against the idea
   - deciding what persuasive techniques you might use (anecdotes, statistics, etc.)
   - deciding how you will structure your text.

2. Begin by spending five minutes generating ideas, using a grid with points for and against. Alternatively, use a spider diagram or list to quickly jot down your main ideas in the order you might use them. If you are short of time, this could help you bypass stage 3 below.

3. Now decide how you will structure your paragraphs.

4. Finally, draft your article.

Reflecting on your progress

Read the following plan and extract from a response to the practice task by one student, then look at the comments below.

> **Plan 1**
>
> *Points for (digital only):*
> - *Books get tatty.*
> - *Not enough of them (have to share sometimes).*
> - *Books can be free online.*
>
> *Points against:*
> - *Libraries are pleasant spaces.*
> - *Feel like a grown-up reading books.*
> - *Nice to hold/touch.*
> - *Too much screen time already.*

Response 1

> *I remember the first time I went into our school library – it was really special. All those books which seemed to welcome me.* [1] *They made me feel like I was a grown-up entering big school and that I would learn a lot.*
>
> *But I can see that there are lots of downsides to printed books.* [2] *Over time they become very tatty and they cost a lot to replace. Often we have to share them in class, which is really annoying as I like to have a book all to myself.* [3] *It would be great to have lovely, clean books all the time.*
>
> *On the other hand* [4]*, books are such a joy to hold. It is lovely to turn the pages and see the characters come alive. It would be terrible if children could not do this any more. Besides they get enough of electronic screens as it is. It is not a good idea to have even more. When I interviewed some of my classmates, some of them said they couldn't care less if books were ditched from school, but quite a few were really sad when I told them that it might happen.* [5]
>
> *Digital classrooms might be a good idea. Everyone has to use technology and this means we would all get better at it. Also lots of books are available free on the internet so it would save money, like you can read the classics such as Dickens, if you want and not have to buy a great big paper copy.* [6]

[1] begins with a vivid anecdote to engage the reader

[2] new paragraph introduces other side of argument

[3] develops argument but use of 'we' not appropriate for article in local paper; also mixes first person with third person ('they')

[4] contrasting connective introduces new point

[5] survey to support/expand argument but better with statistics

[6] well-developed new point

Comment on Response 1

The plan (not assessed) clearly sets out points for and against, but might have benefited from deciding on the paragraph structure. This is a *competent* response. It has a reasonably logical structure, moving between points for and against. However, the tone is a bit informal in places and the style does not take account of this being a newspaper article for local people, not other school students. The anecdote is a good way to start, but the argument would be helped by some statistics and more persuasive language.

5 Using the comments above and the list of progress points at the end of this chapter, rewrite this response to improve it.

Now read another student's response to the same practice task, then look at the comments that follow.

Plan 2	
Para 1:	*against: surveys show school children like printed books; for: anti-progress?*
Para 2:	*against: anecdote of being read to; liking the feel of books*
Para 3:	*for: need for instant info; plus desire to be advanced in technology?*
Para 4:	*against: counter-argument of clutter but comfort of being surrounded by real books*
Para 5:	*for: use of visualizers can give impression of looking at real books; against: it is still an impression*
Conclusion:	*keep books but increase access to texts through online subscriptions or borrowing*

Response 2

A recent survey of school children between the ages of 8 and 14 revealed that over 80% liked buying, borrowing or being given real printed books – quite a blow for local government, which is currently proposing a move to an all-digital classroom. [1] But should students stand in the way of progress?

My earliest memory is sitting on my grandmother's knee as she read to me from a picture book. I used to love turning the crumpled pages with my little hand and pointing at the bright pictures. [2] So [3], I cannot imagine a world without printed books, a world in which all we have is a cold screen to swipe.

Yet [3] the truth is people increasingly want to have information and stories at their fingertips, and not have to go to shops or libraries to access texts. [4] Therefore, [3] schools are only reflecting how society is changing. Surely students want their schools to be modern and students at Sunnyville High to be technologically superior? [5]

[1] statistics used to open the argument

[2] vivid, touching anecdote creates emotional effect

[3] connective signposts development of ideas

[4] new paragraph introduces counter-argument

[5] rhetorical question

I'm not so sure. [6] While there are benefits to digital classrooms, such as lack of clutter and access to texts when and where you want them, [7] there is something incredibly comforting [8] about piles of books around you as you learn. It makes you think of all the other learners who have read the same books and been touched or moved by the stories inside. I for one would feel sad to lose that feeling.

[6] short, clear sentence emphasises writer's view

[7] relative clause states counter-argument to be knocked down in rest of sentence

[8] intensifier – 'incredibly' reinforces point of view

Comment on Response 2

The plan is effective in not only setting down some key arguments but also deciding on the way they would be structured. This is also a *superior* response, which demonstrates a measured well-argued case. The tone is appropriate for the form and purpose, and the evidence used (anecdote, statistics, etc.) are well-chosen and reinforce the key point of view. Structurally, the response is sound using a range of connectives and sentences to introduce and answer counter-arguments. The use of a range of sentence styles also helps engage the reader and make an impact, for example the use of the short sentence 'I'm not so sure' makes clear the writer's reflective and considered approach.

Revision tip

Practise using a range of structures for argument essays: for example, ones which deal with paragraphs for and against in turn, but also ones like the above in which for/against points are combined in the same sentence or paragraph.

Check your progress

Competent

- I can understand and 'break down' an argument-style task.
- I can generate ideas to support my point of view.
- I can identify the audience and the purpose of an argument task.
- I can use an appropriate tone to express my viewpoint.
- I can put ideas for an argument into a clear structure.
- I can make my ideas clear through my use of connectives and the sequence of my sentences.

Superior

- I can understand how role, audience and purpose affect my response.
- I can generate arguments and counter-arguments both for and against my point of view.
- I can match the ideas for my argument to the audience and purpose.
- I can adapt and modify tone and style to persuade the reader.
- I can select from a range of structures for my argument.
- I can adapt and modify my argument through using a range of connectives and sentences.

Chapter 5 Practice questions for Paper 2

Introduction

In this section, you will find five practice tasks for Paper 2. Before each task, there is guidance on the question set, including advice on areas to focus on and mark allocations.

Once you have read the instructions for each task carefully, follow the guidance and make sure you stick to the allocated time.

You are advised to take some time to read through and plan your answers.

Paper 2 Section A Guidance

The first question on **Paper 2** is a summary question. You will be given a text to read. Select its key points before writing a summary in a set number of words.

There are **25 marks** available for this question.

- **5 marks** will be for the **five main points** you pick out.
- **20 marks** will be for the **summary** itself.

Of the 20 marks for the summary:

10 will be for **content** and how it is **organised**. Your work will need to:

- include the key points that you selected to begin with
- have the same purpose as the original text, and similar tone/style based on audience
- be clear, concise and sequenced in an orderly way
- have no more than 120 words.

10 marks will be for **language use**. Make sure:

- sentences are complete, clear and match the meaning of the original
- sentences link together fluently
- subjects and verbs agree
- tenses are consistent
- spelling and punctuation are correct.

> ### Remember
>
> For the notes/five points you make:
>
> - You should spend about five minutes reading and *no more than 10 minutes* on the five main points you have picked out, as this part of the exam is worth 5 marks.
> - Write 12–13 words max for each point you pick out.
> - This will leave you 20–25 minutes to write your summary.
> - Your notes can include some words from the original text.
>
> For the summary:
>
> - Use your own words where possible.
> - Think about using your five points to guide the paragraphs you write (although you do not have to).

Summary task

(Suggested time: 40 minutes)

You MUST answer this question.

You may make notes but these will not be marked.

1 Read the following article on sharks in the Caribbean carefully and list FIVE MAIN points discussed, then write a summary of the article in NOT MORE THAN 120 words. If this limit is exceeded, only the first 120 words of your answer will be read and assessed.

As far as possible, use your own words. Your summary must be in continuous prose. You may use your answer booklet to jot down a plan.

In your answer, you will be assessed on how well you:

a) identified the main ideas and opinions in the extract

b) organised and expressed these ideas and opinions in your own words

c) used appropriate grammar, sentence structure, vocabulary, spelling and punctuation.

The Truth About Caribbean Sharks

It's hard not to be scared of sharks – those sharp teeth, the unblinking black eyes, their speed and stealth… But a shark attack isn't something to fear in the Caribbean according to George Burgess, director of the International Shark Attack File (ISAF) at the University of Florida. In fact, you're much more likely to be bitten by a shark in the waters off North America or South Africa. The Caribbean records an average of only one shark bite a year; compare this with the 20–30 shark attacks that take place annually in Florida alone. Burgess explains why this is: 'A combination of cold and warm waters brings a large variety of sharks to South Africa, while a tremendous amount of people and year-round good swimming weather in Florida increase the chances of attacks in North America.'

Sharks have also acquired an unfair reputation when it comes to attacking humans. Burgess explains that close to the shore in places such as California or the Eastern Seaboard, breaking waves create poor visibility for the sharks. They mistake people swimming off the beaches for bait fish. In the Caribbean, where there is less surf along the shore, visibility is better and sharks are more likely to steer clear of humans.

You may still prefer not to wade into Caribbean waters, but there are ways to reduce the risk of a shark attack. To begin with, don't venture out alone. Sharks will usually avoid groups of people. Leave your jewellery at home and don't wear a swimsuit that shimmers and shines – a shark might mistake these glints in the water for the scales of a fish. Remember that sharks can smell blood from many miles away, so don't go spearing fish in the water! It also helps to recognise the signs that a shark is uneasy. Rubbing its belly on the ocean floor, swimming erratically and lowering its pectoral fins are all indicators that a shark may be readying for an attack. If you see this, get out of the water as quickly and as calmly as possible.

'The International Shark Attack File isn't overly concerned about shark attacks in the Caribbean,' says Burgess. 'On a per capita basis, [the Caribbean] isn't where you'd expect to find attacks.'

Total 25 marks

Paper 2 Section B Guidance

The second question on Paper 2 requires you to write an informative text. You will be given a situation and asked to write a particular type of informative text.

There are **30 marks** available for this question.

- **10 marks** will be for the **content of your text and your understanding of the situation**.
- **20 marks** will be for **how you express yourself** in the text.

For the full **10 marks** for **understanding/content**, you will need to:

- use the proper conventions of the given text type (for example, a proper opening for a business letter)
- include relevant information from the given situation in a clear way
- provide the specific information required by the task and make sure it is appropriate.

10 marks will be for **organisation**. Make sure your information is:

- sequenced properly
- coherent – makes sense
- concise and not 'over-wordy'
- appropriate for the audience/reader.

10 marks will be for **language usage**. Make sure:

- sentences are complete, clear and match the purpose of the task
- sentences link together fluently
- subjects and verbs agree
- tenses are consistent
- spelling and punctuation are correct.

Remember

- Spend at least five minutes reading the task and highlighting the core requirements: the task/purpose, audience, form, etc.
- Spend at least five minutes planning your response.
- Spend the remaining time writing your text, and then allow five minutes to check your work at the end.

For your plan:

- Set out the number of points (and paragraphs if possible) that you will make in the sequence you think works best.
- Put the most important information first; supporting information next; and further information/future situation/outcome last.

Informative writing task

(Suggested time: 35 minutes)

2 **Study the situation presented below and then answer the question that follows.**

You went for a day trip to a local beauty spot, helping out a family friend with small children. When you arrived, you realised that it was too dangerous for the children, even though the local tourist office had said it was completely safe and suitable. You returned home without visiting the spot.

Write a letter to the local tourist office or to the local newspaper expressing your concerns about the beauty spot and the original information you received.

Your answer will be assessed on how well you:

- **formatted your letter**
- **selected relevant and complete information**
- **organised and expressed the information in your letter**
- **used appropriate grammar, sentence structure, vocabulary, spelling and punctuation.**

Your letter MUST be in continuous prose.

Make sure to include all the details that would help in highlighting the matter. Your letter should include:

- **Details of the problems/dangers, for example:**

  – **date and time of trip**
  – **where you went**
  – **what you were told originally**
  – **specific dangers or problems you encountered.**

Total 30 marks

Paper 2 Section C Guidance

Questions 3 and 4 on Paper 2 give you the choice of writing a story based on a photograph/picture or one based on a sentence or other written text.

There are **25 marks** available for this question. There are no separate marks for your ideas, organisation or how you express yourself, but it is a good idea to give equal weight to all three.

Here are the areas you should look to address:

Content: story-line, plot and character

Make sure you:

- develop and organise your ideas/events fully and link them appropriately
- create motives for actions, then resolve actions and conflict satisfactorily
- establish a clear setting
- create believable, consistent and developed characters
- create dialogue that is meaningful (it advances the plot or tells us more about the characters).

Language

Make sure you:

- use appropriate vocabulary to create characters, atmosphere and setting
- use language in an economic yet lively way to create the story features above.

Make sure:

- sentences are complete, clear and have a clear purpose (for example, to create tension)
- sentences link together fluently
- subjects and verbs agree
- tenses are consistent
- spelling and punctuation are correct
- paragraphing is clear and useful.

Remember

- Spend 5–10 minutes on your ideas and plan (you can make your plan as detailed or simple as you like but leave yourself time for writing and checking).
- Use any note-making technique which works for you, e.g. numbered list, flow diagram, spider diagram.
- Include ideas in your notes and plan about: the plot structure (the five key points); details about main character, choices/conflicts he/she faces; consequences of choices; any 'hook' to start the story or twists to end or change it.
- Spend around 30 minutes writing your story.
- Spend five minutes proofreading it at the end.

Narrative writing task

(Suggested time: 45 minutes)

You MUST answer ONE question from this section.

Your answer should be approximately 400 to 450 words in length.

You MUST write in Standard English. However, dialect may be used in conversation. You are expected to write within the word limit. You may make notes but these will not be marked.

In your answer, you will be assessed on how well you:

a) **used the stimulus provided**

b) **developed and organised the content of your writing**

c) **used language appropriate to your audience, purpose and content**

d) **used appropriate grammar, sentence structure, paragraphs, vocabulary, spelling and punctuation.**

EITHER

SHORT STORY

3   Write a story based on the picture below.

(25 marks)

OR

4   Write a story that includes these words: 'He opened the letter and began to read. As he did so, his eyes filled with tears.'

(25 marks)

Paper 2 Section D Guidance

Question 5 on Paper 2 requires you to write a text that expresses a particular point of view about a situation or issue. You will need to argue your point of view persuasively.

There are **25 marks** available for this question. There are no separate marks for your ideas, organisation or how you express yourself, but it is a good idea to give equal weight to all three.

Here are the areas you should look to address.

Content: argument and comment

Make sure you:

- include relevant information to the topic
- show awareness of your audience through register and tone
- make your purpose clear and link it to the audience's needs
- support your argument through at least one of the following: illustration, explanation, anecdote or expansion
- use a range of strategies such as use of persuasive language techniques, showing cause and effect, comparing and anticipating opposing arguments
- are consistent in your argument.

Organisation: logical development and reasoning

You must:

- present your ideas in a logical sequence, whether in individual sentences, across or between paragraphs
- sustain your argument over the course of the text
- draw logical, natural conclusions from the points you make.

Language

Make sure:

- sentences are complete, clear and contribute to the persuasive effect
- sentences link together fluently
- subjects and verbs agree
- tenses are consistent
- spelling and punctuation are correct
- paragraphing is clear and useful.

> ### Remember
>
> - Spend five minutes reading the task and highlighting: the task/purpose; the audience; the voice/role; the form you must write in.
> - Spend at least five minutes, possibly as much as 10, noting down your core points for or against the proposal.
> - Jot down how you will present these points, or ideally decide the number and order of paragraphs and the way in which the points will be presented (e.g. paragraph 1: 'for' point; paragraph 2: 'against' point).
> - Spend around 30 minutes writing the text.
> - Spend five minutes at the end proofreading and checking what you have written.

Argumentative writing task

(Suggested time: 45 minutes)

You MUST answer this question.

Your answer should be approximately 250 to 300 words in length.

You MUST write in Standard English. You are expected to write within the word limit. You may make any notes you want to make. This will not be marked.

In your answer you will be assessed on the:

    a) clarity, organisation and development of your argument

    b) correctness of grammar, sentences, paragraphs, vocabulary, spelling and punctuation.

5   You are a student representative for your local area. One school has introduced CCTV throughout the school for security reasons, and local principals are recommending that all schools should have CCTV.

     Write an article for your local newspaper giving your views on the proposal.

(25 marks)

Structure and mechanics: the basics

Why are these important?

In the Paper 2 exam, your use of correct grammar, punctuation and spelling can be worth about 30% of your marks. However good your ideas, you need to ensure you do not make common mistakes.

Sentences

A sentence is usually a *complete idea* or *thought* and contains at the very least a *subject* and a *verb*.

All sentences begin with a word that has an initial capital letter: *His trainers had holes in them.*

They end with a full stop, question mark or exclamation mark.

Subject-verb agreement

The subject and verb must agree. For example:

- *Dwayne goes to the match* = correct
- *Dwayne go to the match* = incorrect ('Dwayne' is the third person form 'he/goes', 'go' can only be used with 'you', 'we' or 'they'.)

However, if the sentence included 'Dwayne and Shelima', 'go to the match' would be correct as this creates a plural form which requires 'go' not the singular 'goes'.

Also watch for number and gender agreement with pronouns and determiners. For example:

> *Dwayne lost his ticket. Shelima blamed herself as she made him hurry. There were many other problems on the way to the stadium too.*

> **Revision tip**
>
> The verbs 'to have' and 'to be' are *auxiliary* verbs – they help to create other tenses. Ensure you use them correctly (for example: 'I was walking', not 'I were walking'; 'they have left' not 'they has left').

Tenses

Tense is the form the verb takes to signal state or the time of the action. For example:

Past tense forms	Present tense forms	Future tense forms
Dwayne watched the match.	*Dwayne watches the match.*	*Dwayne will watch the match.*
Dwayne had watched the match.	*Dwayne is watching the match.*	*Dwayne is going to watch the match.*
Dwayne was watching the match.		*Dwayne may/might/could/ should watch the match.*

There can be subtle differences in meaning or tone between verb tenses. For example, 'will watch the match' suggests certainty (it will happen) whereas 'is going to' suggests intention (Dwayne's desire to watch the match). It is also vital that subject and verb agree. Equally important is ensuring that you do not switch between tenses unless you intend to introduce a new time frame.

For example:

> *Dwayne and Shelima <u>had left</u> at five in the morning. <u>It took</u> them all day to get to the ground.*
>
> NOT: *Dwayne and Shelima had left at five in the morning. <u>It takes</u> them all day to get to the ground.*

1 Correct the subject-verb agreement and tenses in the following paragraph.

> *Dwayne goes to the ticket office but the people there wouldn't let he through without a ticket. He went back to Shelima, who is waiting by the car park and told her the news. She weren't happy and will storm off.*

Punctuation

The main punctuation uses are covered in Topic 2.6 in the Paper 1 section of this book, but here are some key things to remember.

The comma splice: Proofread your work for the comma splice. This is a common mistake where two independent clauses or sentences are joined using a comma or when one sentence 'runs on' into the other. For example: 'We went surfing, it was great.' This should be two separate sentences ('We went surfing. It was great.') or a single sentence with the comma replaced by a conjunction ('We went surfing <u>and</u> it was great.').

Apostrophes: Apostrophes are used for two reasons:

- For *contractions*: when words are shortened and letters omitted. For example, 'It's' = 'It is'; 'They're = they are', etc.
- To show *possession* of something: 'the mother's hopes', 'the boy's bike', 'the twin girls' bikes'.

> **Revision tip**
>
> Remember, if there is just one 'owner' then the apostrophe goes *before* the 's'. If there are two or more 'owners' then the apostrophe comes after the 's' (as in 'the twin girls' bikes').

Colons: Colons are used to introduce a list. For example:

> *Saj checked her bag: purse, hair straighteners, phone, keys – but she couldn't find her watch.*

Or they can be used to introduce a definition, elaboration or explanation:

> *We stared up at it: Pico Duarte, the highest mountain in the Caribbean.*

Semicolons: Can be used to separate items in a list if they are phrases rather than single words:

> *...the burning sands; the dominant sun; the constant flow of tourists.*

Or they can be used instead of a conjunction to separate two main clauses (and to avoid the comma splice):

> *It was the wettest summer on record; people were leaving the city in droves.*

2　Add the correct punctuation to improve the sense of the following paragraph.

> *Emerging from his tent he quickly packed up the camp tent bag damp items of clothing camping stove it all fitted neatly into his rucksack. His passport and partners photograph went into his pocket.*

Paragraphs: Help shape ideas, direct your reader and create impact. In handwritten text and most printed texts they are indented (pushed in) from the left-hand side of the page/margin. For example:

> *The sun rose quickly over the huts. Men came out, wiping their brows in the early morning heat and began to haul the boats down to the shoreline. Then, they were on their way. The oars dipping in the water made hardly a ripple.*

Generally, a shorter paragraph has a focus on one thing, person or set of ideas. However, longer paragraphs may contain a much wider variety of elements. When you change from one paragraph to a new one, there must be a reason. This can be to express a change in *time* or *place*:

> *By the time I was fourteen, and living with my grandparents in Santa Cruz, I was pretty wild. They couldn't control me, and I couldn't control myself.*

To introduce a *new character* or *speaker* in a story or other account.

> *Then I met Danni. She changed my life in so many ways. I remember the time she first spoke to me as if it was yesterday.*
>
> *'Hey! You! What are you doing riding your bike across my father's lawn?*

Short, one or two sentence paragraphs can be used for *dramatic effect*:

> *Danni was fifteen and in a wheelchair.*

In informative or persuasive texts, paragraphs can introduce the other side of an argument:

> *Those who argue that we're harming the planet point to rising water levels. Glaciers are shrinking, too, and average temperatures are up all over the world.*
>
> *However, there are those – sometimes called 'climate deniers' – who insist the planet will heal itself. They say it is useless making short-term judgements.*

EITHER

Write two further paragraphs from the 'Danni' story in which you use them in one of the ways listed above (for change of time, place, person, speech, dramatic effect, etc.).

OR

Write two paragraphs expressing different viewpoints about the good/bad effects of tourism.

School-Based Assessment

This part of the coursebook introduces you to the core skills that you will need to demonstrate in your **School-Based Assessment** (SBA). It also guides you through the tasks you need to perform in order to complete this assessment.

To support and develop your understanding of the skills needed, you should explore a range of discussions of topics that interest or concern you. You might get ideas for these in libraries, through news websites, podcasts or videos, or simply in the conversations you hear around you.

Topic 1.1 introduces you to the core requirements of the SBA, while 1.2 and 1.3 develop skills to help you choose a topic and plan your investigation. You will also learn how to work efficiently as an individual and as part of a team. Units 1.4 and 1.5 help you in identifying and analysing different types of source material, such as opinion pieces or graphs and tables. In 1.6 and 1.7 you will learn how to write reflective pieces based on these sources, including the Group Report for the work your team produces. Topic 1.8 guides you through planning, developing and delivering your spoken presentation. Finally, Topic 1.9 tackles your reflective piece, in which you will examine the lessons you have learned from the SBA, including its contribution to your self-development.

You will encounter challenging and engaging texts on topics including the effects of tourism on the Caribbean environment and the impact of social media, such as cyberbullying, on teenagers. At the same time, this SBA chapter is meant to encourage you to pursue your own interests and to understand how to research them effectively.

Each unit ends with a *Check your progress* feature, so you can assess your progress with the key skills needed for each part of the SBA project. The units are as follows:

1.1 Understanding the School-Based Assessment

Learn how to:

- *secure your understanding of the SBA*
- *begin to explore topics of interest.*

What are the key elements of the School-Based Assessment?

The School-Based Assessment (SBA) consists of a series of tasks and outcomes that will demonstrate your competency in a range of areas. In particular, you will develop research skills, the ability to collect, interpret, analyse and evaluate data, and skills of teamwork and collaboration. You will also develop your ability to present both verbally and in writing.

You will:

- select a theme or topic of interest within a group
- choose some interesting **stimuli** to analyse, research and respond to
- write three pieces of reflection on these stimuli, including what you have learned or gained from the process
- write a report on your team's research with the rest of your group
- present ideas on your specific area of interest within the topic to an audience
- write a creative response (for example, a poem, song, story) to the topic or stimuli.

1 Which of these tasks/outcomes are you most and least confident in completing? Why?

> **Key term**
>
> **stimuli:** materials (e.g. photos, poems, articles) that generate a response in the reader/listener

Pursuing your interests

Think of the SBA as a chance to do something different from what you might usually do in school. You can explore topics you find interesting, and perhaps find interest in things that don't at first seem appealing.

2 Write a brief summary of yourself, your skills and your interests. Use a grid like this one to note down your thoughts.

What sort of person am I? (Shy? Chatty? Confident?)	What am I good at?	What sorts of things do I like or have an interest in?

3 Share your summary with a good friend or your group. Do they agree with you on these points? Sometimes we can be quite hard on ourselves, and it can be useful to hear others' perspectives. Have your friend's or group's views changed your perspective of yourself? Be positive!

How can you manage the challenge of the SBA successfully?

In addition to being assessed for English proficiency, you will also need project management skills. Here is some general advice to bear in mind:

- Keep a clear record or log of what you do and the questions you need to resolve (there is more on this in Topic 1.3).

- Manage your time efficiently: set yourself goals and deadlines, and keep a record of how well you are doing. That way, you can see when you are slipping behind or if you need support in any areas.

- Communicate with others effectively: make sure you communicate with your team, whether that is through a WhatsApp group, texts, regular meet-ups or emails. You will also need to ensure your teacher has a clear picture of how you are getting on.

- Develop an inquiring and curious mind: the more attentive you are to what is going on politically, socially and culturally, the more you will have to contribute to the process. So, read the news – local, national and global – and follow up on your interests.

Approach texts and other sources (in whatever form) with a **critical** mind: don't take things at face value but question their authenticity or reliability. This means asking questions about:

- the writer's purpose
- the information presented (facts, opinions)
- the interpretations/inferences made
- the possible implications
- underlying assumptions
- the writer's point of view
- any bias the writer shows, and whether this is reasonable or excessive.

> *Key term*
>
> *critical: able to interpret, analyse, evaluate and reflect upon an issue*

Apply the skills

What else do you need to find out about the SBA? Make a list of any questions you have and check with your teacher to make sure you are absolutely clear about what you have to do.

Check your progress

Competent progress

- I understand the basic requirements of the SBA, and the skills I need to demonstrate.

Superior progress

- I fully understand all the requirements of the SBA, which skills I already have and which I need to work on.

1.2 Selecting a theme and working as a team

Learn how to:

- *select a topic or theme that interests you*
- *work as part of a team.*

What is a 'topic or theme of interest'?

In the last unit, you began to reflect on the skills and qualities you already have as a person and student. You also began to think about your own hobbies and interests. These personal interests may provide topics that are suitable for SBA selection, but if you are finding it hard to choose, you can seek guidance from your teacher or instructor, who may select some broad themes to consider.

You will need to identify specific related sub-themes or sub-topics of your own. For example, here is a set of detailed areas that could spring from the general topic of 'The impact of social media on teens':

online bullying

how social media damages body-image

social media as a learning tool for teens

how social media helps teens keep connected

how mobile phones help gangs operate

1.   Would all these areas be suitable and fit with the main theme of 'the impact of social media on teens'? Think about:

   - which are strictly relevant and which might lead you 'off track'
   - whether any the ideas could be improved to be more precise or focused (for example, think about gender and age)?

2.   What other areas or ideas could come under this topic? For example, you could consider ideas about money, gambling, shopping, sport, and so on. Try to add at least two further ideas to the list.

As part of the SBA, you will need to say why you chose the topic or theme, so make sure you have a wide range of ideas to choose from.

Working effectively as part of a group

Once you know your overall theme (for the group), you will begin to work with your team members to plan the investigation and carry out your research. Before you do that, however, you need to be clear about your role within the group and what is expected of you. For example, your role might be one of the following:

- Group leader/chair of meetings: someone who will lead the group by making decisions when ideas have been fully discussed and/or (alongside the timekeeper) ensuring that the group stays on track.
- Scribe or recorder: someone who keeps a clear record of what is discussed or decided.
- Timekeeper/manager: someone who makes sure team members remain on track and keep to deadlines, both within meetings and outside of them.
- The writer of the final group report: someone who will **synthesise** everything that has been discussed and put it into words for the report (this might be the same person as the scribe, depending on the size of your group).

> **Key term**
>
> **synthesise:** *bring together in one place various bits of information*

3 Look at the roles above. Discuss with a partner what particular skills each one requires, and make a brief list (rather like a job advertisement). For example:

> **Group leader**
> *Confident*
> *Respected…*

What more general skills do all group members need?

Whether you are leading the group or taking more of a secondary role, it is important that you play an active part. Here are some positive qualities you will need.

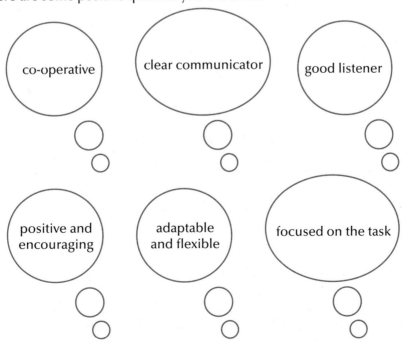

4 Discuss with your group what you think each of these qualities means in the context of good teamwork. What others could you add?

Generating sub-themes

Now that you have a good idea of what skills you will need when you are working with a group, you can think about how this might work in practice.

A group has decided to work with the theme 'Damage to the environment in the Caribbean'. What ideas could you get from this?

One student has used a spider diagram to begin to explore different ideas.

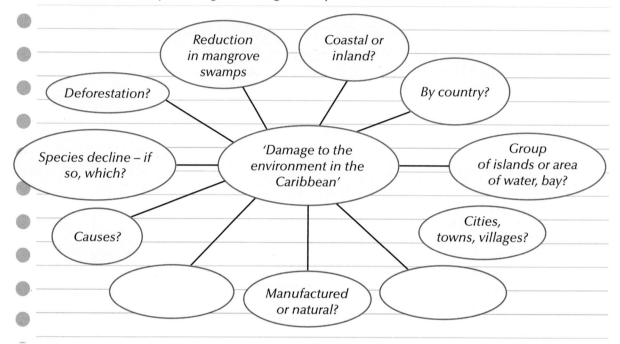

5 Copy and complete the spider diagram, adding your own ideas. Think also about how you could add information to be even more specific. For example:

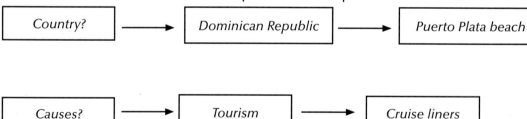

Once you have generated some ideas of your own, possibly deciding on a specific area you would be interested in, you need to share those ideas with the group and, if necessary, modify them.

Assigning roles and planning schedules

Once your group has been established, it is important to assign the roles discussed above. Keep a record of who is doing what, and make sure you fulfil the role required of you.

Another important step is to set up proper communication channels and a time schedule. Consider these questions:

• What will be your communication channel?

• When and where will you meet? Will you have a regular/fixed meeting in the same time or place? How many meetings? For how long?

1.2 Selecting a theme and working as a team

Developing ideas further as a group

Read the following extract from one group discussion.

A: So, we're looking at environmental damage in the Caribbean? What have you got, D?

D: Well, I'd like to look at over-development – y'know like the way there's loads of building…

C: Great. But where? You mean here – Tobago?

D: It's a problem all over the island. There's even a Critical Eco-system Partnership Fund – like, to protect against it across the whole Caribbean.

A: Wow, that sounds great – but it might help to narrow your focus to specific areas, yeah?

D: Um, OK, I'll think about that.

C: Er – I've got an idea…

A: Go on.

C: Have you read about the plans for a massive five-star hotel here? You could find out about that.

D: OK, cool.

B: So, I've noted down your general area of interest. What are you going to do next? And by when?

6 Think about how the group worked.
   a) How well did the group help D with his ideas?
   b) Who seemed to be listening well and suggesting ideas?
   c) Were you able to recognise who was leading the discussion, and who the note-taker was?

Apply the skills

Think carefully about the general theme which your group has decided to explore and research. Before you meet as a group, take the following steps:

- Remind yourself of your own skills as a speaker/listener and note down at least one target for what you will need to do to improve your performance in a group.

- Use a spider diagram like the one in this unit to identify particular areas of interest that you could explore within the given theme. Then make some brief notes about how you could refine this further.

Check your progress

Competent

- I understand which skills are useful in group situations.
- I can work out some of my own ideas from a given theme.

Superior

- I can evaluate my own group skills and put them into practice effectively.
- I can generate a range of appropriate ideas from a given theme.

1.3 Planning your Investigation

Learn how to:

- *give reasons for the topic you have chosen and its benefits to you*
- *plan your research and the sorts of materials you might use.*

Introducing the Plan of Investigation

As part of the School-Based Assessment, you will need to write a 'Plan of Investigation'. This addresses the following three key areas:

- what your topic is and why you chose it
- what its benefits are to you as a student
- how you will go about researching it.

It is not a long document – it should ideally be no more than 100 words. However, this is part of the larger process in which you refine and develop ideas both on your own and with your group. In either case, you need to start by judging the potential of your selected topic of interest.

1 What topic or area of interest do you have in mind?

    a) Write it down in a succinct form (for example, 'damage to our coastline by tourist development').

    b) Now, try to come up with at least two reasons why this topic interests you. You could think about:

        • how it connects to you personally ('I live near the coast and have seen how…')

        • what it makes you want to find out ('I'd like to know what the long-term effects of…').

> **Remember**
>
> Consider whether your ideas are too close to, or blurring into, another group member's work. Discuss your findings with your group to ensure that each person's work remains distinct but related to the overall theme that your group has selected.

Finding appropriate materials for your analysis and research

The syllabus mentions the following material for your research and it is worth bearing in mind the full range of stimuli. However, it is important to consider which are the best ones to use for your research:

- Print: books (fiction and non-fiction), manuals, articles, speeches, leaflets, blogs.
- Visual: photographs, paintings, pictures, cartoons.
- Moving images: video clips, music, features and audio clips.
- People's views/data: from friends, family with expert knowledge or memories, eye-witness reports.

2 Where are you going to find some or all of these materials? Here is a list of potential sources or locations. Copy this out and next to each one, jot down which form (or forms) from the list above would be found here. Many of these are likely to be found on the internet.

Sources		
newspaper (e.g. article)	**general interest magazine**	**specialist magazine**
art gallery or museum	podcast provider radio	television channel
app live event	school library public library	YouTube
friend or other student	family teacher	college/university
business organisation	shop market/stall	travel agency

general interest magazine: a full magazine or a supplement in a paper or a magazine covering lots of topics and issues

specialist magazine: a magazine dedicated to a more narrow or specific area, such as motorbikes or 'hip-hop'

3 **a)** Which of these sources would be better if:
- accessed online
- accessed in physical or other form (e.g. printed book or in person)?

b) What might be the advantages/disadvantages of accessing sources in one way rather than the other?

Selecting initial materials for a topic

One student is looking for potential pieces of stimulus material to show to her group based on the topics from Topic 1.2.

The *group theme* is 'Damage to the environment in the Caribbean'.

The *student's individual topic* is 'Effects of tourist development on nature in island coastlines'.

On the next page are five pieces of material she has found that she might bring to the group. Which *three* of these seem to offer the most potential for investigation? You should think about:

- whether they will provide interesting language usage
- if they are relevant to the topic or could be linked to it
- if they sound up-to-date
- whether they could generate further research.

(You will learn more about reliability of material and sources in Topic 1.4.)

The student has noted her ideas down in a grid.

Form and source	Title or focus	Further details
An online opinion piece/article from Trinidad and Tobago Newsday website. https://newsday.co.tt	Save a 100-million-year-old legacy (and more) by Elspeth Duncan, 7 June 2020	The plight of leatherback turtles in Tobago, threatened by further building of hotels and facilities for the tourist trade.
Podcast: The World Nomads – insurance/travel company website https://www.worldnomads.com/explore/caribbean/the-world-nomads-podcast-the-caribbean	'Saving the sea turtles', 6-minute section in a podcast called 'The Caribbean'; interview with conservationist on programme part funded by World Nomads.	Problems facing sea turtles in Costa Rica, especially fishing techniques, climate change and a few comments on development/building.
Poem: On pages 70–71 of this book.	'Skeete's Bay, Barbados' by Robert Lee	Explores how a bay is unspoilt but will change in the future.
TV programme: Wild Caribbean – school DVD from library.	Episode 1, 'Treasure Islands', BBC nature programme from 2007	Overview of the rich natural history and animal life on several Caribbean islands.
Report: extract from online report from CEPF (Critical Eco-system Partnership Fund) https://www.cepf.net/our-work/biodiversity-hotspots/caribbean-islands/threats	'Caribbean Islands' – threats; a 300-word extract from longer report.	Summary of main threats to islands, especially pollution and overdevelopment.

4 Discuss with a partner your three choices from the student's list – judging only from the information above.

- What other obvious sources of information can you think of for this topic?
- Where might you find them?

Planning the investigation

Now think about the topic *you* are considering. Have you refined it with your group so the title is right? If so, you will now need to think about the potential benefits to you as a student. For example, how could the investigation help you:

- understand and analyse complex and diverse texts and other sources
- inform yourself on societal and other issues
- develop your own voice and viewpoint/opinion on issues
- appreciate and respond to sources
- evaluate and assess the reliability of sources
- use standard English
- develop general writing skills, such as spelling, paragraphing, vocabulary, etc.
- structure writing concisely and clearly
- edit and assess your own work.

5 Rank these benefits from 1 (top) to 9 (bottom) in terms of how important or relevant you think they are to your development. You will mention two or three of these in your plan, so make sure you carefully choose the benefits that will bring you rewards.

You may not have finally decided on your chosen pieces yet, but you will need to say in your plan what these are, and how you intend to use them.

You will also need to say which specific English and language skills you will use as part of your investigation. This will be linked to what you think the main benefits will be, but you need to be precise about *how* you will use certain skills. For example:

> *Through reading my chosen poem, I will use inference skills to read between the lines and explore the writer's viewpoint.*

6 What particular language skills, specific to your topic and sources, will you use? Write 25–30 words explaining your views now. Use this framework:

> *Through my topic of…*
> *I will use…*

Apply the skills

Write your draft Plan of Investigation. It should be no more than 100 words and should address the three key areas you have looked at. You can use the following prompts and fill in ideas as you refine them.

> *I chose the topic of…with the title…because…*
>
> *The benefits I hope to gain from this investigation are…*
>
> *The materials I have chosen are…*
>
> *They will be sourced from…*
>
> *The language skills I hope to use in my investigation are…because…*

Check your progress

Competent

- I understand what I need to include in my Plan of Investigation and have started to consider possible source materials.

Superior

- I have begun to draft my Plan of Investigation and have a clear idea of the sort of sources I wish to include and where I will get them from.

1.4 Analysing and reflecting on print materials

Learn how to:

- *explore and **deconstruct** how printed materials work*
- *evaluate them and begin to reflect on the issues raised.*

When you view or listen to any piece of material selected for your topic, you need to make sure you fully understand what makes it work. This means deconstructing its constituent parts and the effect it has or message it carries. For written texts, it is natural that much of the focus will be on the language, although you may also have to pay attention to visual elements such as layout or use of images as well.

> **Key term**
>
> **deconstruct:** *to take something apart in order to understand how it works*

A process for deconstructing written texts

When you have identified a printed piece for your investigation, you can apply this deconstruction process, by asking the following questions:

- What is its form and audience (E.g. is it a magazine article, an advert, for teenagers, for children)?
- What is the gist or main focus of the article (E.g. ethical fashion, travel tips, social media issues)?
- What are its key features? How does it work? (E.g. does it use particular language devices or techniques? Is it structured in a particular way?)
- What does this reveal about the writer's or producer's viewpoint or perspective (E.g. are they arguing a particular point of view, promoting something or explaining or describing)?
- Is it effective? Why, or why not? (E.g. does the text fulfil its purpose as far as the intended audience is concerned?)
- Can you trust it? (E.g. given the viewpoint, is it biased? Does it use convincing evidence? Is the source or context it comes from trustworthy or reliable?)

Form and audience

1. What might be the general advantages and disadvantages of using each of the following sources for material (whatever the topic)?

   a) Newspaper website

   b) Personal blog

   c) Academic report

A student has identified the following text to help with his investigation 'Effects of tourist development on nature on island coastlines'.

Title	Author	Source//context	When
'Save a 100-million-year-old legacy (and more)'	Elspeth Duncan	www.newsday.co.tt website	7 June 2020

He has started to make the following notes before he has read the rest of the text.

Title: sounds like a **call to action**: 'Save' – save what? Sounds like a strong message.

Author: named writer – she writes lots of pieces – so a sort of journalist.

Key term

call to action: *an instruction or incentive that encourages immediate action, such as making a phone call to support a cause*

2 Based on these details alone, answer the following items:

   a) What *form* of text do you think this is likely to be? (You may already know the website.)

   b) What audience do you think such a text would be typically aimed at? (You could think first of age groups, then interests.)

You can verify whether your initial thoughts about the form and audience are right when you read the whole text.

Now, read the text extract below. Using the skills you have learned about identifying key points, as well as some of the initial annotations made by a student, answer the items that follow.

Save a 100-million-year-old legacy (and more)

By Elspeth Duncan

[…]

For Tara Short, founder of US-based **Green Edventures**, 'every leatherback encounter [1] is life-changing' – the reason why she started bringing her international tours to **TT** almost annually. Leatherback turtles are the largest turtles on earth [1], capable of growing up to ten feet and weighing as much as 2,000 pounds. Over 100 million years ago [2] their ancestors traversed this planet's oceans. In current times, leatherbacks grace [3] us [4] with their presence, annually swimming thousands of miles from as far afield as Europe and Canada to our shores [4] – one of their most important nesting grounds.

It is important for us to deeply consider these treasures [5] from the deep and the immense value they bring to Trinidad and Tobago – a nation that strives to make a significant mark on the world through tourism. Natural assets, such as these phenomenal beings, should be protected and nurtured at all costs.

Locally, leatherbacks and four other species of turtles are listed and protected as environmentally sensitive species and are further protected by international environmental conventions. Many of us are aware of the range of threats (mainly human-related) that contribute to decreasing global turtle populations – from overharvesting for shells, meat and eggs…to pollution, fatal plastic **ingestion**, boat collisions, **bycatch** in **gillinets**, and more.

Trinidad and Tobago Newsday,
7 June 2020

[1] 'leatherback turtles' mentioned regularly – main focus?

[2] link to title – legacy of turtles

[3] verb suggests a gift which we must be thankful for

[4] pronouns link to TT readers

[5] connotes idea of preciousness and richness

Green Edventures: a US-based travel company specialising in eco-tours for women and student groups
TT: Trinidad and Tobago
ingestion: swallowing or absorbing things down the throat
bycatch: fish or other creatures caught by accident alongside the main catch
gillnets: (or gill nets) vertical panels of fishing nets that are hung in a line across the water

3 Work with a partner to answer these items about the text and its language.

  a) What does the writer say about the value to the islands of the turtles?

  b) In the second paragraph, identify language choices (particular words or expressions) that build on how the writer has described the turtles and the situation in the opening paragraph.

  c) What is the purpose of these language choices (for example, are they designed to create an emotional reaction, to explain things factually, or something else)?

  d) What is the function of the final paragraph here? What new direction, or information, does it introduce?

  e) What more negative uses of language can you identify in the final paragraph?

The writer's viewpoint or perspective

You probably now have a fairly good idea of the writer's overall focus and a sense of her viewpoint.

4 Look at these four statements, noted down by a student about the text. Which do you think best sums up the writer's opinion? Why?

  a) *Leatherback turtles are vitally important to the economy of the islands.*

  b) *Leatherback turtles are endangered and need protecting from threats from humans.*

  c) *Leatherback turtles are an endangered, precious resource that should be protected both for their own sake and for the island economy.*

  d) *Everyone should have a chance to witness the life-changing experience of seeing the turtles.*

Is the text effective?

To answer the question of whether or not the text is effective, you need to understand that its purpose is to *persuade* the reader.

5 In pairs, share your views on whether the text is persuasive.

  • Does the writer provide key points and evidence to support her view?

  • Is the language persuasive?

Can the text be trusted?

You should consider a range of aspects to decide whether or not a text is reliable. Some key aspects are outlined in the table below.

Aspect	Reliable or not?
Date and source: Written in 2020, so recent, and from a national news site.	The content seems up-to-date, and the site is reputable, so yes.
Writer and context: The writer is a regular columnist for a trusted national news site, and therefore a local person herself. But she is not an eco-specialist or scientist.	On balance, given she is an employed journalist who is subject to some ethics and need to tell the truth, yes.
Evidence: The quoted 'expert' is a representative of an eco-tours company, but could be said to have a **vested interest** in the turtles. The evidence about the threats to turtles is not supported by any specific references, so would have to be verified.	Difficult to say – probably more research needed, especially about specific evidence of pollution or other threats.

> **vested interest:** to be personally involved or affected by a situation

6 Write a paragraph summing up the writer's view, any specific language features you noticed and your judgement about whether or not the text can be trusted.

Apply the skills

The following is an extended extract from a text on the general topic of 'Social media and young people'. Details of the piece – where it comes from – are given at the end. Read the extract, and as you do so, begin to think about the focus of the text and the sort of language being used.

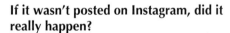

How social media is affecting the health of young people

With Meisha-Gay Mattis

[…]

If it wasn't posted on Instagram, did it really happen?

To many **Millennials** and **Gen Zeros**, the answer would be *no*. The obsession with sharing every aspect of life and **curating** perfection has led many young people to think that their lives are meaningless because they don't have access or proximity to the lavish or adventurous life-styles they see on their screens courtesy of their favourite celebs and influencers, or even their friends – the fun, fashion, food, and travel. This constant obsession with keeping up with the Joneses or creating our own picture-perfect lives has been taxing on our health, but are we ignoring these implications?

There is this constant fear of missing out (FOMO) that gets people so caught up in documenting and sharing the moment that they don't truly experience it. Just pay keen attention the next time you go out. At dinner, there are people trying to find the best angle of their meals before they take a bite. At concerts, there are people more concerned with recording the artiste on stage than actually singing and dancing along. In fact, you'd be lucky to see the stage with all the cell phones in the air, either streaming the show to their followers or recording snippets **to drop** later – all to prove they were there and had the time of their lives.

The pressures of wanting to keep up and thinking that everyone is doing so much more or better than you are leading to feelings of depression and anxiety, and many young people are spending beyond their means to ensure they, too, can enjoy, snap and share the 'perfect' experience.

What many people don't understand is that these celebrities and influencers, who earn millions to their hundreds, are oftentimes given for free what they have to shell out thousands of dollars to purchase – all to chase the almighty 'like'.

In a recent poll that was running on Twitter and on Instagram, 65 per cent of Twitter respondents said that social media did not impact their spending habits, 19 per cent said it did, and 16 per cent said it did somewhat. However, the Instagram respondents gave a completely different result with 65 per cent agreeing that it does impact their spending habits. The main difference here is showing how persuasive pictures can be.

Psychological research has shown that constant comparison can result in acute stress and anxiety. According to Dr Tara Swart, a neuroscientist and lecturer at MIT: 'Your brain is looking for a threat... so it will look at the image and think: 's this as good as me, better than me or less good than me?'

From https://www.loopjamaica.com/content/how-social-media-affecting-health-young-people

---

Millennials: people born between the early 1980s and the early 2000s

Gen Zeros: people born in the mid to late 1990s to the early 2010s

curating: selecting carefully

to drop: to post something noteworthy online

Following the process set out at the start, make your own notes on the text. Remember, you need to as yourself the following:

- What is its form and audience?
- What is the gist or main focus of the article?
- What are its key language features? How does it work?
- What does this reveal about the writer's viewpoint or perspective?
- Is it effective? Why, or why not?
- Can you trust it? Why, or why not?

Check your progress

Competent

- I understand the basic ideas in a text and how a writer puts across their ideas.
- I can make a straightforward judgement as to whether the text is useful and reliable.

Superior

- I understand the form, purpose and audience of a text, and a range of ways in which it works.
- I can make thoughtful judgements about a text's impact, effectiveness and reliability.

1.5 Analysing and evaluating data and images

Learn how to:

- *explore and deconstruct how visual sources, data and other pieces of material work*
- *evaluate this material and begin to reflect on issues raised.*

Exploring verbal and visual pieces

Many of the approaches you adopt when you look at print-only pieces also apply to material that uses data, images or other media, such as sound, to convey ideas. However, in these cases, there are additional aspects to look out for and consider. For example, one way to make sure you capture each aspect of a visual piece is to ask these questions:

- What images have been selected?
- What information is presented and how is it sequenced? What draws the eye? Is there a particular order to the way you are meant to look at the source?
- What, if any, text is there? How is it presented (for example, size, colour, style of language)?
- Are there any other features (for example, logos, design styles, use of grids, boxes)?

You could call this the 'descriptive' stage or the 'What?' stage.

A student has found this text to support her work on the effect of social media on teenagers' well-being. She has begun to make notes describing its features.

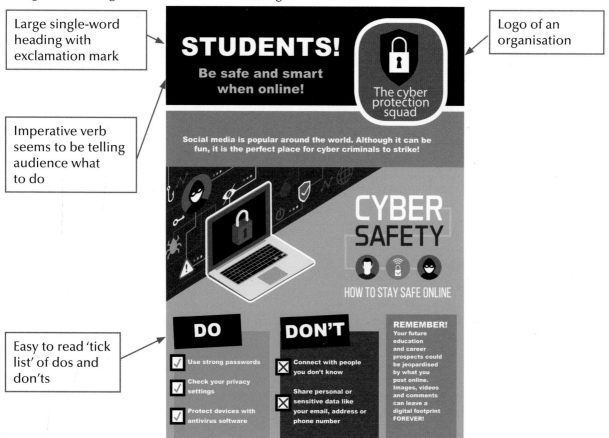

Large single-word heading with exclamation mark

Imperative verb seems to be telling audience what to do

Logo of an organisation

Easy to read 'tick list' of dos and don'ts

1.   Complete the process, either annotating a copy of this online safety text, or by making a list of all the features that have been used in it. Make sure you mention everything you can see.

Deconstructing and analysing pieces

Once you have described the contents of the piece, you can further deconstruct it by thinking about its purpose and effects – the *how* and the *why*.

2.   Using the same process you learned about in Topic 1.4, answer the following questions.

   a) What is the text's form and audience?

   b) What is its gist or main focus (what is it about)?

   c) Does the poster have a specific viewpoint or perspective? If so, what?

   d) Is it effective in its aim? Why, or why not?

Development and reconstruction

Remember that the selected piece is only useful if it helps you explore and respond to your core topic. So, the final stage of the process requires you to evaluate the piece, and recognise its weaknesses or strengths. For example:

- Can you trust it as a source of information or as evidence for the argument it promotes?
- What questions might it raise in your mind?
- Where might it lead you in terms of further research?
- How has it changed or developed your thinking on your topic, if at all?

The same student has made these notes reflecting on this source:

My informative piece uses authoritative, bold tick and cross bullets and logos to give guidance on how to stay safe online. It has made me think about whether it is possible to keep all this in mind when you are surfing the internet.

3.   Although the focus of this unit is on exploring the sources, ask yourself what elements of the source and which of the four bulleted questions above she has commented on.

Remember

Images can be manipulated in the same way as text can. For example, just because a poster or leaflet features photos of 'real people' doesn't mean you should take it at face value. Consider:

- the age and ethnicity of the people
- the clothes they are wearing
- the setting and lifestyle conveyed
- what they are doing
- how they are placed within the frame – for example, foreground, background

All these factors convey a message to the reader or viewer which can reveal the target audience and the purpose of the image.

Same message, different means?

Similar messages can be conveyed in different ways. Another organisation has produced a video called the 'What if rap' about using social media irresponsibly. Here is a screenshot from the video, which features a teacher rapping in front of a class of students, who are dancing and singing along.

From https://www.getsafeonline.org.jm/video/

The rap begins with these lines sung by a teacher to the class (and to the camera):

Watch

Watch yourself online, that's what my crew say

Make it a new day

I'm reminded by the Broadcasting Commission, by the BCJ,

What if

What if it was your friend in the mix?

What if it was your sis in the pix?

4   You may not have the opportunity to watch the whole video, but from the information given here, what *different* techniques are being used to achieve its purpose? Discuss the following aspects with a partner.

   • the title of the video

   • the image you can see

   • the use of text on the screen

   • the lyrics in the rap – the rhythm, rhyme, repetition, etc.

One key difference you might have noticed is the tone of the message.

5   How are the register and style different from the poster? Think about:

   • words like 'my crew', 'mix' and 'pix'

   • the use of rap music

   • the class singing and dancing along.

Data and statistics

Oral and visual media such as podcasts, interviews, videos and advertisements are very rich sources for your topic. However, you should also think about other forms of information and data you can collect and analyse. This might involve questioning people – at home, school or in your local community – or looking at material that has come from similar questioning or surveys.

For example, look at the graph on the right, again related to the topic of the effect of social media on teenagers' wellbeing.

This piece is sourced from an organisation called Ditch the Label, which categorises information about the effects of cyberbullying.

Making sense of such graphs or tables of information, even apparently simple ones like this, is vital in developing your understanding of your topic. For example, there is nothing in this source that defines what 'kids' means, in terms of age or age range, which might be an issue if the topic is focused entirely on teenagers.

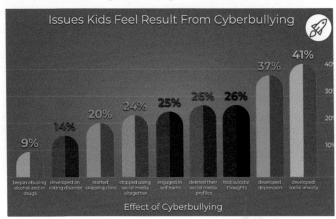

6 Discuss the following items with a partner.

   a) What is the main focus of the graph?

   b) In what way is the focus slightly different to that of the poster and the video?

   c) What information does it reveal? How is it presented?

   d) Who do you think it is aimed at? Is it the same audience as for the other pieces?

   e) What is the graph's purpose? Is it the same as for the other two pieces?

   f) What information is missing from this piece? What else do you need to know?

Apply the skills

How have any of the pieces in this section changed or made you rethink your ideas about social media and teenage wellbeing?

Write a paragraph on **one** of the pieces.

- Describe briefly how it works and any particular language, data, visual or presentational features that stood out.

- Explain its purpose and effectiveness.

- Finish by writing about any questions the piece raised in your mind, or what it made you want to explore in more detail.

Check your progress

Competent

- I can identify key features of presentation in graphic and oral materials.
- I can explain the purpose of these pieces.

Superior

- I can deconstruct a variety of details in the presentation of graphic and oral pieces.
- I can analyse the effectiveness of the pieces and explore any questions they raise.

1.6 Writing reflections on themes and use of language

Learn how to:

- *write and reflect on themes in a concise, interesting way*
- *reflect on the language used and its effects.*

You have already started reflecting on the sample pieces you have looked at over the course of the chapter. This section shows you how to write up your reflections in a simple, clear and relevant way.

Summing up themes

In your first reflective entry, you need to:

- introduce your theme and how it is presented or portrayed in each piece, which you should name or describe simply
- explain why and how the piece is relevant and how it has influenced your thoughts or ideas.

You only have a limited number of words (150 words maximum) to reflect, so you will need to be very efficient and economical with what you say.

Look at the opening section below from one student's reflection, based on the three pieces in the previous unit.

> *The topic I selected was the effect of social media on teenagers' wellbeing. [1]*
> *My informative piece [2] was a chart from a report by pressure group 'Ditch the Label' [3]. It used statistical data to show the effects of cyberbullying. [4] It revealed to me that this is one of social media's main problems and how it has many harmful outcomes. [5]*

[1] clear opening statement of what topic/issue is

[2] states the text type/purpose of the first piece

[3] states the sort of information and where it came from

[4] details of what the chart showed

[5] explains what the student learned or found out

1 Using a similar model, write your own opening (50–55 words) on your first informative or graphic piece. You could use these prompts:

The topic I selected was…/My chosen theme was…

My informative piece/graphic was…

It used/presented…

It revealed to me/I learned that…

If you are not ready to write up your reflections, use one of the other pieces in Topic 1.5 to write an opening paragraph to a written reflection.

Writing about language

In the rest of the reflection, you will need to be just as efficient in covering the different uses of language in the other two pieces. As you saw in Topics 1.4 and 1.5, this might include:

- emotive vocabulary – for example, strong positive or negative verbs and adjectives ('grace us', 'phenomenal', etc.)
- powerful imagery – sensory descriptions that evoke images and settings
- figurative or metaphorical language – for example, 'curating perfection'.

It might also include:

- lists of facts and figures, or specialist language (for example, to convey authority)
- register – formal, informal, use of idiom
- imperative language – 'Do', 'Don't', 'Remember', etc.
- rhythm, rhyme, repetition – for example, in song or poetry.

You can use Paper 2, Chapters 4 and 5 to check your knowledge of these and other relevant language features.

 2   Read this paragraph from a reflection by another student, writing about the 'What if?' rap video from Topic 1.5.

> *The rap used a number of poetic devices to engage the viewer and link to the imagery on the screen. For example, the repetition of 'what if' stressed the questions you needed to ask yourself around social media use, while the informal vocabulary – 'your sis', and 'in the pix' was designed to connect with the teen audience. It spoke very directly to the audience.*

    a)   What two language features does the student mention?

    b)   What purpose is identified for the use of these features?

Apply the skills

Write a brief reflection, of about the same length, about any of the other texts from this chapter. You could use the following prompts to help you:

The article/leaflet used…   *While/and another was…*

One example of this was…   *The effect of these were to…*

Alternatively, draft your own reflective section based on one of the pieces you are working on for your SBA. You can use the same prompts to help you.

Check your progress

Competent

- I can explain how my selected pieces link to my theme.
- I can make a general comment about language use in my chosen pieces.

Superior

- I can link my selected pieces to my theme in a coherent, fluent way.
- I can make focused, clear and concise comments about language use and its impact.

1.7 Writing the Group Report

Learn how to:

- *contribute effectively to the content of the Group Report*
- *draft a fluent, well-written written report.*

The Written (Group) Report brings together many aspects of the learning that are central to the SBA – collaboration, research, analysis and expression of your own ideas.

Contributing to the Group Report

While only one person will scribe the report, every member of your group will contribute to what it says and how it is written. You should be ready to talk about the pieces you have selected and researched, summarising their content and citing their sources accurately. You should talk honestly about your own and your group's pieces, but in a positive way. Through this process, make sure you are keeping notes about your own and others' responses to all the pieces put forward for discussion.

1   Check the notes you have made so far. Have you accurately recorded the pieces you selected? You could use a version of the table on page 259, adding a further column to include your views or thoughts.

Creating a successful Group Report

There are three main elements that the report will need to address, and on which your group will be marked. These are outlined in the table below.

Element of report	Explanation
Content of the report – what you actually include	The overall context for the issue, the particular pieces of material, the issues you addressed and explored, and the tasks each student undertook.
Evidence of **investigation/inquiry/ research** – how you use your pieces	The actual analysis of the pieces, how well these are summed up, and how well you can show evidence of research.
Use of **language and vocabulary** – how you express your ideas	the organisation and structure of the report, how clearly expressed the ideas are, the quality of the language, clear sentencing and paragraphing.

2   As a group, use this table to make sure you are all clear about the requirements of the task and what needs to be included in the report. Then check in with your teacher to show them your progress with the report so far.

Structuring the Group Report

Here is one suggested way of structuring the report. Remember that anything you include must fall within the word count of 250–300 words.

- Paragraph 1: Introduce your topic or issue, saying why it was chosen. You could also comment on how and when the group met, and the ease or difficulty you had in finding particular material.

- Paragraph 2: You could explain which three pieces put forward by group members were chosen for the report. Give titles and, if important, the source/context, and most importantly, say why they were chosen.

- Paragraph 3: Explain concisely how each piece connects to the larger theme. Draw conclusions, for example, explaining if it refers to particular causes and effects or draws meaningful comparisons between things.

Remember

Do not write too much about the pieces and where they came from – keep it brief, clear and concise, bearing in mind the overall word limit.

Read the following sample Group Report.

Group Report: Drug-taking in sport

The chosen topic for our SBA was 'Drug-taking in sport'. In this topic, the recent background to drug-taking in sport (for example, in athletics and cycling), social pressures on young athletes, and the psychological effect on sportspeople and their families was analysed. All five members of the group collected three pieces each, focused on their own sub-topic, and met regularly once a week to discuss and select materials. We set deadlines, had a chairperson for meetings, and made sure notes were taken by the designated scribe. The research done led to our own individual oral presentations.

We decided as a group that the most representative pieces are an article about Jamaican-born athlete Ben Johnson called 'Hero or Villain?' on the CNN news site, an extract from a documentary film called 'Icarus', about Russian doping, and an infographic showing doping statistics over the last three Olympics. After the table had been analysed by the group, we realised that drug-taking in sport hasn't gone away. Despite high-profile cases such as Lance Armstrong's, there are still states or nations where efforts to prevent it have had been scaled back due to cost and political pressure.

The CNN article gives Johnson a chance to explain his reasons for drug-taking and shows how difficult it was to reject the rewards it offered. The 'Icarus' film clip showed that some countries would go to extreme lengths to win at all costs; it made us wonder whether any sport could be seen as completely 'clean'? The final infographic showed that drug-cheats are still being caught, and made us want to check Jamaica's record in sprinting: while Usain Bolt remains innocent, several athletes have been caught. Analysing and discussing these pieces made us realise that we need to make sure that if we compete in sport, we all do so fairly.

3 How effective is this report in terms of what it covers? Decide if:

   a) it covers all the suggested content (are the three pieces all different in content and form?)

   b) it shows analysis of the pieces and their sources, and how they were used/what they revealed

   c) it provides pieces that differ in perspective or viewpoint

   d) it offers sufficient information that clearly sets out group roles and how these helped with the process of the investigation

   e) the final conclusion is logical or not, or whether a more appropriate one could be drawn.

If the answer to any of these is 'no' or 'partly', make a note of what you think could have been done better.

For example, in response to a), you might say:

Yes, there is an article, a video clip and an infographic. Each deal with

different information although there is possibly some cross-over between

the video and the infographic. So, the group possibly might have chosen a

more different third piece.

For b), you could focus on whether each of the sources made the group re-assess their views – was there one that didn't do this (Or, if it did, have the group said how it did so?)

Effective language

Another aspect for which you can gain marks is the effective use of language and vocabulary in the report.

4 Answer these items about the sample report.

    a) Does each paragraph tackle a separate part of the report so that it is easy to follow?

    b) Which word in this sentence makes the sequence of learning clear (e.g. what happened first and next)? *After the table had been analysed by the group, we realised that drug-taking in sport hasn't gone away.*

    c) In the same sentence, which clause of the sentence deals with 'effect' rather than 'cause'?

    d) In several places, the writer of the report used the word 'showed'. What alternative words or phrases could have been used instead to give the report more precision?

    e) In the following sentence, the use of tenses is not consistent. Identify the verbs used and rewrite the sentence so it fits the rest of the paragraph.

We decided as a group that the most representative pieces are an article about Jamaican-born athlete Ben Johnson called 'Hero or villain?' from the CNN news site, an extract from a documentary film called 'Icarus', about Russian doping, and an infographic showing doping statistics over the last three Olympics.

Apply the skills

Although only one of you will be writing up the final report, you all have to contribute to how it is written. Draft your own version of your group report based on the three pieces selected by your group.

Remember

- Give details about the selected theme, the three pieces chosen, where they came from, what they showed and what the group learned from them.
- Include details about how the group was organised and how the process was structured.
- Write in paragraphs, setting out what you and the group discussed and decided in clear sentences and precise vocabulary.

Check your progress

Competent

- I can contribute to the Group Report by explaining why I chose my pieces and by listening to others.

Superior

- I can help make the Group Report highly effective by tracking what is required, contributing ideas and improving expression.

1.8 Planning and delivering the Oral Presentation

Learn how to:
* *plan and structure your oral presentation*
* *deliver an effective oral presentation and creative response.*

Introducing the Oral Presentation

As part of the SBA, you will make a presentation of about four minutes, to a group or your class, based on the sub-topic you explored. You will complete a written plan for your presentation too, which will form part of the written element of the SBA portfolio.

The presentation plan

In the written plan, you should:

* state what form your presentation will take? (Will it be a speech or a **dramatic monologue**? Or a song or poem? Or something else?)
* explain what ideas you will cover in your presentation: you might define some key concepts, or explain causes and effects, or say what perspective is represented
* explain how your chosen pieces have assisted you – for example, how they link to what you will say or do in the presentation, or how you emulated a particular style or form of writing that you used.

> **Key term**
>
> **dramatic monologue:** *a single, fictionalised speech, as if from a play, made by one character*

Read the following sample presentation plan. It is based on one student's sub-topic from the main topic of social media that her group explored.

My presentation will consist of a dramatic monologue [1] based on the theme of cyberbullying [2]; it will be spoken by someone who is suffering from it. I chose this form because I wanted to make a strong, emotional impact on the audience, and show how bullying problems can escalate. [3] I collected three pieces that helped me understand the theme. The first piece, an infographic on effects of cyberbullying from the Ditch the Label website showed me what the largest impact on teenagers was – general social anxiety, which I have included in what my character says. The second piece was an extract from a play called *Mugged* by Andrew Payne, which was more about general bullying but helped me learn how to present a spoken monologue, and express emotional, informal thoughts. The third piece was a video called 'What if rap' from the Safe Schools website, which gave me ideas about how thoughtless actions can lead to people suffering.

[1] form chosen

[2] her chosen sub-topic

[3] why this form was chosen

1 How did each of the student's three pieces help her create her monologue? Think about:
* what particular effect of bullying she deals with in her monologue
* how the monologue is spoken
* what else happens or is talked about in the monologue.

Here is a very short extract from the student's monologue.

> [...] So, you see – it was all my sister's fault really. Yeah, she think she cool making fun my new haircut an' posting, like, on Instagram. 'Do it for the Gram!' everyone say, but what she don't realise is she didn't get like a million comments. 'You ugly, girl!' 'LOL!' Course, when you read 'em out they don't seem like much, but it had a massive effect on me, right. I hated that haircut. I didn't go to school for a week.

2 How did the 'What if rap' help the student create this part of the creative response/ monologue?

3 How could you use dramatic monologue (taking on the role of a particular character or person) for your theme? What sort of person or role could you use? (Remember, it does not have to be someone of your age or background.)

Developing a presentation

A monologue is just one way of developing your presentation. You might prefer to prepare a speech that explains what you have learned from the research you carried out, and your views on the topic you selected.

Here is one possible structure for a speech. This could be seen as an expanded version of the 'presentation plan', but the key thing is to develop your points to ensure the speech is four minutes long.

Speech sections	Details to consider
Introduction	• Explain your theme and why it interested you. • State the focus of your speech. • Briefly sum up the pieces you researched and where they came from. • State what your feelings or knowledge about the topic were before you researched it • Explain what you expected or hoped to find out
Body of speech: part 1	• What you learned from each of the pieces you found. • How each piece presented the theme – what it had to say, or how it was said. • How the pieces confirmed or challenged what you originally thought, or what new or unexpected information you found out. • How this made you feel or react.
Body of speech: part 2	• Your thoughts now, taking into account what you have learned. • What message you would like the audience to take from your speech, if any. • What changes – if changes are needed – you would like to see around this issue/topic. • How this project might affect your life in the future.
Conclusion	• Sum up the core ideas/points you have learned. • If suitable, end with a 'call to action' – something you would like your audience to do or change. • Thank your audience for attending/listening/watching

4 Using this template, draft your own ideas for a speech on your theme.

Starting your speech

Think carefully about your first sentence or two, as this can give your audience a clear idea of your focus and thinking. For example, address your audience directly:

I want to talk to you about how/why/the ways in which…

In this speech, I want to focus on the issue/problem/challenge/topic of…

Consider adding a further phrase to highlight your thought processes, such as:

…and persuade you that we should…

…and explain to you how we can solve…

…and ask you to change the ways you…

…and argue that we all need to…

For example:

In this speech I want to focus on the problem of cyberbullying, and argue that we all need to take more care in our social media behaviour.

5 Write the first sentence or two of your speech using some of the phrases above. If you haven't yet chosen your final topic, it is worth practising with the general theme you are working on.

Body paragraphs of your speech

The main part of your speech should consist of clear sections where you explain your thinking and what you learned from the sources. One way to do this is to use paragraphs with a four-part structure. For example:

Paragraph structure

Part 1: a topic sentence that tells the reader the focus of your paragraph/ section of speech.

Part 2: a descriptive sentence giving details about a piece and what it consisted of.

Part 3: an explanatory or analytical sentence that reveals how the piece worked.

Part 4: a concluding sentence about what you learned or how you felt as a result.

Read this example from the main part of one student's speech.

> I would like to talk to you about one particular effect of cyberbullying on teenage girls – social exclusion. The piece I identified was a letter to a counsellor in a teen magazine in which a teenage girl described how she had become a recluse because of social anxiety caused by cyberbullies. The piece was incredibly powerful because of the emotive language used by the writer, for example describing herself as 'desperate' and 'hopeless' until she saw 'the light at the end of the tunnel'. This affected me profoundly as the girl was exactly the same age as me, so I was able to empathise with her.

6 Answer these items.

    a) What does the opening topic sentence reveal is the focus of the speaker's point?

    b) What was the source/piece she got her information from?

    c) How does the speaker indicate the words or phrases that have been directly taken from the piece?

    d) What was the effect on the speaker of reading the piece?

Signposting language and punctuation

In the model paragraph above, the student uses a number of 'signposts' to help signal her ideas clearly:

- The dash adds precise detail at the end of the first sentence (' – social exclusion').
- The conjunction 'because' is used to explain cause and effect ('become a recluse because of social anxiety').
- The phrase 'for example' introduces the clause that gives more information ('for example, describing herself as…').
- The conjunction 'until' is used to show a sequence of events in time ('until she saw…').
- The conjunction 'so' is used to mean 'as a result' or 'as a consequence'.

7 Write a body paragraph for your own theme. If you don't have enough information to do this yet, try practising by writing one on the same topic as the student above. For example, imagine you have read a leaflet offering a helpline to students who have been bullied online. Use the four-part paragraph structure to help you, and any useful signposting words, phrases or punctuation.

Conclusions

You will need a strong conclusion that leaves a lasting impact on your audience. Part of this can sum up your key points or feelings, but at the very end you could use one of these techniques:

- A call to action: this is when you ask your audience to act or think differently. For example: *Make sure you let others know how you are feeling when social media posts upset you. Otherwise you will bottle up emotions until they damage your mental health.*
- A rhetorical statement or question: this is a provoking statement, often expressed as a question that implies an answer. For example: *Do you really want social media to become the dominant force in your life? I certainly don't!*
- A powerful image or imagined situation. For example: *Let's all hope for a time when we can sit in the classroom at the start of the day, our screens safely put on one side, speaking and listening to each other – with real, authentic voices.*

8 Think of a good sentence or two that could end your concluding paragraph. Try to use one of the three techniques above, or even consider combining them in some way.

Delivering the presentation

Once you have planned and drafted the content of your presentation, think about *how* you deliver it. The table below contains some key pointers to bear in mind. For each one, give yourself a mark out of 10 in terms of your *current* performance (before you have practised).

Feature	Explanation	Mark out of 10
clarity	How clearly do you speak? Can a listener hear each word or do you mumble and fail to project? Do you talk too quickly, so listeners miss vital points?	
fluency	How well does your speech or performance flow? Are there awkward pauses and chopping/changing, or is it smooth and easy to listen to?	
variety	How well can you vary the tone, pace and emphasis of your speech or performance? Do you stress important ideas, or allow your voice to rise for questions?	
non-verbal skills	How animated are you when you speak? Do you have an open body stance, or use your hands to mirror what you are saying (for example, palms open when asking a question)? Do you look at your audience confidently or stare at your feet?	
overall performance	How do you rate your overall performance? Are you broadly confident about your presentation, or do you have a lot of work still to do?	

Revision tip

You can make a strong impact on your audience through the use of non-verbal skills and paralanguage. For example, hesitation noises ('err', 'um') can disrupt your flow – but pausing for effect can be used to emphasise a point; equally, a vocal sound like 'hmm' might convey thoughtfulness.

9 Share your marks with a partner. Talk about your performance strengths and weaknesses, and discuss what you could do to improve. (For example, what would boost your confidence more – practice on your own, or practice with friends and family?)

10 To improve your oral and presentational skills, you can practise in other ways. Try one of these activities.

    a) Talk to a friend for one minute about your favourite film, trying to persuade them that it is worth seeing. Ask them to give you a mark out of 10 for each of the elements in the grid.

    b) Record yourself on your phone or laptop camera, describing something that you have done that day and making it sound as interesting as possible. Use non-verbal gestures to make it more engaging.

    c) Learn a short poem and then perform/speak it aloud without prompts. How easy did you find it?

Apply the skills

If you haven't completed your presentation plan, now is the time to draft it. Remember:

- Write your presentation out in full: you can reduce it to prompt cards or notes later.
- Structure it carefully, making sure that the links between the sources you used and your final presentation are clear.
- Pay attention to the introduction and conclusion (whether it is a speech or the start/end of a poem or monologue) so that these make an impact on your audience.
- Decide where and how you can make the spoken delivery engaging – for example, highlight words or phrases in a speech or poem which could be stressed, or note where you might speak more slowly to emphasise a point and give it impact.
- Consider how you could use non-verbal skills and paralanguage to keep your audience interested.

Finally, have some strategies in place in case you get stage fright. These might include taking a sip of water or taking some slow, deep breaths. Most important of all, remain positive – you are a good speaker!

Check your progress

Competent

- I can plan a clear presentation, drawing on the sources I selected.
- I can deliver a presentation that is easy to follow and gets my main points across.

Superior

- I can plan a clear presentation that shows the different ways I have used the sources.
- I can deliver a fluent, engaging and thought-provoking presentation using a range of skills.

1.9 Final Reflections

Learn how to:

* *reflect on all the work you have done*
* *write up your reflections in a clear and thoughtful way.*

The process of reflection

What is a reflection? Literally, it means the image that stares back at you when you look into a still pool or a mirror. This gives us a clue, because when you reflect, you have to look at yourself almost objectively – with honesty and positivity. Reflection is about moving forward. Even though this is the third, and 'final' reflection, it is really part of a process that started before you began the SBA and which will continue long after you have submitted your portfolio.

1 Without looking back at any notes, spend five minutes quickly noting down everything you have learned from your SBA. Once you have finished, divide your notes into categories:

* the skills you have developed
* the new knowledge you have gained
* how you have changed.

Did you have at least one point for all of these? Share your notes with your 'theme' group. Are there any aspects that you all wrote down?

Knowing what to write about

There is a huge amount you could include in your final reflection, but you must focus on the core things you have learned. The table below outlines some possible areas to reflect on.

How the SBA helped you…	Questions to ask yourself
as a person	How did the process change you? Did it make you more sensitive, or raise your awareness of something? Did it make you look at things from a new perspective? Did you become more empathetic?
as a group or team member	What leadership skills, if any, did you develop? How co-operative were you? Did you improve your listening skills? How did you contribute to the group/work? How did it make you more confident?
as a reader/researcher	What did you learn about how to evaluate pieces, their sources and evidence? Did it improve your critical thinking and analysis? Did you improve your time-management and record-keeping?
as a performer/presenter	How confident were you? Did it help you develop your creative side? Did you improve speaking and presenting skills? How far out of your comfort zone did it take you?
when looking to the future	Has it made you an advocate for change – if so, in what way and in what respect? Has your attitude to the issue changed? Has it made you reconsider your own choices or paths?

Remember

You do not have to cover all the questions in the rows above, and some will naturally overlap, so be selective.

2 Read this short extract from one reflection by a student on his theme, then answer the items below.

> *Through the project, I have altered my perspective on business development on our island, as I now see it has both positive and negative impacts. In the future, I will listen to all opinions, even those that I initially find problematic or troubling.*

a) How has the student changed in terms of his views about business development on the island?

b) How has it changed his views going forward?

c) Which rows/questions from the table above has the student addressed?

3 You can now begin to draft your final reflective piece, which should be around 150 words. You might want to use some of these connective words and prompt phrases to help you reflect.

Prompt phrases to begin or explain ideas	Connective words or phrases
I learned that/how…	also, in addition, moreover, furthermore, and
I began to appreciate that/how/why…	
I altered my perspective on…	but, however, yet, although, even though
I was surprised to learn that/about/how…	
I developed my skills in…	because, as a result of, from this, so that
I now see that…	
I became more aware of…	for example, as is shown by, which can be seen in
I feel strongly that…	
It is vital that…	first, initially, beforehand, before, next, then, later, afterwards, finally, in the end

Apply the skills

Check your draft against the table on page 280. Have you covered at least one reflective question from each section?

Write up your final reflection on your topic or theme.

Check your progress

Competent progress

• I can reflect in a general way on the main things I have learned from my SBA.

Superior

• I can reflect carefully on my SBA, drawing out key elements that I have learned or ways in which I have changed or developed.

CSEC® English A Answers to Paper 1

Chapter 1 Understanding meaning: Looking at word choice and idiom

1.1 Introducing literal meaning

1 b)

2 Predominated means were the most frequently seen; paucity means a lack of; construct means to build.

1.2 Introducing non-literal language

1 a) Sensory appeal due to the onomatopoeia; also alliteration.

   b) Emotion – the idea of an oasis suggests that the character seeks refuge or feels endangered and is relieved to see it.

   c) Impact created by the use of hyperbole.

2 and 3

'forced on you every five minutes': hyperbole, which creates humour and thus has impact
'What is her solution?': personification makes Jamaica seem alive and wanting to please you
'float your boat': idiom that creates impact by seeming informal and trustworthy
'sparkle like diamonds': simile that creates a sensory image of brightness and light
'keep your wits about you': idiom, as if offering friendly advice

1.3 Understanding nuance

1–3 Answers will vary.

4

Word	Sensory associations (linked to sight, sound, touch, taste)	Emotional associations (linked to feelings)
hideous	deformity	fear
gorgeous	beauty, everything in proportion	admiration, affection, attraction, happiness
spacious	airy, roomy, bright and light	relaxed, carefree
cramped	dark shadows, full of furniture	tense, nervous, irritable

5 Answers will vary.

6 c) – it is less formal than the others and continues the nuance of playfulness.

7 b) – it continues the formal register of 'immaculately'.

8 d) – the idea of a bouquet links with 'gift' and the other choices suggest a retreat or refuge, which is not the implication of the sentence.

9 b) – 'sprang' continues the animation created by the bat imagery.

10 b) – this continues the informal and child like register.

1.4 Understanding register

1 Answers will vary but might include: 'goodbye, bye, see ya'; 'Mother, Mum, Ma'; 'hound, dog, mutt'.

2 may/might; will/would; shall/should

3 Answers will vary but might include: 'Give me a hand'; 'Bring me my coat'; 'Put it in the bin'.

4 Answers will vary.

5

MESSY [1] PLAY DAY!

Hey! [1] Don't [2] sit at home whilst the kids grizzle [1] around you!

Join us for a messy play day – and we'll [2] even clean up afterwards.

Everything provided – just bring your budding artists! [3]

11am Community Hall Friday 7th June

[1] short, informal vocabulary

[2] abbreviations

[3] slightly light-hearted

---

6 b)

7 b)

8 c)

9 d)

10 b)

1.5 Identifying synonyms

1 c)

2 d)

3 c)

1.6 Identifying antonyms

1 a)

2 wild; dramatic; unruly; extreme

3 arid; barren; dry; parched

4 stay; keep; remain; maintain

1.7 Identifying clichés and idioms

1 **a)** She is a constant source of discomfort.
   b) I'm feeling uncomfortable about this.
   c) I'm listening keenly.

2 **a)** The expression does not give any detail about how each side will benefit and so is too general.
   b) This metaphor does not make any sense, meaning that it is probably an idiom, and also a well-known phrase, which means it is a cliché too.
   c) This expression does not give any detail about the precise events that have led to a problem.

3 All of them except h).

4 Answers will vary.

5 **a)** *It has been* <u>the day from hell</u> *for everyone at the funeral home.* The reference to hell, when linked with the concept of death, is unfortunate here.
   b) *The nanny said that completing the crossword was like* <u>taking candy from a baby</u>. Taking anything from a baby is not a good image for a nanny.
   c) *You could* <u>cut the air with a knife</u> *when the twins were around.* Cutting with a knife sounds inappropriate when children are around.
   d) *Reaching this trial verdict is as* <u>easy as pie</u> *for the jury!* This suggests a light-heartedness that is not appropriate when considering the role of a jury.

1.8 Recognising redundancies

1 a variety of different items; the most important, vital; combine together; delicious tasty; final result; while at the same time

2 a), c), d), f), h), j)

3 Answers will vary.

4 a)

5 d)

6 a)

7 a)

Chapter 2 Understanding meaning: Looking at grammar and syntax

2.1 Introducing grammar – parts of speech

1 Answers will vary.

2 'slithy' = adjective; 'toves' = noun; 'gyre' = verb.

3 **a)** Using 'the' implies that no other book would be as effective; 'a' suggests it will be a good book for you, but it is less forceful than the first sentence.
   b) The effect of 'around' and 'over' is more vague and general than 'across', while 'towards' seems threatening.

4 b)

5 a)

6 a)

7 b)

2.2 Introducing syntax and structure

1 a) 'and or 'but'; c) 'if'; e) 'but' or 'however'

2 a) *To what extent is Shakespeare still relevant to the modern world<u>?</u>*
   c) *Why* <u>are</u> *we still arguing about this same point?*
   d) *What a terrible waste of a day that was<u>!</u>*

3 a), d), e) and f)

4 The following words and connectives help the paragraphs link: pronoun 'they' is used to refer to 'school uniforms'; the idea of discipline problems is picked up from the first paragraph and developed in the second and then the concept of rebellions is taken from the end of the second paragraph and developed in the third.

5 *She paused for breath, looking around to check where she was now. Suddenly she realised she didn't know this place at all; she'd never been there before. Panic gripped her and she didn't know what to do next. Who could help her? Glancing around, she saw a woman with a small child and decided to ask her for directions.*

6 **i)** b)
   ii) c)
   iii) c)

2.3 Understanding pronouns

1

first person	singular	to refer to just yourself	I
first person	plural	to refer to a group that includes you	we
second person	singular	to refer to another person whom you are talking to/addressing directly	you
second person	plural	To refer to a group of people whom you are talking to/addressing directly	you
third person	singular masculine	To refer to a single male person you are talking about	he
third person	singular feminine	To refer to a single female person you are talking about	she
third person	singular neutral	To refer to a single thing or animal you are talking about	it
third person	plural	To refer to a group you are talking about (rather than to)	they

2 **a)** The man turned towards them. <u>He</u> looked like he wanted to speak but didn't know what to say.
   b) Levi, Brianna and I are coming this afternoon. <u>We</u> will be arriving at about three.
   c) Jodi, Lisa and Leanne all have driving tests next month. <u>They</u> could all be on the road soon.

3 b) *<u>He</u> ate the chicken really fast.*
   c) *I saw <u>her</u> yesterday.*
   e) *<u>They</u> are going to the party with us.*

4 **i)** c)
   ii) a)
   iii) d)

2.4 Understanding verbs and tenses

1 a)

2 **a)** *He talks so quickly.*
   b) *She is a pretty girl.*
   c) *There are many problems.*

3 **a)** *If I had more money, I could do more interesting things.*
   b) *If I had had more money, I could have done more interesting things.*
   c) *If I get more money, I will do more interesting things.*

4 c)

2.5 Understanding prepositions

1 *Mrs Shelley works <u>in</u> the accounting department <u>at</u> Fitzgerald & Millers, the law firm <u>in</u> town. Her walk there every morning, <u>along</u> busy roads, takes 20 minutes. She always goes <u>to</u> the coffee shop next door <u>to</u> get her lunch, as she says their coffee is the finest <u>on</u> the island.*

2 a), c), d) and f)

3 **a)** <u>on</u> foot/the bus/the train (but <u>by</u> bus/train/plane)
   b) <u>on</u> the radio/TV/internet/phone

4 b), c) and d)

5 **a)** The first implies someone used a rock to kill the bird; the second suggests the rock itself did it.
   b) The first suggests visiting the area; the second implies physically going into the lake.
   c) The first implies running in a straight line through the middle of the park; the second suggests going all the way around the outside of it.

6 **a)** c)
   b) b)
   c) a)

2.6 Understanding punctuation

1 Answers will vary but should follow the model answer provided.

2 **a)** The goat hurt <u>its</u> leg.
   b) Joelle and Deneice both play for the local <u>girls'</u> soccer team.
   c) He <u>wouldn't</u> have gone if she <u>hadn't</u> sent him 17 texts.

3 **i)** c)
   ii) a)
   iii) b)
   iv) c)

2.7 Developing spelling skills

1 Answers will vary.

2 a) *If <u>they're</u> not going to check every single one, <u>there</u> is no point checking any.*
   c) *If only he'd listened to me, he <u>too</u> would have avoided this.*

3 **a)** a)
   b) b)
   c) d)
   d) b)

Chapter 3 Extracting information from information texts

3.1 Recognising facts and other types of information

1 Any four from these six facts:

- '75 per cent of phone owners have reported this as an issue'
- 'survey...commissioned by local telephone provider GreenRing'
- 'While the number looks like an innocent three-digit area code for the Caribbean it's actually a premium-rate line.'
- 'they only ever let the phone ring once before disconnecting'
- 'that it's a robo caller on the other end of the line'
- 'you're 65 per cent more likely to return a missed call than you are to ring them if they leave a message'

2
- '75 per cent of phone owners have reported this as an issue'. This statement mentions home owners who are real people, and the statistic shows that this is a fact that can be proven.
- 'survey … commissioned by local telephone provider GreenRing'. This statement is also specific about where the information is from. If necessary you could prove that they commissioned the survey.
- 'While the number looks like an innocent three-digit area code for the Caribbean it's actually a premium-rate line.' This statement has a clear 'what', as it is about a number. It is possible to prove that the three-digit number is the same as a Caribbean one, but links to a high-cost line.
- 'they only ever let the phone ring once before disconnecting'. Again, there is a clear event stated here – the one-ring call. This could be proven by monitoring calls from the number.
- 'that it's a robo caller on the other end of the line'. By telling us clearly who the caller is (or in this case, what), this could be proved by monitoring calls.
- 'you're 65 per cent more likely to return a missed call than you are to ring them if they leave a message'. Here, the statistic is something that could be verified by research.

3 a) and b)
- 'you'll only come across one in the Caribbean if you're travelling in Trinidad.'
- 'These bloodsuckers may be small (only about 3 inches long).' This can be proved by research.
- 'weighing 1.5 ounces.' This can be proved by research.

- 'they'll still try to attack you (or any other mammal) in your sleep.' This can be proved by a behavioural study.
- 'They can only drink about an ounce of blood in one sitting.' This can be proved by measurement.

3.2 Extracting literal information from a text

1 Under the subheading 'Habitat'.
2 'height'
3 b)
4 b)
5 b)
6 c)

3.3 Using implicit information

1 Aruba or Barbados in December.
2 'dump' is quite an informal word, suggesting a large unwanted volume but not a threat to life; 'entangled' suggests being inconvenienced but not in extreme danger, as the word is not about being trapped and unable to avoid the storms.
3 c)
4 a) Europe is the most popular destination for tourists; Africa is also shown to be the least visited continent.
   b) France is the most popular destination within Europe, receiving more than twice as many tourists as any other European country.

3.4 Extracting information from a non-prose source

1 26 per cent like swimming/beach, 7 per cent like fishing, 22 per cent like social networking, 15 per cent like computer games.
   63 per cent enjoy outdoor hobbies and 37% enjoy indoor hobbies.
   37 per cent use technology in their hobbies.
2 Athletics is the most popular hobby.
3 All the percentages of each hobby for both male and female students.
4 The most and least popular hobbies for both male and female students. The most popular hobby across both genders overall.
5 The reader cannot tell the exact figure for each export.
6 Canada
7 That increases in visitor numbers are not linked to extremes of high or low temperature (i.e. information is inferred using the data from both the charts).

3.5 Recognising main and subordinate ideas

1 Cars and other vehicles are the cause of the pollution.

2 Example of a completed model:
   The first sentence repeats the main idea.
   The second sentence echoes the subordinate idea.
   Then the author adds detail to flesh out the main idea followed by details to back up the subordinate idea.

3 c)

4 The heading is general and makes it clear that the focus will be on travelling around Grenada. The subheadings then each introduce a specific mode of travel: Local buses, Ferries and Water taxis.

5 a) For example: Local buses: main idea is that they are a friendly, comprehensive and easy to use service. Subordinate ideas are the details of different journeys, how to use the buses and examples of how much journeys will cost.
   b) The subordinate ideas add detail to the main ones or offer examples to make the main ideas clearer.

3.6 Identifying sequences in a text

1 1900s, 2001, late 2000s. They tell us that the text is organised chronologically.

2 Words signalling tense are: 'were', 'has led', 'has to be', 'is', 'looks'

3 Words and phrases indicating a sequence of cause and effect are: 'To start with'; 'An equally serious issue'; 'As a result'; 'in turn'; 'But even worse'; 'knock-on effect'; 'Plus'

4 c)

5 b)

Chapter 4 Gaining insights from literature: Poetry

4.1 Understanding literal language in poetry

1 Word meanings:
   Embattled – under attack, or in the midst of a conflict
   furious – angry, maddened
   spikes – sharp points, often metal

2 a) All three are right but Frankie's definition misses the inference that the tree is personified and like a creature of myth or legend.
   b) Students own response: but they may think of giants being capable of good as well as bad as here, protecting the speaker.

3 It is used primarily for sensory appeal and impact, although the poet does convey how small he feels and perhaps his sense of protection under the giants shelter.

4

Word: 'stolen'	Alternatives: 'thieved', 'taken without permission'
Impact	The precise meaning of this word suggests an unsavoury immoral character to the cat.
Sensory appeal	
Emotion conveyed	Creates a sense of dislike/fear towards the cat.

Word: 'Gaze'	Alternatives: 'look intensely', 'stare'
Impact	The precise meaning of this word suggests the cat is very focused and determined.
Sensory appeal	Leads us to imagine that the cat is extremely aggressive.
Emotion conveyed	Creates a sense of awe and perhaps even dislike towards the cat.

Word: 'bright languid segments'	Alternatives: 'shiny pieces'
Impact	The precise meaning of this phrase suggests the eyes are of a specific shape and very animated and shiny, but not very alive.
Sensory appeal	Leads us to imagine eyes of a very specific shape.
Emotion conveyed	Creates a sense of awe/fear towards the cat.

Word: 'velvet'	Alternatives: 'smooth cloth'
Impact	The precise meaning of this word suggests a degree of smoothness which is pleasant and an attractive sheen.
Sensory appeal	Leads us to imagine that the cat is very soft and shiny.
Emotion conveyed	Creates a sense of awe and perhaps admiration towards the cat.

Word: 'latent'	Alternatives: 'not fully utilized', 'held in reserve'
Impact	The precise meaning of this word suggests potential destruction, as if the cat is holding back.
Sensory appeal	Leads us to imagine that the cat is potentially aggressive.
Emotion conveyed	Creates a sense of awe, fear and perhaps even dislike towards the cat.

Word: 'frays'	Alternatives: 'fight' or 'altercation'
Impact	The precise meaning of this word suggests the cat is often in fights and is aggressive.
Sensory appeal	Leads us to imagine that the cat is extremely aggressive.
Emotion conveyed	Creates a sense of awe and perhaps even dislike towards the cat.

Word: 'dainty'	Alternatives: 'delicate', 'fragile-looking', 'neat'
Impact	The precise meaning of this word suggests that the cat is physically small and appealing.
Sensory appeal	Leads us to imagine that the cat is beautiful.
Emotion conveyed	Creates a sense of awe and perhaps admiration towards the cat.

Word: 'wheezy'	Alternatives: 'laboured breathing'
Impact	The precise meaning of this word suggests the cat is not in good health or is old.
Sensory appeal	Leads us to imagine that the cat is old.
Emotion conveyed	Creates a sense of sympathy towards the cat and confusion that it is old and yet such a predator.

Word: 'maul'	Alternatives: 'smack', 'battering'
Impact	The precise meaning of this word suggests the cat gets ill-treated by humans.
Sensory appeal	Leads us to imagine that the cat is vulnerable in some ways.
Emotion conveyed	Creates a sense of awe, sympathy and perhaps admiration towards the cat.

   c) Two patterns that seem to emerge are ideas and images relating to fighting and those relating to smoothness and neatness and the cat's appearance.

5 c)

6 b)

7 c)

8 d)

4.2 Understanding figurative language in poetry

1 a) imagery and metaphor
    b) imagery the carousel/roundabout may in fact be real but the word carousel brings to mind children's colourful playground attractions.
    c) simile

2 Students own responses

3 Walcott may have chosen the power lines image because this fits with the earlier images of violence and the final references to slavery, itself a violent act it suggests that the power lines are criss-crossing and almost doing battle with each other, too.

4 Figurative techniques: (line 2) 'seven notes dance in his throat'= personification; (line 3) 'like seven tame birds' = simile; (line 3) 'His voice is a sharp sword' = metaphor; (line 5) 'darts like lightning'; (line 6) 'He sets deadly traps for himself, then cuts them away' = extended metaphor.

5 a) The similes reveal the different aspects of the singer's voice and his skill in performing a technically difficult song.
    b) Connotations of the four images about the singing voice: 'tame birds' carries with it the idea of beautiful song, but also captivity and vulnerability; 'sharp sword slicing and thrusting' implies the almost violent and energetic nature of the voice and contrasts with the image of beauty; 'darts like lightning' is light and dynamic, but also carries with it ideas of power and danger; 'sets deadly traps' conveys the idea of the voice's skilfulness in overcoming any difficulty but also implies the risk being taken and the consequences of failing.
    c) Emotions: awe and admiration; concern that he might fail.

6 Students may mention that the singer's voice is often described as powerful and awe inspiring, but with a hint of danger and violence. This might be to hint at the power of the words that he sings, or the vulnerability of his situation, where he must entertain, or die.

7 a) literal meaning – a sun that is fading or going down
    b) figurative – could be dying, ageing, losing power or bringing darkness

8 d)

9 d)

10 b)

11 c)

12 c)

4.3 Understanding sound effects in poetry

1 Answers/ examples given will vary.

2 Sound effects include: (line 3 and line 4) 'rolls' and 'clashing' = onomatopoeia; (line 2) 'Giant and grey' = alliteration; (line 9) 'greasy paws' = sibilance; (line 11) 'moon rocks in the stormy cloud' = assonance; (line 14) 'And howls and hollos long and loud' = specific use of rhythm; (lines 15–17) 'June/dune/tune' = rhyme enhancing meaning.

3 **a)** they are slow and drawn out too
   b) that it repeats in loops, and even has an 's' shape

4 Possible examples of alliteration: 'Giant and grey'; 'Hour upon hour'; 'Bones, bones, bones, bones!'; 'snuffs and sniffs'; 'Shaking his wet sides'; 'howls and hollos'; 'sandy shores'; 'scarcely snores'

5 Answers will vary.

6 Answers will vary.

7 At first there are sound effects such as onomatopoeia to help us imagine a noisy lively dog. Then the sounds become softer to show the dog sniffing. There is assonance to show the slow howl of the dog. The final section of the poem is slower and has less rhyme and fewer sound effects to reflect the dog being quiet and inactive.

8 • The words 'rippling tide' rhythmically imitates the action and sound of the water, a form of onomatopoeia; 'glisten' with its sharp s seems to reflect the sparkling sound and look too.
   • The assonance of 'hollows echo' with the three repeated o vowels reflect the sounds of the birds cries in the holes in the cliffs.

9 The sound echoes and patterns mimic the repeated bird calls, the echoes in the cliffs, and perhaps even the repetitive action of the waves. Phrases like 'white wings glancing' have a dipping high and low sound like the swooping birds.

10 **a) and b)** Answers will vary.

11 c)

12 a)

13 b)

14 a)

15 b)

4.4 Understanding structure in poetry

1 **a)** Suggested verse headings: Setting the scene; How I felt about lessons; More about that; Sent out but drawing; Always drawing; Doing well in art class; Moral of the story
   b) Each new verse is used to signal a change or time or topic.

2 'Six year old' stands out because it is as if the poet is saying it loudly. 'But one time' also stands out as if it is special, which it was to the poet.

3 **a)** There are fewer words and syllables in most of the lines here.
   b) It sounds more positive and upbeat because of the rhythm.

4 It brings the 'story' from the poet's childhood to a close.

5 c)

6 b)

7 c)

4.5 Identifying themes in poetry

1 (1) c); (2) d); (3) a); (4) b)

2 (1) matches with d); (2) matches with c); (3) matches with a); (4) matches with b)

3 Theme = sadness; sub-theme = the transience (or eventual passing) of sadness

4 (1) matches with b); (2) matches with a); (3) matches with d); (4) matches with c)

5 **a)** 'bright' and 'fade' are a contrast, which suggests something being lost.
   b) 'Stars' and 'flower' in lines 5–6 seem to suggest it is about nature.
   c) 'Hearts' and 'ties' in lines 7–12 seem to suggest it is about people's relationships.

6 It creates an image of light flying, which suggests a religious/spiritual sub-theme.

7 d)

Chapter 5 Gaining insights from literature: Prose

5.1 Understanding figurative language in prose

1 **a)** simile: when one thing is compared to another using the words 'as' or 'like'
   b) metaphor: when one thing is compared to another without a comparative word such as 'as' or 'like'
   c) personification: when an inanimate object is described with human-like qualities
   d) symbolism: when an object is used consistently to represent a concept or theme
   e) pathetic fallacy: using the natural world to reflect human experiences and feelings

2 Any five of the following:

   the damp 'lying'/'hanging' – personification

   'as if some goblin' – simile

   'like a coarser sort of spider's webs' – simile

   'like a phantom' – simile

   'everything seemed to run at me' – pathetic fallacy

   'The gate and dykes…bursting at me…as if they cried' – personification

'One black ox, with a white cravat on' – personification

3 a) The mist is made to seem omnipresent and malicious. This is unusual and draws the reader into the landscape and Pip's experience of it.
   b) The description visualizes the effect of the damp through details like the cobwebs, the cloud of smoke out of the ox's nose. The reader also feels the damp with phrases like 'wet lay clammy' and can imagine how it affects Pip.
   c) The connotations are negative: 'lying', 'goblin', 'crying', 'hanging', 'phantom' all suggest a supernatural experience with danger, punishment and the unexpected very close by.

4 The techniques may make the reader feel scared for Pip and empathize with his fear and guilt.

5 b)

6 b)

7 a)

8 d)

5.2 Identifying tone in prose

1 a) melancholic: sad and depressed
   b) ironic: wry amusement at something that happens in a contrary/unexpected way
   c) sarcastic: given to using irony in order to mock or show contempt
   d) condescending: having a manner of superiority; patronizing

2 a) The tone is melancholic.

3 It develops the melancholic tone, but it is also concise and economical, picking out these small details about the simple, rather poor house to build up a picture.

4 a) 'expectancy'
   b) Changes in the man, i.e. he does not look as he did the last time they saw him.
   c) gold, green and red
   d) 'no longer the colourless and larva-like figure we had known', 'superb metamorphosis', 'It was difficult to believe that it was the same man.'

5 a) He looks pale and featureless, perhaps fat.
   b) No – these are not very nice ways to describe him. It also implies that he was not notable as a person before his promotion.

6 The final sentence sums up the reactions of the narrator, who seems to think that the proconsular has dressed up for effect and is not being true to himself. c)

7 a)

8 d)

9 c)

5.3 Understanding structure in prose

1 Chapter IX is likely to be organised **by location** and **chronologically**.

2 simple, compound, complex, simple, simple

3 The writer chooses to begin each paragraph to highlight the narrator's next moment of realisation.

4 a) To emphasise the fact that he was crying.
   b) This order makes the reader focus on the narrator's thoughts, not his tears. The reverse would be true if he had written: 'I thought of him never eating … and tears poured down my face.'

5 b)

6 d)

7 b)

5.4 Identifying themes in prose

1 Themes suggested by the other highlighted sections might be freedom/contentment.

2 In the rest of the story Meryl might find happiness/fulfilment.

3 Birth/moved home/played baseball then basketball/cut from team/practised hard and grew/selected for a team. Events relate to early years of Michael Jordan's life, which involved lots of change and practice.

4 a) The Jordans want the best for their family and so chose to move to North Carolina.
   b) Jordan keeps on going with his sport even when he does not succeed.
   c) He and his parents want to do well and take their future into their own hands.

5 b)

6 Answers will vary.

7 a)

8 d)

9 b)

Chapter 6 Recognising and evaluating opinion

6.1 Recognising implicit meaning

1 A negative, critical attitude to this dangerous sport
   A sarcastic and critical attitude
   A shocked and negative attitude

2 To suggest a different attitude, each topic sentence could start like this:
   Some say that sports such as…
   Clearly, divers gain…
   Exaggerated statistics reveal…

3 **a)** A man is jumping off a cliff wearing a children's inflatable swimming aid.
   b) Tom Brady, the American football player. He looks carefree.
   c) He is stating that he is safer doing this than playing American football.

4 The cartoonist appears to be 'for', but may in fact be 'against' both American football and cliff jumping!

5

Negative	Neutral	Positive
dull	light	bright
rainy	dry	sunny
dank	moist	humid
tense	carefree	relaxing
ramshackle	unsound	rustic
unkempt	well-maintained	pristine
littered	neat	immaculate

6 'exceptionally'; 'really'; 'excellent'; 'extremely'; 'big'; 'terrifically'; 'crystal'

7 d)

8 c)

9 b), c) and d)

6.2 Understanding assertion and bias

1 b) and c) are assertions; the others are facts.

2 A is better because it expands on the assertions, providing both detail and proof.

3 The headlines seek to have maximum impact on readers.

4 *Close result for the Troopers:* 'close' is quite factual and suggests a neutral stance.
   Tragic blow for the Troopers: 'tragic' evokes sympathy as it suggests a major blow to their chances. From this it appears the writer is on the side of the Troopers.
   Shame on you Troopers: 'Shame on you' is a strong criticism and evokes a sense of moral outrage. It suggests the writer is disgusted by the team's performance.

5 b)

6 c)

7 c)

8 b)

9 b) and d)

6.3 Understanding persuasive techniques

1 Here is the letter annotated with letters from the PERSUADER mnemonic to show the persuasive techniques being used:

I am writing to complain about the slow internet service currently available to me and to demand that the installation of fibre to my district is brought forward. Unbelievably, internet speed here is currently averaging 256 kbps, (E2) which is about as fast as a snail goes! (D) Honestly, could you cope with this kind of service? (R1)

In order for my island to be able to compete in the modern world of business we need to be quick, efficient and effective. (D) We cannot do this when an email takes two weeks to load! (D)

Picture the scene: I am sitting in my home-office, fingers poised above the keys. An order comes in for my Mam's Original Bammy, which she makes fresh every day. I reply to the enquiry, offer to ship that afternoon. (A) And then I wait…and wait…and wait. (R2) The bread would be mouldy before they received my reply! (E1) This is not good enough! It is a disgrace!

If I could reply swiftly, I could employ more people like my Mum – honest, good people who want to work and have unique skills to offer. I could build my business and start giving something back to my community. (S)

I know you (P) will say that you've been working on this. (U) I know that my cousin on the Caymans has a full 10 mps. Well is that any use to me? When is fibre coming to my town? When will I be allowed to join the twenty-first century? When? (R1 and 2)

2

Effect	Analysis
impact	*Personal Address: The advert seems to be sending out a dare, which gets the reader's attention.*
sensory appeal	*I can almost taste the food because the picture is so vivid.*
conveying emotion	*The beach scene makes us feel comfortable and positive.* *The tornado suggests drama and the power of the sauce.*

3

Technique	Effect
Evidence: 'internet speed here is currently averaging 256kbps'	Facts reinforce the impact of the argument.
Device – exaggeration (hyperbole): 'which is about as fast as a snail goes'	This creates a visual picture which in turn reinforces the argument.
Rhetorical question: 'Honestly, could you cope with this kind of service?'	This engages the reader.
Device – power of three: 'quick efficient, and effective'	This reinforces the key idea of what the writer wants.
Device – exaggeration: 'when an email takes two weeks to load!'	This adds impact to the key idea of slowness, which is at the centre of the writer's complaint.
Anecdote: 'Picture the scene'	This helps us to visualize the issue and empathise.
Repetition: 'And then I wait…and wait…and wait.'	This emphasises the key idea of slowness.
Emotive images: 'The bread would be mouldy before they received my reply!'	Strong visual image which evokes disgust and emphasises the key idea of the slowness.
So what?: 'If I could…'	This helps the reader to see the impact of the issue by imagining what things would be like if it was not a problem.
Personal address: 'I know you will say'	Makes the reader sit up and take notice.
Undercut your opposition: 'I know you will say that you've been working on this.'	Mention an argument the reader might want to use themselves and takes the power from them.
Rhetorical question: 'When will I be allowed to join the twenty-first century? When?'	Re-engages the reader and shows strength of feeling.

4 c)

5 a)

6 b)

7 c)

8 b)

6.4 Understanding presentation in adverts

1 The font used in the advert is simple but quite formal, suggesting calm but also high standards. Even the curly brackets imply 'high quality'. The font matches the emphasis on being a 'better' type of tourist (so having high standards). It also matches the idea of being calm and then being 'at one' with the place.

2 The blue and white colours suggest freshness and clarity – a sense of healthy and natural wellbeing.

3 This advert appeals to our sense of wanting to fit in, using the idea of belonging and also of doing our best – in this case for the environment. The picture also suggests that it is a healthy place to go, which appeals to our sense of health and well-being.

4 The heading plays with the word 'golden' which describes the sand and sun literally, but in its other sense, refers to the 'moments' which will be treasured and valuable, like gold. The third meaning refers to the top awards the company has won– 'gold' being associated with winning a top medal or prize.

5

Effect	Questions to ask yourself
Impact	*The header is big and it makes me understand that the resort will be welcoming and be somewhere I will want to be and perhaps return to, because I can relax there.*
Sensory appeal	*The picture of the resort and the gentle colour palette of blues, whites and greens to help me to visualize and even 'hear' the quiet calm resort.*
Conveying emotion	*The wordplay and the images make me want to be there, which makes me feel a kind of longing myself.*

6 c)

7 b)

8 c)

Practice questions for Paper 1 marking guidance

Question	Correct answer	Question	Correct answer
1	b)	31	b)
2	c)	32	b)
3	a)	33	d)
4	d)	34	d)
5	b)	35	b)
6	b)	36	c)
7	c)	37	d)
8	a)	38	b)
9	b)	39	b)
10	c)	40	c)
11	c)	41	c)
12	b)	42	d)
13	d)	43	d)
14	a)	44	a)
15	a)	45	c)
16	c)	46	c)
17	a)	47	b)
18	d)	48	b)
19	c)	49	b)
20	b)	50	b)
21	a)	51	c)
22	a)	52	c)
23	c)	53	c)
24	c)	54	b)
25	d)	55	d)
26	c)	56	c)
27	b)	57	d)
28	d)	58	b)
29	c)	59	b)
30	a)	60	d)

Answers to Paper 2

Chapter 1 Writing a summary

1.1 Identifying the main ideas

1 a) A person, probably someone famous: his best moments or perhaps music

   b) Nature article – mentions 'killer whales'

   c) Celebrity article

   d) News article – dramatic

2 c) and d)

3 d)

4 It deals with cats not people.

5 We learn that there was an inspection, who did it and how the cats had died.

6 Statistics (eights cats poisoned and four unexplained) and specific names, as well as a comment from a witness.

7 For example: *Poison is the main cause of death but four fatalities are still unexplained.*

8 a)

9 The abilities the ocelot has which help them catch prey.

10 The last sentence is the topic sentence because it mentions the ocelot's features and links them to its prey.

11 Paragraph 1: Navassa has not had a very happy or productive history; people have fought and died over it.
Paragraph 2: It has become a National Wildlife Refuge; it has a very varied, rich underwater life.

1.2 Identifying opinions

1 Fact: *The Bahamas have traditionally been the strongest team in the men's CBC championship with seven gold medals.*
Opinion: *They have great coaches and great individual players.*
Fact: *In addition, in the 2015 women's tournament final, the Bahamas beat Jamaica 55–51.*
Opinion: *Every man, woman and child in the Bahamas will be desperate for their teams to continue their dominance.*

2 b)

3 c)

4 Local dialects have enriched pop music.

5 100 years ago, working-class children were dominant in competitive sport while upper-class children did non-competitive activities. After World War II, middle-class and upper-class children began to overtake those from the working classes in competitive sport. The implied opinion is that this is unequal and unfair.

6 Poorer children do not have the same opportunities as middle- and upper-class children in many areas of life.

7 Competitive sport is very popular among children in the USA, especially the middle classes. Fact. About 100 years ago, lower-class children dominated competitive sport. Fact.
After World War II, middle- and upper-class children began to dominate in sport, as they do in other areas of life. Fact.

8 Sample answer: *About a century ago, in the USA, lower-class children, especially those from migrant families, participated in competitive sport. However, after World War II, middle- and upper-class children began dominating sport. Nowadays this has spread to a range of areas of life, such as work and education.*

1.3 Paraphrasing and using your own words

1 Suggested synonyms: fur = hair; stripe = line or band; paw = foot; fang = tooth; scent = odour; prey = quarry; habitat = home

2 *Gifts* are a(n) <u>key/important/unmissable</u> part of any party. But they can <u>burden</u> us, too. For example, the cost can be <u>unaffordable/ridiculous/out of reach</u>; nowadays, people <u>demand</u> more and more, and it can be <u>humiliating/upsetting</u> if you can't afford something <u>wonderful/fabulous</u> or <u>special/original</u>.

3 *<u>A huge number of sportsmen and women</u> gathered at the island's annual awards ceremony last night. <u>Drink</u> was flowing as the speeches carried on into the night. Finally, when it was all done, people spilled out of the hotel and awaited <u>vehicles</u> that carried them off into the night.*

4 a)

Original version	Gina's version
This endangered species, like so many others, is quite stunning to look at. Twice the size of an average domestic cat, it has sleek, smooth fur, which can vary in colour and pattern from cream to reddish-brown, with highly visible black patches, which often come together to form curved stripes. The face is also striped, lined in black on either side – like a wonderful miniature leopard or panther. Visually, the ocelot is highly attractive to poachers.	Though under threat, it is an impressive creature. It is double the size of a house cat with soft hair and colourful stripes and notable black spots. Its appearance attracts hunters.

b) 'Size', 'cat', 'stripes', 'black'

c) She leaves out the comparison with the leopard, as it does not add anything important.

5 a) <u>Giving food</u> to animals at the zoo is not advisable unless monitored by staff.

b) <u>Where extinction has occurred</u>, 'rewilding' or reintroducing species is one solution.

6 Possible response: *Numbers are rising because of efforts to limit threats such as predators, poachers and loss of habitat.*

7 heavy = weighty; easier = simpler; incredibly difficult = extremely hard; attempting = efforts; favourite = preferred; trade = market/business; accept = agree to/take in; survive = live/keep going.

8 Paragraph 1: Caimans are mostly water-based creatures; similar to crocodiles, they are powerful and can swim well.

Paragraph 2: Very difficult to raise in captivity, but many now sold privately despite rearing problems.

9 Students own response.

1.4 Structuring a summary

1 Bahamian music and its history.

2 'Proximity to the US' ('nearness' in original), 'power of empires', 'troubles and triumphs'.

3 It is quite accurate but does not mention the 700 islands or the way influences have merged.

4 Possible response: *Storytelling at heart of Bahamian music; lots of well-known songs and artists have their roots in Bahamian music.*

5 Possible response: *Storytelling is at the heart of Bahamian music, drawing on biblical and historical accounts; furthermore many well-known songs and popular artists have their roots in Bahamian music.*

6 <u>After that</u> black power was less prominent, and the election of President Obama <u>masked</u> the problems in society. The killing of Trayvon Martin <u>changed</u> everything. <u>From that time onwards</u> black people fought to get their voices heard.

7 The end.

8 Possible response: *In the future, world powers must address fairness for black people, otherwise having a black US president was in vain. 'Black Power' demonstrated people would not put up with ill-treatment.*

Chapter 2 Writing an informative text

2.1 Understanding the conventions of informative texts

1 It tells the reader the situation/the letter's purpose; it is clear that the letter is intended to tell the employer he is not coming to the interview.

2 The letter needs to be set out in a more formal, recognisable way. It should include clearer information about time, date and purpose of writing. The tone should be more polite and respectful.

3 This version of the letter is set out in a more recognisable, formal way. It offers information about time, date, purpose of writing. It uses a polite and respectful tone.

4 In the first sentence. The letter begins by thanking the reader, which is not the most important information.

5 a) Nothing – We don't find out anything about the writer of the article other than her name.

b) This is different from the letter, which focuses on the writer himself.

6 Both are divided into paragraphs dealing with separate points.

7 a) Newspaper article in local paper. The purpose is to recount what happened on a visit to the centre and why you are concerned.

b) Perspective is that of a reporter, with local people/readers as the audience.

8 Sample grid:

Start	Quick summary of where I went and why, which was new sports centre to report about facilities.
Middle	Specific details about the poor facilities and state of the building and its features.
End	Account of conversation with rude manager, and appeal to those in charge to address the situation.

2.2 Understanding content, audience and purpose

1 c), d) and f)

2 a) disappointed because it was a new restaurant, so the writer might have expected it to be good; cross because no one likes to be spoken to in a nasty way.

3 b) is appropriate.
a) is too impersonal and not local.
c) is too specific/professional – not suitable for people who are not food experts.

4 Possible response: *Compared with the Blue Crab just down the road, the whole place looked drab and unappealing. Pictures on the wall were pale and hung at funny angles and hadn't been dusted. Tables were made of cheap plastic and ours had a cigarette burn in the middle, which was strange as smoking wasn't allowed!*

5 Lack of detail about the food, for example

6 The tone is too chatty/conversational.

7 Possible response: *I hoped dessert would be better, but it turned out to be just as bad. I had ordered Peach Melba, but I was given two very dry slices of*

peach and the raspberry sauce tasted bitter. As for the ice cream, it had completely melted and was like a creamy, grey lake.

8 Possible notes:
- Purpose/audience: to review the festival for readers of the paper.
- Tone: positive, formal but with a friendly tone.
- Factual details: could be names of bands, who the organiser was, what they said.
- Features or conventions: first paragraph should include who, what, where, when and why.

9 Possible opening paragraph: *The Straight-Outa-Jail Festival, which took place last night on Gold Beach, was the brainchild of organiser Jay Taylor and was run by ex-prisoners raising money to help orphans find suitable families. Featuring music from lots of well-known local bands, it was a great event which showed there is life after time inside.*

2.3 Writing clear and accurate sentences

1 Possible response: *The coastal road is full of potholes and <u>boulders often fall from the cliffs</u>. In addition, it is too narrow so buses <u>have to swerve into the middle of the road</u>.*
Although there are plenty of 'slow down' signs, drivers <u>often race at breakneck speeds</u>.
However, the worst spot is the u-bend at the bottom because <u>you cannot see oncoming traffic</u>.

2 Compound: a); Complex: b) and c)

3 Possible final sentence: *If we don't address the problem, it will just get worse.*

4 Future tense

5 *I (attend) the festival on Gold Beach yesterday, which (is) fantastic. The festival was run by ex-prisoners who now call themselves 'JayBirds' rather than 'Jailbirds' after their founder, Jay Taylor, who (does) a stretch inside prison until he was released last year. It (is) his idea to set up the festival.*
<u>The festival featured local artists. There was Mama Rag there. Also, there was reggae group, HiFive.</u>
<u>Officially, it was on from 11 in the morning yesterday till 11 at night. In fact, it finished at past three in the morning!</u> Those tunes are still in my head. It was a really wonderful day and night.
<u>I spoke to organiser Jay. It was when the music had finally stopped.</u> He (says), 'If we get the funding we'll do it next year.' I say 'Amen to that!'.

6 Possible response: *I attended the festival on Gold Beach yesterday, which was fantastic. The festival was run by ex-prisoners who now call themselves 'JayBirds' rather than 'Jailbirds' after their founder, Jay Taylor, who did a stretch inside prison until he was released last year. It was his idea to set up the festival.*

The festival featured local artists such as Mama Rag and reggae group, HiFive. Officially, it was on from 11 in the morning yesterday till 11 at night, but in fact it finished at past three in the morning! Those tunes are still in my head. It was a really wonderful day and night.
I spoke to organiser Jay after the music had finally stopped. He said, 'If we get the funding we'll do it next year.' I say, 'Amen to that!'

2.4 Structuring informative texts

1 Possible plan:
a) *Setting off from Handy Andy's bike hire shop in Bequia by the harbour.*
b) *Noticing the trail entrance, deciding to explore, lovely scenery.*
c) *Going up the trail – wildlife seen.*
d) *Meeting other people – who they were.*
e) *Returning – feelings at end.*

2 Possible next paragraphs:

change of time or location	*The local toilet block wasn't much better. The women's was closed and the men's had not been cleaned. There was no running water or hand-drying facilities.*
change of idea or point being made	*The council have known about this situation for a long time, but nothing has been done. They have promised to tackle the litter problem, but have failed to do so.*
change of person or perspective	*However, when I questioned a local boat owner he told me that the workers responsible for clearing up had all been sacked after a dispute over money. No wonder the place looked so bad!*

3 *<u>Initially</u> I was delighted with the hotel. <u>For a start</u>, the room was spacious <u>and</u> there was an airy balcony running the length of the room. <u>Over</u> the bed were attractive prints of the local area, encouraging me to explore. <u>However</u>, not everything was as it seemed. <u>Under</u> the bed, I could see several large creepy-crawlies, <u>which</u> gave me a shudder. <u>As a result</u>, I rushed to reception <u>and</u> asked to change rooms.*

4 a) *<u>Underneath/below/beneath</u> the bridge, there were huge holes in the road which we had to swerve <u>around</u> to avoid.*
b) *<u>Because/as a result</u> of lack of spending by the government, minor roads are in a terrible state <u>so/which means</u> accidents are frequent.*
c) *<u>However</u>, we all need to take responsibility to improve our environment <u>or</u> we won't be able to enjoy our own sights and sounds.*

5 Possible plan:

Section/paragraph	Focus
1	*Careers meeting with Ms Davenport in school library.*
2	*What I told her about my ambitions – to work in technology, run my own business.*
3	*Our discussion about my skills – good at technology, good at maths and science.*
4	*Specific things I could do – develop my own music or gaming apps.*
5	*Ms Davenport's encouraging response but advice to keep options open.*
6	*Next steps – what college courses would help me develop.*

6 Possible first two paragraphs:
I had a meeting on Tuesday 5 April with Ms Davenport, our careers adviser, in the school library. She had asked me to come prepared to discuss my ambitions and the sorts of careers I thought I was suited to.
At first, I talked rather generally about wanting to work in technology, which was rather vague and aimless. I also mentioned wanting to run my own business, but was not able to say exactly what the business would be.

Chapter 3 Writing a narrative

3.1 Structuring and resolving stories effectively

1 a) He thinks his wallet has been stolen so he cannot pay for the meal.
  b) Conflicts could be with the restaurant because he cannot pay; with the new girl; with his brother.

2 b), d), c), a)

3 He might lose the girl's number. She might refuse to see him again.

4 Leroy's choices: to borrow money from his brother; whether to tell his girlfriend he can't pay; how to deal with the situation of having no money; whether to call his girlfriend to ask for another chance.

Reactions: brother helps Leroy; girlfriend storms off; manager's anger with Leroy

Consequences: Leroy may or may not anger his brother for borrowing money, then losing it or forgetting it; his girlfriend may not forgive him.

5 Students' own choices. They may feel that Hook 4 is slightly less compelling, but it does use speech which makes the opening very immediate.

6 Any reasonable ideas that relate to the character seeming isolated, reflective or sad – staring downwards; mention the bus stop.

7 Any ending that fits and completes the plot sequence.

8 Possible alternative plan:
- **Introduction:** *Older man is sitting at bus stop when he is approached by a young adult.*
- **Complication:** *They start chatting – the young adult realises the older person suffers from memory loss and does not know how to get home.*
- **Rising action:** *Young adult takes the man to his home address.*
- **Climax:** *It is the wrong house! A group of noisy inhabitants tell them to get lost.*
- **Resolution:** *A neighbour comes out and explains the man's family moved many years ago. She has the new address. The young adult is able to take the man back to his home and his family.*

9 Examples in third person:
- *As **he** sat at the bus-stop **he** remembered getting off the plane…*
- *'Is this the place I grew up?' **he** thought as **he** looked around the modern airport…*
- ***He** looked at **his** daughter across the room in her beautiful wedding dress, tears streaming down her face. 'Get out!' she cried.*
- *There he was, **her** father, back after all these years, at **her** wedding!*

10 Any ideas that effectively relate to the given stimulus, provided they use the five-point structure. This could be an *in media res* beginning, for example.

11 Any ideas that effectively reflect the photograph provided are fine, provided they have the five-point structure.

12 Students' own responses.

13 Students' own responses.

3.2 Developing vocabulary for characters and settings

1 b)

2 'rich juicy fruits', 'freshly baked loaves'

3 'lightning', 'snake', 'knives'

4 *Above him, he could see a tiny slit of blue sky like a <u>mirage/oasis/finger/lizard</u> in the side of a wall. He called out for help but the walls answered back, <u>laughing/sneering</u> at him, mocking him. He should never have tried the climb; he didn't have the skills. Shame burned inside him like <u>fire/coals</u>.*

5 a) Where: harbour; weather: hurricane season/ strengthening wind; when: hurricane season; first day back at school.

b) Connections to the plot: His father is 'out at sea' so he is possibly in danger. Jayden's job is to get home and make house safe.

c) Dramatic mood: will Jayden make it in time? His anxiety and the strengthening wind both suggest time is running out.

6 'howled', 'roared', 'grappled', 'rammed', 'flung open', 'rattling', 'forced', 'pricking'.

7 His lips 'sensed salt' so we know the sea has created a flood, it is not just the wind he has to worry about.

8 Possible paragraphs:
She opened the window and climbed out. That was the easy bit – what came next was far more difficult. Three floors below, no one stirred at midnight in the cool, breathless street. She had endured enough: enough of the bullying man and red-faced, cruel-eyed woman. Slowly, she felt her way down the wobbling drain-pipe, her flimsy maid's outfit occasionally getting caught on rusty nails protruding from the shabby apartment block that had been her prison for the last year.

3.3 Effective speech and dialogue in stories

1 *Ray hesitated, clutching the small gift in his hands. He felt ridiculous.*

'I guess you don't want my present then?' he asked.

'The only thing I want from you is for you to leave,' Linda said, wiping away her tears. 'You think one present can make up for all those missing years?'

Ray put the damaged photo frame down on a nearby table.

'Of course not. I'm sorry I spoiled your big day.'

He paused for a moment, then turned and walked out.

2 a) Ray has arrived to surprise his daughter at her wedding. He has been away from her for a long time.

b) Ray thought it was a good idea – but then realises it was not. His daughter is upset as she says him coming and the present do not make up for the past.

3 The final line of speech suggests that Deon did not expect to see the Shana again/alive. Did he arrange for her to be killed?

4 Shana has the most power: Deon's responses show he 'stammers' and is sweating. Clearly he is shocked to see her.

5 Possible rewritten dialogue:
'Thought I'd be driftin' in that boat out in the storm until a big wave came and knocked me overboard?' Shana grabbed Deon's hair and pulled his head back. 'You'd have liked that?'
'That wasn't my intention, honest!' Deon struggled to free himself, but Shana's powerful fist held firm. 'I meant to tell you about the smuggling...I didn't know the boat would sink...'

6 Formal, standard English is used to convey politeness/class of man getting off the boat.

More informal, chatty language and dialect convey the local man's speech.

7 The lines of dialogue produced should reflect the styles of the two characters as noted above.

8 Possible dialogue:
The mother wandered in a half-mad daze from counter to counter, finally stopping at the perfume section where a neatly manicured woman filed her nails.
'Can I help, madam?' said the woman, without taking her eyes off her hand.
'My child! My only child...five years old, she's gone missing,' cried the mother.
The assistant finally looked up. She seemed bored; this happened all the time.
'What does she look like?' she asked, eventually.
'Tiny, small for her age. Ringlets. She...she had a doll, though maybe she dropped it...I don't know. Please...'
Tears ran down her face, smudging a sample of foundation on the counter.

3.4 Writing meaningful sentences and paragraphs

1 We are told that the girl puts the ring in her pocket, which suggests that she wants to hide it and not show she is engaged.

2 The word 'slyly' means in a cunning, rather underhand way, which suggests that the girl is acting in a deceitful way.

3 a) She has a boyfriend/fiancé called Robbie. She just got engaged.

b) She is misleading Robbie, perhaps.

4 Possible response: *Robbie watched Shelley from the shadows, even though he found it difficult to believe she was betraying him.*

5 a) She originally looked down on Robbie. She has changed – now she loves him, although she cannot understand it.

b) Two longer multi-clause sentences are followed by two short ones.

c) The short penultimate sentence emphasises the surprise – her sudden realisation. It is final.

6 'After several minutes of silence', 'Finally', 'However'

7 'Again'. It tells us that she keeps falling asleep – perhaps she has been drugged?

8 *After a while, Deonte awoke again, properly this time. She got out of the bed and checked the door but it was locked. During the next few minutes she banged on it again and again, shouting to be released. Yet/But/However no one came.*

9 Possible answer: *She had been working in the luxury spa treatment room when the rumour that pirates were alongside the ship started spreading. At first she hadn't believed it, but suddenly, her colleague Lucy rushed into the room and cried, 'Hide! They've boarded!' That was the beginning of the nightmare.*

10 Possible response:

Stuttering and juddering through the air, the little plane rocked and rolled in the storm. It was no good. He could no longer control the plane and he had no choice. He would have to crash land. He cut the motor and went into a controlled dive. Even though the water rushed up to meet him, he wasn't scared. He had done everything he could, but now it was in the hands of God. The plane skidded on the water, and flipped over, and he felt the world turned upside down. The dark blue water flooded in, but he pulled himself clear through the smashed side-window. He had crashed on the shoreline. He emerged from the wreckage and looked around. He was safe, but utterly alone.

Chapter 4 Writing an argumentative text

4.1 Effective ways of arguing a point of view

1 c)

2 a)

3 d)

4 Purpose: give view on how donation should be spent; role: student councillor; audience: school council

5 Against the ban.

6 Possible further arguments:
- Why pick on fast-food outlets? What about shops that sell cigarettes?
- Fast-food can be healthy and nutritious – it is better to educate the businesses.
- It is better to educate students to eat healthily, not ban things that just makes them rebel.

7 The first counters point c) from the original list. The second counters point b) about taxes.

8 Students often make choices based on poor information; if left to their own devices they will not discriminate between good and unhealthy food.

9 Possible other ways donation could be spent (students can suggest any within limits of amount available):
- buying some up-to-date tablets for poorer or disadvantaged students to use
- restocking the school library with books chosen by students
- bringing in a motivational speaker or speakers to inspire students
- improving the 'look' of the school: displays, signage, flowers in entrance, etc.

10 Answers will vary.

4.2 Using an appropriate tone and language

1 **a)** The letter opening is good because the student mentions the purpose for writing to the principal. He also gives a reason: 'I learn better from doing things'.

b) The letter sounds almost disrespectful and too familiar/personal – 'you probably don't have time for anything enjoyable'. The student also says that 'school isn't so important' to him, which is likely to irritate the principal.

2 The student:
- acknowledges the importance of study and school as a place of learning
- puts forward the idea that his own development will make him a better member of the school community
- flatters the principal with the idea of the school getting some reflected glory through the school flag being shown publically.

3 'wiser, brighter and better'

4 'imagine me proudly planting the school flag at the top of an icy peak'. This is effective because it is the school flag that is being displayed.

5 'surely the student who returns will be twice the one who left?'

6 The first text is informal: it features abbreviations 'gotta', 'cos', etc., and also some informal vocabulary – 'grouse'; it is grammatically incorrect: 'no one' instead of 'anyone'.

7 The tone could be seen as urgent and emotive in the first – a sense of personal engagement; in the second, the tone could be seen as authoritative and clear, but it lacks the same sense of emotive power.

8 Possible opening paragraph:

Dear Mr Martinez,

As you know, I have always loved music. Well, the opportunity has arisen for me to pursue this passion for a very short period of time. As you know, I value my work for you and I would like to thank you for employing me, but this chance to tour the Caribbean with my band for six months is a once-in-a-lifetime event. I hope you won't feel I am letting you down by leaving, will you?

9 Possible words relating to each topic:

Healthy eating	Dangerous dogs	Designer brands	Homelessness
diet, well-being, fibre, organic produce, fitness, calories, carbohydrate, balance	*muzzle (concrete), aggression (abstract), snarl, jaw, chain, coat, anger, thug*	*logo, fashion, style, trend, suit, catwalk, mannequin, season, flair, unique, glamour, retail*	*shelter, humanity, donation, food-bank, pity, empathy, winter, desperation*

10 Any relevant examples of the four language features.

11 Possible responses (first paragraph of each):
   a) FOR (relatively formal in tone, authoritative)
      The well-being of students must be paramount in our schools. It is for this reason that I recommend adopting the idea of compulsory self-defence classes for all students. For too long, students have been powerless, weak and fragile in the face of aggression from adults and other students. Who would deny them the chance to lead a peaceful existence?
   b) AGAINST (tone – is formal, but less so than for the above, possibly more personal/emotive)
   So, the idea that we all need to take self-defence classes has been proposed. I am utterly against this ridiculous idea. I mean, can you really believe it? By making us act aggressively, the school board thinks it will stop violence. Are they out of their minds? I can just imagine what would happen if I laid my weak little hands on some lout who was attacking another person; it would mean me getting hurt, too. Far better to call for help from professionals, don't you think?

4.3 Explaining, expanding and illustrating an argument

1 c)

2 Statistics from a survey are used.

3 Possible responses:
   a) *In my school, <u>60 out of 75 students questioned</u> told me that they had visited a fast-food outlet in the past week. That is an incredible <u>50%</u> increase on last year when I carried out the same survey.*
   b) *Fast-food now accounts for <u>around half</u> of the average teenager's diet, according to <u>Doctor Phil McBelly</u> of the <u>National Eat Well</u> Institute*

4 It suggests that not having a 'permanent home' also defines homelessness; if you are moving from place to place, always in temporary accommodation, this can also mean being 'without a home'.

5 Possible response: *I am sure you all agree that healthy eating is a 'good thing', but what exactly is it? Well, my definition is eating food that is fresh and ideally without harmful additives to enhance shape or colour. But fresh food alone isn't enough.*

6 The writer contrasts the image of New York we usually think of (with modern buildings and exciting experiences) with a ramshackle, run-down place overcome by water. The article might be about global warming and the problems of rising water levels worldwide.

7 Causes given for disappearing coral reefs: increase in sponges, result of over-fishing which means they have no predators.
   Effect: they destroy other life forms on coral reefs.

8 Some possible responses:
   a) *People's busy lives have meant that when it comes to food they are much more likely to <u>select processed foods that need little preparation, but which have increased preservatives and chemicals.</u>*
   b) *The popularity of basketball is hardly surprising when you consider <u>that all you need is a ball and a small backyard, corner of a street or wall in which to bounce it.</u>*
   c) *The West Indies cricket team's success in the 2016 World 2020 has led to <u>a renewed interest in the islands' cricket teams and support for less well-known players.</u>*

9 Arguments for/against mobile phone-free weekends:
   For: encourage more talking/discussion; less need to 'keep up' with friends and feel envy at what they are doing; better for eyes and brain to do something physical or active; increase family social interaction.
   Against: less security if children are out and about, and out of contact; miss out on latest gossip, sport or news; can't take pictures/photos easily of special moments or events.

10 Possible response:
   Last weekend I lost my mobile phone. It was my own stupid fault. For some reason I had decided to tidy my room and rearrange the furniture and that's when it happened: the phone disappeared, as if into a black hole, and try as I might, I couldn't find it.

   Instead of having the latest hits playing in my head as I walked along the street to do the shopping, I had the drone of cars and lorries, the screech of brakes and the shouts and cries of noisy gangs and groups by the side of the road.

   It was like losing a close friend for 24 hours, losing the thing that was most precious to me, and the thing I depended on for my news, my social life and my entertainment.

4.4 Structuring an argument

1 The point of view relates to not having access to a mobile phone, and addresses both sides of the debate. It uses counter-argument (not having a phone's benefits) to introduce the real point of view – the problems it causes.

2 The 'all together' structure.

3 b) is the best option to complete the sentence because it contains the specific 'follow-up' details to support the topic sentence.

4 *I personally have no objection to having an iconic modern celebrity as a statue in the main square, <u>although</u> I think a statue has to be one that everyone accepts, young or old. <u>Furthermore</u>, I would select a figure from Caribbean history <u>as it</u> should be someone who has had a real impact on the way we are viewed by the world.*

5 Key words: *You are the <u>member of a local youth group</u> who have been asked to give their views <u>to the regional corporation</u> on a <u>proposal to open a new facility for young people in your area</u>. One proposal is to <u>build a new skateboarding park.</u>*

Write the speech you would give to the corporation, outlining your views on the proposal.

6 **For:** quite popular amongst young people; active/ healthy; attract sporty people, but also those who think it's cool; let off steam/energy. **Against:** not accessible to everyone – what about disabled? Not universally popular. Tends to be more popular (though not exclusively) with boys. Encourage gangs who use it as meeting point?

7 Any appropriate set of points and organisation is acceptable.

8 Any appropriate method of organisation or structuring is acceptable.

9 **Possible paragraph:** *Firstly, having a place to let off steam and physical energy is vital for young people. They need this because so many other outdoor activities are now closed off to them due to cost or access, such as cricket. In addition, it is a place where new friendships can be forged and different ages can meet and chat, all with a common interest.*

Chapter 5 Practice questions for Paper 2

1 Summary task

Plan: five main points

1 Shark attacks are more likely in North America and South Africa than the Caribbean

2 Sharks often mistake humans for fish due to poor visibility in those areas

3 You can reduce attacks by swimming in groups

4 Wear things that don't glitter or shine

5 Learn to recognise a shark's behaviour when it is uneasy

Sample summary response

Sharks' physical abilities and appearance are scary but research by the University of Florida has shown attacks in the Caribbean are rare compared with North America and South Africa. This is partly due to the contrasting cold and warm water conditions, which attract a variety of sharks to South Africa, and higher numbers of people swimming throughout the year in North America. Also, in those areas sharks often mistake humans for fish due to poor visibility but less surf in the Caribbean means sharks avoid people. In any case, you can avoid attack by swimming in groups, avoiding clothing that gleams or shines, and learning to recognise a shark's potentially threatening behaviour, such as darting swimming movements.

Comment

The five key points broadly cover the content of the original text and the summary mostly manages to convert these into longer, more detailed sentences using synonyms and paraphrasing.

2 Letter task

Sample notes/plan

My address/address sent to

Greeting

Para 1 Give reason for writing and situation – beauty spot, dangers

Para 2 Develop – more details about what happened

Para 3 Conclude – what I feel needs to be done – better security, inspection, etc.

Sign-off

Sample letter response

7, Greenway Drive
Kingshill

The Manager
Kingshill Tourist Office
Bay Road
Kingshill
June 30th, 2021

Dear Sir/Madam,

I am writing to express my concern regarding safety at one of our most popular beauty spots, Rock Hill Look-out. I visited it yesterday at 3 p.m. with a friend and her family but was especially troubled by two aspects; the information provided in advance, and the actual safety issues at the site.

The leaflet I picked up from your office stated that Rock Hill Look-out was 'ideal for small children to explore', which was clearly not the case. For example, there was no hand-rail on the worn stone steps down to the beach. In addition, there were no changing or toilet facilities for families, and the picnic-site was far too small for the number of visitors. We were very disappointed and returned home but not before my friend's little girl tripped going up the uneven steps from the beach.

I would like to suggest that your leaflet is updated to reflect the fact that the site is not currently suitable for families with young children. Moreover, the facilities need to be improved to make Rock Hill more accessible and welcoming for family groups.

I look forward to receiving your response.

Yours sincerely,

Leticia Floyd

Comment

The plan is very basic – more of a structure but does the job of providing a simple pathway. The letter itself is very well-structured, uses the right register and tone and is clear and concise. The format is correct, and all core details from the task are addressed.

3 Picture prompt: Short story

Possible plan

Plot: mother agrees to allow son (aged 8) to walk to school on own for first time/terrible storm/she searches for him/sees child in river – dives in saves it/ not her son, but he's safe. Hook – story will open with storm starting.

Sample story response

No one had predicted the storm. So, when the black clouds swept across the bay, her heart sank. She should never have let him walk on his own to school! But Trey had been asking and asking and in the end she had given in. Now, school had finished and he wasn't back. The thin fence in front of the house had blown over like a cheap pack of cards, and the drains were overflowing with stinking, grey water. The wind howled like a furious beast and thunder rumbled on the horizon.

She reversed the car out of the drive, and slowly crawled up the street which was more like a river than a road. Figures passed her, hunched over like ghosts, and she had to screw her eyes up to see her way. At one point, she came across a figure she recognised – her neighbour Rita with a tiny, drenched rat by her side.

'Have you seen Trey?' she cried, leaning out.

'No,' said Rita, 'playground was empty when I got there except for Grace.' Her daughter smiled at her through the barrage of rain.

Mrs Lamont carried on to the bridge near the school, and parked up. Getting out, she was almost knocked off her feet by the gale, but steadied herself on the steel railing. Beneath her, the river was a frothing monster. If Trey…no, it didn't bear thinking about.

Then, she saw it – a boy in the river below! Surely she'd imagined it? No – after disappearing under a swell, he popped up again. She raced along the bridge, and half-slid down the muddy bank to the water's edge. The river was rising rapidly and waves kept slamming into her.

'Here!' she shouted, wading out. By complete chance, the current was bringing the child her way, and as the figure floundered near her, she grabbed an arm. For a moment, the current threatened to win the battle and drag him off, but she held tight and yanked him out. They both flopped down on the bank, exhausted. It wasn't Trey, but Sam, one of Trey's friends.

'What happened Sam?' she asked, helping him up. 'Where's Trey?'

The boy spat out some water, and half-sobbing told her.

'We was walking home, holding each other, but I… I slipped and fell down the bank. I couldn't help it, promise! I…I don't know where Trey is…Maybe, maybe he fell in too…or went to get help…'

It was a miracle she'd been there to save Sam, but two miracles were impossible. They slowly clambered further up. And then she saw him. Trey. He was huddled, sheltering under the bridge.

'Mama!' he cried.

He was safe.

Comment

The plan works well and it's helpful to think of the 'hook' before beginning. The story itself is managed very well with dialogue, action and description all dovetailing nicely together. The use of time at the start with the switch between tenses is impressive. The character of the mother is convincing, and the tension well-managed with a dramatic climax and resolution.

Written prompt: Short story

'As he did so, his eyes filled with tears'

Possible plan

'He' – older man surprised by kind act?

Conflict: narrator finds old man grumpy, irritable

Choices: will narrator's act of kindness turn sour?

Consequences – total shut off from old man, rejection

Other characters – not sure, possibly old man's daughter?

Plot – old, irritable man next door seems to reject friendship. Narrator finds out about estranged daughter, tries to bring them back together.

Possible story response

Most days he ignored me, but over time I got a gruff nod of the head when we couldn't avoid each other on the path by his shack. Sometimes, a delivery for him would come to me and, I might get a quick 'Thanks' when I dropped it round. We lived at the end of the same dusty old street and I'd heard on the grapevine that he'd once lived with his daughter but they'd fallen out years ago.

One day, a letter arrived for him. He never got any personal mail so I guess they just put it in with mine. I flipped over the pale blue envelope – on the back was a name and address – a nearby island, but not far. When I went round, the old man was out back, pulling out weeds from the sun-baked soil.

'Looks hard work,' I said.

Under his floppy hat, his face was lined with pain, and he rubbed his hand against his hip. He was like some wiry old root himself.

'Want somethin' sonny?' he asked.

'Here,' I handed him the envelope.

He took it and ripped it open. He glanced at it briefly. As he did so, his eyes filled with tears, or so it seemed. Maybe it was just sweat. Suddenly, he scrunched it up and threw it to one side.

'Junk mail' he growled, and stomped off into his shack.

When he was out of sight, I retrieved the screwed-up letter and smoothed it out. It was from her – his daughter. She wanted to make amends – she didn't say what for. And she wanted to visit. She'd left a number for him to phone, if he wanted to. I knew what I had to do.

A few weeks later, a grey jeep pulled up. A young woman in red-patterned trousers and a white top hopped out, holding a large bundle.

'Hey, you must be Sheryl,' I said.

'How is he?' she asked.

'Well, he's been having trouble getting around. I asked him if he wanted a doctor, but he told me to mind my own business.'

'Sounds like dad!' she said.

I walked with her to the door of the shack. I felt – well, responsible. When he opened the door, the shock on his face was palpable.

'Hello, dad,' his daughter said. 'I brought something for you.'

She pulled back the cover from the bundle, and a tiny, scrunched-up face stared out. 'Your grand-daughter'. The old man looked from me to her, and back.

'This your doing?' he glowered at me. I nodded. He paused as if unsure what to do. Finally he reached out, and took the bundle. He looked at his daughter again.

'I suppose you might as well come in, seein' as you've come all this way.'

Comment

The plan here is very effective, setting out some of the core storytelling aspects. The story itself establishes the character of the old man convincingly, though we learn less about the narrator. The dialogue advances the story well, and though there are not many of them, the uses of imagery help add detail and impact. The structure works well too, with a satisfying conclusion.

5 Persuasive article taks

Possible plan

Pts for: be able to keep closer track of students; will be a deterrent to bad behaviour; has been recommended by respected figures (local principals); CCTV common-place in city centres and shops; useful for evidence in a crime

Pts against: students need to be seen as learners, not prisoners; CCTV can be used to control not just deter crimes; there are other ways of improving security; costs a lot to implement and manage; students and other teachers need to be asked not just principals; too much surveillance in society already

Possible article response

WATCH OUT

Just the other day I was in a local sports shop checking out some new trainers when I suddenly heard a camera whizz and tilt towards me. Immediately I reddened as if I'd committed a crime. Who was watching me? There was no way of knowing. I left the shop without buying anything.

Now, principals of local schools are recommending we introduce CCTV on school sites but I think this would be a wrong move for several reasons: for the atmosphere they create, for their exorbitant costs and for their effectiveness – or lack of it.

Firstly, is it really right that a place of learning, where thought should be free, looks more like a prison than a school? A place where you constantly feel guilty even when you haven't done anything? I don't think so. We need to preserve the idea that schools are open, honest and personal, not the opposite.

Another consideration is cost. Some may claim that it is money well spent but just think of what else that money could be spent on. Surely new programmes of education or sporting or creative opportunities are more worthy of the expense? Crime and bad behaviour happen when students are bored. CCTV won't stop that – all it will do is move crime into the shadows, into the dark places where even cameras can't go.

Finally, I for one cannot support a move which will further develop our surveillance society. So much of our lives are now on show both on our phones or laptops that adding yet another prying eye seems an unnecessary and backward step. Please do not support this step towards even greater surveillance. Contact your children's schools. Reject the proposal. Chose freedom.

Comment

The basic plan of listing points for/against works well. The article itself is very effective in arguing a point of view, anticipating counter-arguments and using a number of persuasive devices such as rhetorical questions, anecdote, etc. The structure is clear with paragraphs used to signal the different points being made, and the call to action at the end provides a powerful conclusion.

Structure and mechanics: the basics

1 *Dwayne* <u>went</u> *to the ticket office but the people there wouldn't let* <u>him</u> *through without a ticket. He went back to Shelima, who* <u>was</u> *waiting by the car park and told her the news. She* <u>wasn't</u> *happy and* <u>stormed</u> *off.*

2 *Emerging from his tent, he quickly packed up the camp: tent bag; damp items of clothing; camping stove. It all fitted neatly into his ruck sack. His passport and partner's photograph went into his pocket.*

3 Either: a continuation of the story that effectively reflects the 'Danni' stimulus, provided one of the ways listed has been used (for change of time, place, person, speech, dramatic effect).

Or: two effective paragraphs expressing two different viewpoints about the good/bad effects of tourism.

Answers to SBA

1.1 Understanding the School-Based Assessment

Apply the skills: questions to the teacher about the SBA might include: how much time students will have, how many pieces of written work, whether they can choose their groups, what the deadlines are etc.

1.2 Selecting a theme and working as a team

1 The most relevant areas: *How social media damages body-image*; *Social media as a learning tool for teens*; *How social media helps teens keep connected* and *Online bullying*

   How mobile phones help gangs operate could relate to social media but 'gangs' may not include teens, and it may focus more on the use of mobile phones in general – untraceable numbers, etc.

   Online bullying could be improved by referencing teens in particular – 'effect of online bullying on teens'.

2 Students' own responses: two possible ideas – 'how companies use social media to target vulnerable users – for example, gamblers or 'shopaholics' who do not have money to spend so get into debt. 'how social media is used for 'gas lighting' and stalking – people using social media as a way to follow and control their partners' lives.

3 Students' own responses:

   Group leader: confident, respected and respectful, strong voice, clear-sighted, good listener

   Scribe/recorder: good listener, able to multi-task (listen, speak and make notes), good vocabulary, quick typist or quick, but clear handwriting.

   Time-keeper/manager: organised, mathematical (?), encouraging, good enforcer

   Report writer: good listener, fluent, skilled writer, co-operative with all of group

4 Possible definitions:

   Co-operative: able to work well with others

   Clear communicator: explains things or speaks in a way people can easily understand

   Good listener: listen to what others say without getting side-tracked, losing interest or making instant judgements.

   Positive and encouraging: seeing the best in things rather than the worst; ready to boost people's confidence by showing interest and highlighting good elements or aspects.

Focused on the task in hand: not distracted by irrelevant information or other issues that arise suddenly.

Could add: well-organised; reflective – able to evaluate performance of self or the group; 'finisher' – someone who is good at completing tasks – can help round things off, or write them up when needed.

5 There are many possible responses. Two further elements that could be added are:

   Environment – air and water quality?

   Box 2: [Damage– loss of diverse landscapes]

   One example of developing the diagram further: [species decline] – [fish] – [blue-fin tuna; red snapper]

6 a) They encourage D and help him to explain his idea, and suggest ways to focus it further.

   b) A seems to listen well – C perhaps interrupts before D can complete his initial points.

   c) A is also the leader, asking questions, encouraging both C and D. B is the note-taker.

Apply the skills: students' own responses

1.3 Planning your investigation

1 Students' own responses

2 There is no absolute fixed response here, but here are some matches:

   Print: books (fiction and non-fiction), manuals, articles, speeches, leaflets, blogs: newspaper, general interest or specialist magazine, school and public library, travel agency, shop.

   Visual: photographs, paintings, pictures, cartoons: newspaper, magazines, art gallery, app, shop, businesses.

   Moving image: video clips, music, features, and audio clips: art gallery/museum, television channel, app, live event, shop, market/stall.

   People: friends, family, teachers, college staff, etc can be sources for all the above but more particularly useful for interviews, surveys, oral evidence.

3 a) Most moving and still imagery is best accessed online, due to technological advantages There are some advantages to having physical copies of books or speaking to people in person – for example, experience of reading material in book form might help you engage with the material. Also some printed material is designed for physical use – such as posters or leaflets in public places.

   b) Advantages and disadvantages might revolve around availability and access, time to search or source specific information, portability, personal versus virtual engagement with material, sensory experiences, primary versus secondary evidence, etc.

4   Students' own responses could make an argument for any of these sources. However, the television programme in particular may be less suitable given its wide scope and the fact it is from 2007, so not very current.

Other sources of information might be direct evidence gained from talking to people who live or are affected by changes on the coastline. Another source would be contacting local agencies or charities who are involved with protecting the island environment.

5   Students' own responses: some may feel that the wider personal benefits – developing one's own voice/viewpoint and becoming informed about key issues, are towards the top of the list as opposed to the slightly narrower skills such as editing and assessing work.

6   Students' own responses

Apply the skills: students' own response using the prompts given.

1.4 Analysing and reflecting on print materials

1   In all these cases it very much depends on the specific piece, so these are just general points

   a)   **Newspaper website:** articles can be authoritative – will have gone through an editorial process – but writers can still have their own agendas, perspectives. Newspapers as a whole can also be biased or support one way of looking at things (e.g. support business).

   b)   **Personal blog:** as writer is also the publisher, it's very much one person's view – and not necessarily supported by academic or authoritative background. However, can provide first-hand evidence and witness to events or experiences.

   c)   **Academic report:** may be authoritative and useful for statistical data and evidence-based information, but may lack the personal, 'on the ground', perspective or the emotional perspective.

2   **Named writer** – so could be book or article. 'Newsday' address suggests something related to news online. The title – 'Save the…' sounds like an opinion – so the form is likely to be an online newspaper or magazine article, probably an 'opinion piece'.

   Audience would depend on knowing more but the title with its vocabulary, e.g. 'legacy', and the fact it is probably a news site suggests an adult audience.

3   a)   The turtles bring value in the form of tourism in Trinidad and Tobago.

   b)   Language choices in second paragraph: 'deep and immense value', 'natural assets', 'phenomenal beings', 'protected and nurtured'.

   c)   The main purpose is to create an emotional connection which goes beyond financial value (though also includes this) through the use of highly positive nouns and adjectives – 'deep and immense' suggests their loss would be profound. The use of the adjective 'phenomenal' suggests the turtles are unique and awe-inspiring. The verbs 'protected' and 'nurtured' are intended to suggest readers have a duty of care for them.

   d)   The purpose is to stimulate action (remember the title) on behalf of the reader and to create both an emotional reaction and a sense of action being needed to counter the range of threats.

   e)   The semantic field (negative terms related to threat or danger) is key: e.g. 'environmentally sensitive', 'range of threats', 'decreasing… populations', 'overharvesting', 'pollution', 'fatal… ingestions'.

4   c)   'Leatherback turtles are an endangered, precious resource which should be protected both for themselves and for the island economy.' (The other options are too narrow and address only one aspect of the article.)

5   Students' own response, but answer should probably be 'yes' as both evidence and persuasive language are present. The evidence – e.g reference to 'overharvesting' – is used to support the idea of threats, positive language such as 'grace us' and 'phenomenal' in praise of the turtles as rare and special; also, direct appeal to the reader (e.g. 'our shores') makes issue relevant to them.

6   Students' own responses. Possible response:

The writer's view is that the turtles represent something very precious to the islands both in terms of the 'significant mark' they make through tourism and their uniqueness, how 'phenomenal' they are. The writer uses emotive language referring to 'fatal… ingestion'; and the need to 'nurture' the turtles which supports her perspective. Quoting a tourism company leader might suggest they have a vested interest in protecting the turtles, but as the writer herself is a regular columnist who is presumably independent we can broadly trust her views.

Apply the skills

Form: is an online article; audience is probably 'Millennials' and 'Gen Zeros' judging by the fact the writer refers to both 'them' and 'us' so might be including herself in the comments she makes.

Focus of article: the different sorts of negative impact social media can have on young people, rather than (say) a specific focus on 'FOMO'.

Language: perhaps pick out vocabulary from, semantic field of social media: 'Millennials', 'influencers', 'curating', 'drop', 'like'. Also negative vocabulary around social media use: 'obsession', 'meaningless', 'taxing on our health', 'constant fear', 'pressures', 'depression', 'anxiety', etc. Later in article, more statistical and technical language: 'recent poll', 'respondents', 'result', 'research', 'neuroscientist', 'acute', etc.

The writer's perspective: it reveals the writer's view that constant social media use is damaging.

Effective qualities: it could be seen as effective in providing some 'real life' examples (people at gigs not enjoying the moment) and pressing emotional buttons in the reader with the constant references to the damage caused. Also, by including expert evidence at the end, this supports the argument made.

Level of trustworthiness: whilst the author is an online journalist, there is no sense they have a vested interest, except in perhaps being of a similar age to the people she talks about. There are a range of examples given of situations where social media is damaging but these are assertions and the claims are not supported until the second half of the extract in which the surveys are referred to and the expert witness from MIT is quoted. Overall, it is relatively trustworthy.

1.5 Analysing and evaluating data and images

1   Other potential features of the poster to note:
- Further imperative statements 'Use', 'Check', 'Protect', 'Do', 'Don't', 'Remember', etc.
- Sub-headings– 'Remember', 'Do', 'Don't', 'Be safe and smart online'
- Direct address: use of 'you', 'your', etc.
- Sequence: eye-catching single word title ('Students!') and subhead imperative statement/
- Introductory sentence giving the context re. popularity of social media and further explanation re. criminal activity
- Under this: two sets of bulleted (tick and cross) key advice and parallel 'Remember' panel
- Images of laptop screen, various symbols denoting threats (hooded face) or online related content
- Blue panel on right exhorting students to take care.
- General style is reasonably formal and authoritative, but also direct and clear – using short sentences and giving tips.

2 a) It is a poster or leaflet presented online; its audience is school students, probably aged between 9–10 to 16.
   b) To advise students of online dangers and how to protect themselves
   c) Possibly that the online world is a dangerous place if students do not take steps to protect themselves. Implies the responsibility is theirs.

   d) Broadly, yes. The poster provides clear information about steps to take. Because of the short format it doesn't have space to argue the points in detail but, as it is authoritative, it assumes reader will take advice as correct and that it will be trusted.

3   Possible answer: the sample touches on whether the poster source is trustworthy – the student talks about the 'authoritative, bold tick and cross bullets' and also how the source has developed her thinking – 'made me think is it possible to keep all this in mind, etc.'

4 • The title of the video: 'What if rap' is short and because it is a rap might engage viewers.
   • The image you can see links to the intended audience: a class of children, mostly looking up engaged with the singer/speaker (who is off screen).
   • The use of text on the screen: the 'What if?' title appears large and clear on the screen and is mirrored in the lyrics, so that it stresses the key message.
   • The lyrics in the rap – the rhythm, rhyme, repetition, etc: the repeated words and phrases(Watch/What?/What if?) are alliterative and so make it memorable. The rhymes (say/day; mix/pix) also make it easy to remember and stick in your mind; the rhythm is also fairly regular – the last two lines have the same number of syllables help to drum the message home.

5   The video uses terms familiar to young people, and a form of music they would listen to or enjoy. The class swaying/dancing sends an upbeat message so that it suggests everyone is in harmony and agrees with the warnings being offered.

6 a) The focus is on what children believe to be the main effects of cyberbullying.
   b) Its focus is more narrowly on cyberbullying but is wider in terms of who it might be about (no implied or direct references to local situation).
   c) It reveals which of the issues is most and least mentioned by children – and the types of cyberbullying. It's presented in the bar graph format with the issues in ascending order from left to right.
   d) The use of the word 'kids' rather than 'you' suggests this is not for 'kids' but possibly for adults. The fairly formal language of the bar titles – 'eating disorder', etc. also suggests this.
   e) The purpose is to inform about the issues rather than persuade, although one might argue the effect is also to lead to efforts to reduce them.
   f) There is no detail about the exact age range, gender, the nationality, the numbers surveyed or when the survey took place. This information would be helpful for more detailed analysis.

Apply the skills: students' own responses using the prompts given.

1.6 Writing reflections on themes and use of language

1 Students' own responses

2 a) The two language features mentioned: repetition and informal vocabulary

  b) The purposes are: repetition stresses or emphasised the key questions; the informal vocabulary engages the teen audience

Apply the skills: students' own response using the prompts given.

1.7 Writing the group report

1 Students' own responses

2 Students' own responses

3 a) Yes – there is an article, a video clip and an infographic. Each deal with different information although there is possibly cross-over between the video and the infographic.

  b) Yes, in the main, although the first source didn't make the group re-assess their views.

  c) Yes: Johnson's perspective; film report's perspective on specific doping issue; infographic gives wider perspective of historical problems of doping.

  d) Yes, it mentions the use of a Chair, a scribe and the deadlines and group meetings

  e) While the conclusion is logical, in the sense that it follows on from the issues, a better conclusion might have commented on how complex the issues around drug-taking are (for example, why someone like Ben Jonson was tempted to take drugs for performance).

4 a) Yes: para 1 = introduces topic, scheduling, etc.; para 2 = what the three stimuli pieces were; para 3- = the perspectives, how each piece linked to the theme, what was learned

  b) Word signalling sequence of learning: 'After'

  c) Clause dealing with effect: *we realised that drug-taking in sport hasn't gone away.*

  d) Alternatives to the word 'show': 'demonstrated', 'indicated', 'signalled'

  e) *We decided as a group that the most representative pieces were an article about Jamaican-born athlete Ben Johnson called 'Hero or villain?' from the CNN news site, an extract from a documentary film called 'Icarus' about Russian doping, and an infographic showing (could be 'which showed') doping statistics over the last three Olympics.*

Apply the skills: students' own responses

1.8 Planning and delivering the Oral Presentation

1 Particular effect mentioned: Social anxiety brought on by bullying problems escalating seems to be the particular focus of the monologue

  How the monologue is spoken: The student takes on the role of a victim of bullying and expresses herself in an emotional way and in an informal style

  Other point covered in monologue: How thoughtless actions lead to people suffering from the bullying

2 The student copied the informal style of the 'What if rap' and also takes up the key idea that a thoughtless action can have damaging effects.

3 Students' own responses

4 and 5: Students' own responses

6 a) Speaker's focus: how cyberbullying leads to social exclusion

  b) Her source: a letter to a counsellor in a teen magazine from a teenage girl

  c) The student has put the words taken from the source in speech/quotation marks

  d) The effect on the student: she was able to empathise with her due to their similar age

7–10 Students' own responses

Apply the skills: students' own responses

1.9 Final Reflections

1 Students' own responses

2 a) He now understands both the positive and negative impacts of business development.

  b) He will engage with a range of opinions and not dismiss things just because they are challenging.

  c) Row addressed from table: as a person; when looking to the future.

3 Students' own responses

Apply the skills: students' own responses

Glossary

abstract noun: a noun that expresses an idea of feeling, not a physical object, for example 'fear', 'spirit', 'politics'

accent: the way someone pronounces something, often linked to region (e.g. 'Yuh' rather than 'You', pronounced 'yoo')

adjective: a word that describes or adds more detail to a noun (e.g. 'This is my <u>lucky</u> coin.')

adverb: a word that adds detail to a verb or a whole sentence (e.g. '<u>Luckily</u> she arrived on time.')

alliteration: when words close to each other have the same initial letter

anecdote: a short account of something that happened to you, or which you have heard or read about elsewhere

antonym: a word with the opposite meaning to the original word

apostrophe: the punctuation mark used to show either omission or possession with a noun (e.g. 'Joanne's phone' or 'I've lost my phone.')

assertion: a strong statement of a view or belief, often without evidence to support it

assonance: when words close to each other repeat the same vowel sound

attitude: a writer's feelings and point of view towards their subject or topic

auxiliary verb: a verb that helps indicate the tense of another verb (e.g. 'was' in 'She <u>was</u> leaving.')

bias: a strong favouring of one side of an argument or debate, often without representing the other side of it

body text: the text in an advertisement that expands on the main qualities and appeal of the product

brackets: the punctuation marks (used in pairs) used to separate a clause or phrase in a sentence

call to action: an instruction or incentive that encourages immediate action, such making a phone call to support a cause or a shopping trip, so as not to miss out on the deal/a product

chronological order: the time order in which events occurred, one after the other

cliché: an unoriginal expression that has lost its effectiveness through overuse

cohesion: the successful linking of ideas in a text so that it flows well

colon: the punctuation mark used to introduce a list or an idea (e.g. 'I've got everything, I think: purse, keys and phone.'); also used in some case to separate clauses (e.g. 'I've eaten it all: everything that was left for me.')

comma: the punctuation mark used to separate items in lists or in pairs to mark off a clause within a sentence (e.g. 'I think, but I might be wrong, that we should take this path.')

complex sentence: a longer sentence consisting of a main clause and a subordinate clause

compound sentence: a sentence consisting of two simple sentences (main clauses) that are closely related in content, joined by a conjunction

concrete noun: a noun that relates to a physical thing (e.g. 'building', 'ladder', 'bucket')

conjunction: a word that joins items, phrases or whole clauses (e.g. 'They bought mangoes, pineapples <u>and</u> pomegranates'; 'She went home early <u>because</u> she was tired.')

connectives: words or phrases that link ideas between sentences and across paragraphs – these may be connectives of time ('initially', 'secondly', 'then'), place ('between', 'over', 'by'), cause and effect ('due to' or 'as a result'), contrast or development ('conversely' or 'similarly') or linking clauses ('while', 'which')

connotation: a sensory or emotional association that a word or phrase has in addition to its literal meaning

consonance: the repetition of the same consonant sound in words close to each other

context: the position, setting or background for a word, phrase or idea

counter-argument: a point that is opposite to the one you are making

critical: able to interpret, analyse, evaluate and reflect upon an issue

dash: the punctuation mark used singly to add information at the end of a sentence (e.g. 'The day was over – just the evening to come.'); also used in pairs to separate a clause or phrase in a sentence (e.g. 'We gathered around the table – friends and family – for a meal never to be forgotten.')

deconstruct: to take something apart in order to understand how it works

definite article: the word 'the', which signals a particular noun (e.g. '<u>the</u> tree in my garden')

definition: an explanation of the meaning of an object, idea or argument

determiner: a word that helps determine the nature of a noun or noun phrase; determiners can be the definite or indefinite articles 'the' or 'a' or may be possessive, such as 'her' or 'their'

dialect: the different vocabulary and grammar used in particular places or by specific groups

dialogue: a conversation between two or more characters

direct speech: the actual words spoken by someone, indicated by use of speech marks

dramatic monologue: a single, fictionalised speech, as if from a play, made by one character

exclamation mark: the punctuation mark used to indicate the end of a sentence that is an exclamation (e.g. 'Well, I never knew that!')

explicit meaning: the direct statement of an idea or viewpoint

extended metaphor: when a comparison is repeated or developed in a text (e.g. the image of a bird for hope used throughout Emily Dickenson's poem 'Hope')

facts: pieces of information that can be proven with evidence

figurative language: words or phrases that prompt ideas or create rich images in the reader's mind and that are not intended to be taken literally

finite verb: a verb that has been conjugated for tense and subject agreement (and is therefore limited in terms of time and person it can refer to)

first person: when a story is told or an account is given from the point of view of the person or people who had the experience (using 'I' or 'we')

five-stage narrative structure: a structure consisting of an introduction, problem, rising action, climax and a resolution

flashback: part of the narrative that takes the reader back to past events

font: a particular design or size of lettering used in print text

full stop: the punctuation mark used to indicate the end of a sentence that is a statement (e.g. 'The tiger is an endangered species.')

header: a memorable statement, usually placed at the top of the page to catch the reader's eye

hyperbole: exaggerated expression (e.g. 'I've told you a thousand times not to exaggerate.')

idiom: a well-known phrase or wise saying, sometimes involving a metaphor that may not be easy to understand

imagery: vivid word pictures that are a key element of figurative language

impact: the overall impression left by a piece of writing due to the writer's choices in making it precise, appealing or memorable

implicit information: information that has to be inferred or worked out from the information given; it often suggests opinions or feelings or can lead you to draw a conclusion

implicit meaning: meaning that has to be inferred or deduced; implicit meaning often reveals opinions or feelings or can lead you to draw a conclusion about an author's intention or viewpoint

implied: an idea or viewpoint that is suggested/ indicated in an indirect or less obvious way

inclusive language: the use of 'we' and 'us' in persuasive texts to make the reader feel valued and involved

indefinite article: the words 'a' or 'an', which signal a non-specific noun (e.g. '<u>a</u> tree in my garden')

in media res: when a story does not start by 'setting the scene' but plunges right into the action

intensifiers: words that are not strictly necessary in a sentence, but which add emotion to the word they modify (e.g. 'He <u>really</u> wanted that ice cream.')

literal information: information that is factual or without any implied meaning

literal meaning: the dictionary definition of a word without any nuance or connotation taken into account

main clause: the clause in a sentence that contains the main verb and which makes sense on its own

main verb: in a multi-verb phrase, the verb that reveals what action or process is happening (e.g. 'She was <u>leaving</u>.')

metaphor: a comparison in which one thing is said to actually *be* another

minor sentence: a fragment of a complete sentence, often missing the main verb (e.g. 'Her own nervous footsteps.' is a fragment of '<u>It was</u> her own nervous footsteps.'

mood: the atmosphere or 'feel' in a story, for example tense, joyful, peaceful, etc.

narrative hook: any technique the writer uses at the start of a story to interest the reader

non-finite verb: a verb that is not conjugated to agree with a subject; infinitives (e.g. 'to eat', 'to dance') and participles (e.g. '<u>Dancing </u>his way to the table…') are non-finite

non-literal language: also called figurative language, this is used in ways that go beyond a literal meaning to create an additional effect

noun: a person, place or thing; types of nouns include concrete or common nouns, proper nouns, abstract nouns and collective nouns

noun phrase: a noun that is modified by additional information, often adjectives (e.g. 'hollow eye-sockets')

nuance: the precise meaning of a word; this may be very subtly or slightly different from that of another similar word (e.g. consider the difference between 'large' and 'enormous' or 'pleasant' and 'delightful')

onomatopoeia: where a word's sound reflects the actual sound that it is describing

paragraph: a distinct section in a piece of writing that signals a change of idea or point being made, change of person or perspective or a change of time or location

paraphrase: to turn a longer piece of writing into something that broadly sums up what has been said

personal address: the use of 'you' in a persuasive text to make a direct appeal to the reader

personification: when an inanimate object is described with human-like qualities (e.g. 'The wind raged, shattering illusions.')

persuasive techniques: language effects that help a speaker or writer state a point of view strongly in order to change their listener's or reader's opinion or influence their actions

plot reversals: events that block or create problems for the main character

predictive and retrospective reading: the ability to look ahead to what is coming next when reading as well as considering what has just been read

preposition: a word that indicates the (literal or metaphorical) position of an object or the relationship between objects (e.g. 'under', 'between', 'in')

pronoun: a word that replaces a noun or a noun phrase; types of pronoun include subject pronouns (e.g. 'he, 'she', 'it') and object pronouns (e.g. 'him', 'her')

pun: creating humorous effect by exploiting different meanings of words

purpose: the main aim of a piece of speech or writing

question mark: the punctuation mark used to indicate the end of a sentence that is a question (e.g. 'How did that parcel end up here?')

redundancy: when more than one word is used even though the meaning is already clearly made by the first word (e.g. 'an added bonus')

register: degree of formality or informality in language, or the typical language used by a particular group, or in a particular situation

repetition: repeating words and phrases to emphasise a point or convince the reader or listener; patterns of three are an example of this (e.g. 'I came, I saw, I conquered.')

reported speech: someone else's account of what was said, without speech marks

rhetorical: written or spoken to produce an effect rather than to convey information

rhetorical question: a question to engage a reader or audience rather than expecting an answer (e.g. 'Who could really argue with that?')

rhyme: where sounds used in two or more words match

rhythm: where the length of words, the number of stressed syllables in a word or a line, or the punctuation used creates a regular pattern

semantic field: a group or set of words that relate to a topic or subject

semicolon: the punctuation mark used to separate longer items in a list (e.g. 'the shifting sands; the unrelenting sun; and the crowds of tourists'); also used to link clauses closely related in meaning or evenly balanced (e.g. 'It was the hottest summer on record; I had had enough of it.')

sensory details: references to sight, sound, smell, taste or touch

sensory language: language that stimulates your senses and adds nuances that help a reader visualize or relate to taste or smell

sibilance: when the repetition of 's' sounds in words close together creates a 'hiss' effect

simile: a comparison in which one thing is said to be like another, using the words 'as' or 'like'

simple sentence: a sentence made up of just one main, independent clause

sound effect: the rhythms and sounds by which letters within words, whole words and combinations of words create meanings

speech: any spoken language

statistics: numerical data that is drawn from surveys or 'expert' sources and which is often used as supporting evidence

status: power or control in a dialogue or a dramatic situation; this can alter during a conversation so that the balance shifts from one character to another

stimuli: materials (e.g. photos, poems, articles) that generate a response in the reader/listener

structure: the way that writing is arranged; in the case of poetry, the order of words, the way they are punctuated and organised into lines

subordinate clause: a clause that is secondary to the main clause in a sentence and which does not make complete sense on its own

subordinate idea: an idea that is an example or part of a bigger or main idea (also called a secondary idea)

symbolism: when something is used consistently to represent a concept or theme (e.g. the daffodils in Wordsworth's poem 'I Wandered Lonely as a Cloud')

synonym: a word with a very similar meaning to the original

syntax: the arrangement of words and phrases to create well-formed sentences

synthesise: bring together in one place various bits of information

theme: a topic or idea that is explored in a piece of writing

third person: when a story is told or an account is given from the point of view of a person relating the experiences of others (using 'he' or 'she')

tone: a writer's attitude or their 'voice' in a piece of writing; for example, the tone of writing could be negative, sour or jovial

topic sentence: the sentence that sums up the main idea of a paragraph; the topic sentence is often, but not always, at the start of the paragraph

verb: a word or words indicating a state, action, thought or process

verb tense: defines *when* an action is happening (e.g. present tense: 'I arrive at 11 a.m.'; past tense: 'I arrived at 11 a.m.'; future tense: 'I will arrive at 11 a.m.')

wh word: one of a set of pronouns and adverbs used to form questions; pronouns: who, which, what; adverbs: where, why, when, how

Acknowledgements

Collins Concise Course for CSEC English by Julia Burchell, Mike Gould and Beth Kemp, 978-0008-458577.
Acknowledgements prepared 28th January 2021.
We are grateful to the following for permission to reproduce copyright material:

Figures
Graph on p.52, "Average Caribbean Weather", copyright © 2015 by Scott Bateman. Reproduced with kind permission; Bar chart on p.53, "International Average Arrivals" from http://mecometer.com/topic/international-tourism-number-of-arrivals/, created by mecometer.com; Pie chart on p.55, "U.S. Agricultural Exports to Dominican Republic", 2014, The Foreign Agricultural Service (FAS); and bar charts on p.55, "Jamaica Tourism Statistics", copyright © 2015 by Scott Bateman. Reproduced with kind permission;

Text
Extracts on pp.8, 9 from "Insight Guides" https://www.insightguides.com/inspire-me/blog/caribbean-architecture, APA Publications (UK) Limited. Reproduced with permission; Extract on p.59 from "Sea Change: The Ecological Disaster That Nobody Sees" by Richard Schiffman, 18/09/2014, *Truthout*, http://www.truth-out.org/news/ item/26202-sea-change-the-ecological-disaster-that-nobody-sees. Reproduced with permission of Truthout and YES!; Extract on p.60 from "U.S. mosquitos spreading Chikungunya, the excruciatingly painful disease that tore through the Caribbean", 21/07/2014, The Associated Press. Reproduced with permission of Wrights Media; Poem excerpt on p.68 "Laventille" by Derek Walcott, first published in *The Castaway*, Faber & Faber Ltd, 1965. Reproduced with permission of the publisher and Farrar, Straus & Giroux; A screenshot and excerpt lines on p.70 from "What if?" https://www.getsafeonline.org.jm/video/, Broadcasting Commission / Get safe Online. Reproduced courtesy of Broadcasting Commission of Jamaica, www.broadcom.org; Poem on pp.70-71, "Skeete's Bay, Barbados" by Robert Lee, from *Elemental: New and selected poems 1975–2007*, Peepal Tree, 2008. Reproduced with permission of Peepal Tree Press; Poem on p.75, "The Sea", by James Reeves, from *Complete Poems for Children*, Faber & Faber. Reproduced with permission of David Higham Associates; Poem on pp.76-77, "Wind-rush" by James Berry, from *A Story I am In: Selected Poems* by James Berry, Bloodaxe Books, 2011, p.144. Reproduced by permission of Bloodaxe Books; Poem on pp.80-81, "Well done" by Dreadlock Alien. Reproduced with kind permission of Richard Grant; Poems on pp.85, 86, "Grandfather;" "I'm pillowed;" "Winters after me;" "My man saws the wind blows" and "Sorrow moves" by Lorine Neidecker, from *Lorine Niedecker: Collected Works*, edited by Jenny Penberthy, copyright © 2002 by the Regents of the University of California. Published by the University of California Press; Poem on p.88, "Valentine" by Carol Ann Duffy, from *Mean Time*, Anvil Press Poetry, copyright © Carol Ann Duffy. Reproduced with permission of the author c/o Rogers, Coleridge & White Ltd., 20 Powis Mews, London W11 1JN; Extracts on pp.95, 96 from *The Traveller's Tree: A Journey through the Caribbean Islands* by Patrick Leigh Fermor, copyright © Patrick Leigh Fermor, 2010. Reproduced with permission of Hodder and Stoughton Limited; Extract on p.100 from *Breathe: A Ghost Story* by Cliff McNish, Orion Children's Books, 2007. Reproduced with kind permission of Cliff McNish; Extract on p.104 from *The Royal Diaries: Anacaona, Golden Flower* by Edwidge Danticat. Copyright © 2005 by Edwidge Danticat. Used with permission of Scholastic Inc and The Aragi Agency; Extract on p.105 from "Amellia at Devil's Bridge" by Joanne, C. Hill House, from *Pepperpot Best New Stories from The Caribbean*, Peekash Press, 2014. Reproduced with kind permission of Joanne C. Hill; Letter on pp.122-123 from "#nonamechange for Denbigh High", 28/06/2016, Mario Raphael Boothe, Jamaican, Advocate, Political Activist and Blogger. Reproduced with kind permission of Mario Raphael Boothe; Extract on pp.135-136 from *Please Don't Take My Baby* by Cathy Glass, Harper Element, 2015, copyright © 2015 Cathy Glass. Reproduced with permission of HarperCollins Publishers Ltd; Extract on p.150 from "Strangest island in the Caribbean may be a sanctuary for critically-endangered coral" by Julian Smith, 16/07/2012, https://news.mongabay.com/2012/07/ strangest-island-in-the-caribbean-may-be-a-sanctuary-for-critically-endangered-coral/, copyright © 2012 Mongabay.com. Reproduced with permission; Extract on pp.154, 155 from "When did competitive sports take over American childhood" by Hilary Levey Friedman, 20/09/2013, copyright © 2016 by The Atlantic Monthly Group. All Rights Reserved; Reproduced by permission of Atlantic Media; Extract on p.160 from "Islands of Song", Smithsonian Folkways, copyright © Smithsonian Institute. Reproduced with permission; Extract on p.241 from "The Truth About Caribbean Sharks". Reproduced with permission of Gavin Naylor, Florida Program for Shark Research Curator, International Shark Attack File, https://www.floridamuseum.ufl.edu/sharks/; An extract on pp.266-267 from "How social media is affecting the health of young people" by Meisha-Gay Mattis, 16/01/2020, https://www.loopjamaica.com/content/how-social-media-affecting-health-young-people. Reproduced by kind permission of Meisha-Gay Mattis; and statistics on p.271 from "From those who have experienced cyberbullying, what impact did it have on you?"

from *The Annual Bullying Survey 2017*, Ditch the Label, DitchtheLabel.org. Reproduced with permission. In some instances we have been unable to trace the owners of copyright material, and we would appreciate any information that would enable us to do so.

Photos

P6–7: Meryll/Shutterstock, p9: Patrick Donovan/Getty Images, p11: Chris Howes/Wild Places Photography/Alamy Stock Photo, p14: Syda Productions/Shutterstock, p15: Gerisima/Shutterstock, p16: Seaphotoart/Shutterstock, p19: Angela Rohde/Shutterstock, p20: Jan Stromme/The Image Bank/Getty Images, p22: Eye Ubiquitous/Alamy Stock Photo, p23: OlegDoroshin/Shutterstock, p24: Nikkolia/Shutterstock, p25: Ammit Jack/Shutterstock, p26: Ajayptp/Shutterstock, p29: Galyna Andrushko/Shutterstock, p30: Boris15/Shutterstock, p31: Sean Drakes/Alamy Stock Photo, p33: Wwing/Getty Images, P34: Shamleen/Shutterstock, p35: photopixel/Shutterstock, p36: Djjis/Shutterstock, p37: Hill Street Studios/Gary Kious/Blend Images/Getty Images, p39: Kumar Sriskandan/Alamy Stock Photo, p41: Roberto Machado Noa/LightRocket/Getty Images, p42: Pascal Deloche/Getty Images, p43: Alexandr Junek Imaging s.r.o/Shutterstock, p45: Banana Republic images/Shutterstock, p48: Kovalchuk Oleksandr/Shutterstock, p49: Belizar/Shutterstock, p51: James A Hancock/Getty Images, p51: Tom Uhlman/Alamy Stock Photo, p59: Arthit Chamsat/Shutterstock, p60: Dimijana/Shutterstock, p65: Allen Paul Photography/Shutterstock, p66: SJDuran/Shutterstock, p68: Bill WASSMAN/Contributor/Getty Images, p70: Smebeesley/Shutterstock, p71: PHB.cz (Richard Semik)/Shutterstock, p72: Styve Reineck/Shuttertock, p75: F9photos/Shutterstock, p77: Arndale/Shutterstock, p78: Sakon Jamroekjeang/Shutterstock p78: Iren Key/Shutterstock, p81: 9george/Shutterstock, p83: Denis Sv/Shutterstock, p84: VanderWolf Images/Shutterstock, p85: Jeffrey Isaac Greenberg 3+/Alamy Stock Photo, p86: Guentermanaus/Shutterstock, p87: Akhenaton Images/Shutterstock, p88: Oraveepix/Shutterstock, p91: PatriciaDz/Shutterstock, p93: Everett Collection/Shutterstock, p95: Ajax News & Feature Service/Alamy Stock Photo, p96: Binh Thanh Bui/Shutterstock, p97: Harvey Meston/Archive Photos/Getty Images, p98: Universal History Archive/Getty Images, p100: Lisa Hagan/Alamy Stock Photo, p100: Lario Tus/Shutterstock, p102: pikcha/Shutterstock, p103: pp1/Shutterstock, p109: Politicalcartoons/www.politicalcartoons.com, p111: Tequiero/Shutterstock, p112: Tim UR/Shutterstock, p114: CLIMATE/MANGROVES REUTERS/Gerardo Garcia/Alamy Stock Photo, p115: Ivan Cholakov/Shutterstock, p117: Blend Images/Shutterstock, p118: Matt Antonino/Shutterstock, P118: Sergey Khandogin, p120: Advertising Archives, p124: Fotografen GmbH/Alamy Stock Photo, p129: Air Images/Shutterstock, p130: Africa Studio/Shutterstock, p132: Alexandra Astaleks/Shutterstock, p133: Elena Shashkina/Shutterstock, p138: Naeblys/Shutterstock, p140: Sylvie Bouchard/Shutterstock, p140: Africa Studio/Shutterstock, p140: Sylvie Bouchard/Shutterstock, p142: Elena Shashkina/Shutterstock, p143: Viktor Kochetkov/Shutterstock, p144–145: NakoPhotography/Shutterstock, p146: Xavier MARCHANT/Shutterstock, p147: Dima Sobko/Shutterstock, p149: US Fish and Wildlife Services, p150: ARENA Creative/Shutterstock, p151: Venturelli Luca/Shutterstock, p152: Alistair Berg/DigitalVision/Getty Images, p154: Africa Studio/Shutterstock, p154: Volodymyr Burdiak/Shutterstock, p156: Michael Potter11/Shutterstock, p157: Dorling Kindersley ltd/Alamy Stock Photo, p158: Timothy O'Keefe/Photolibrary/Getty Images, p161: Mark Wilson/Getty Images, p163: De Agostini/A. Dagli Orti/Getty Images, p166: Ray Bond/Shutterstock, p167: Pressmaster/Sutterstock, p169: BluIz60/Shutterstock, p171: Chudovska/Shutterstock, p172: Westend61/Getty Images, p173: Kevin Britland/Alamy Stock Photo, p175: Sergey Kelin/Shutterstock, p177: Lawrence Manning/Corbis/Getty Images, p178: Yut4ta/Shutterstock, p180: Akos Nagy/Shutterstock, p180: Andrey_Popov/Shutterstock, p183: Brent Winebrenner/Getty Images, p186: James Schwabel/Alamy Stock Photo, p189: alexmillos/Shutterstock, p190: David Grossman/Alamy Stock Photo, p192: HECTOR RETAMAL/AFP/Getty Images, p195: oOhyperblaster/Shutterstock, p196: Ariadne Van Zandbergen/Alamy Stock Photo, p198: Jupiterimages/Getty Images, p199: David Hyde/Shutterstock, p200: Suti Stock Photo/Shutterstock, p202: Bryon Palmer/Shutterstock, p204: Alexandra Lande/Shutterstock, p206: Corbis/VCG/Corbis/Getty Images, p209: Mimagephotography/Shutterstock, p214: Richard Levine/Alamy Stock Photo, p215: Myrleen Pearson/Alamy Stock Photo, p216: Andrey Armyagov/Shutterstock, p218: HolyCrazyLazy/Shutterstock, p220: Arif Ali/AFP/Getty Images, p221: Jupiterimages/Getty Images, p222: Kypros/Alamy, p223: Joshua Resnick/Shutterstock, p224: ozgun evren erturk/Shutterstock, p226: Antoniodiaz/Shutterstock, p227: S_bukley/Shutterstock, p228: Barry vanwagner/Alamy, p229: Filipe Frazao/Shutterstock, p230: Don Pablo/Shutterstock, p230: JGA/Shutterstock, p232: Ammentorp Photography/Alamy Stock Photo, p233: Alex and Laila/Getty Images, p234: John Birdsall/Alamy Stock Photo, p237: Matt9122/Shutterstock, p239: Golden Pixels LLC/Shutterstock, p241: Tejas Tripathi/Shutterstock, p243: Titikul_B/Shutterstock, p246: daraka/Shutterstock, p249: Jacob Lund/Shutterstock, p250: Darren Baker/Shutterstock, p254: Juice Flair/Shutterstock, p255: Rawpixel.com/Shutterstock, p255: jakkaje879/Shutterstock, p255: jakkaje879/Shutterstock, p255: Monkey Business Images/Shutterstock, p257: Ollyy/Shutterstock, p258: Kreminska/Shutterstock, p259: fizkes/Shutterstock, p260: AVETPHOTOS/Shutterstock, p262: Iryna Inshyna/Shutterstock, p265: fizkes/Shutterstock p266: https://www.getsafeonline.org.jm/video/, P268: fizkes/Shutterstock, p270: Daniel M Ernst/Shutterstock, p272: Professional Sport/Contributor/Getty Images, p276: wavebreakmedia/Shutterstock, p278: Monkey Business Images/Shutterstock, p279: Daniel M Ernst/Shutterstock, p281: Gorodenkoff/Shutterstock